POSITIVE TRA

for Aggressive and Reactive Dogs

Dedication

For my heart dog, Echo—what a gift you were.
And for Jeff Hebert, the best man in the world. I'm lucky to share this life with you.

Positive Training for Aggressive and Reactive Dogs

CompanionHouse Books™ is an imprint of Fox Chapel Publishing.

Project Team
Managing Editor: Gretchen Bacon
Editors: Sherry Vitolo and Amy Deputato
Designer: Mary Ann Kahn
Proofreader: Kurt Conley
Indexer: Jay Kreider

ISBN 978-1-62187-198-9

Library of Congress Control Number: 2023931386

This book has been published with the intent to provide accurate and authoritative information in regard to the subject matter within. While every precaution has been taken in the preparation of this book, the author and publisher expressly disclaim any responsibility for any errors, omissions, or adverse effects arising from the use or application of the information contained herein. The techniques and suggestions are used at the reader's discretion and are not to be considered a substitute for veterinary care. If you suspect a medical problem, consult your veterinarian.

Fox Chapel Publishing
903 Square Street
Mount Joy, PA 17552

We are always looking for talented authors. To submit an idea, please send a brief inquiry to acquisitions@foxchapelpublishing.com.

Printed in the United States
Second printing

POSITIVE TRAINING
for Aggressive and
Reactive Dogs

Proven Techniques to Help Your Dog
Overcome Fear and Anxiety

ANNIE PHENIX,
FEAR FREE CERTIFIED PROFESSIONAL & CERTIFIED CANINE BEHAVIORIST

Contents

How well do we really understand the dogs with whom we share our homes? Dogs are complex beings with species-specific needs and motivations.

Introduction

I wrote this how-to-help-your-troubled-dog book for two audiences. The first audience can't read, of course, but they need our help. The second and most important audience is you—the caring dog guardian facing a serious canine behavior concern. These very real problems can result in a life-or-death decision for the dog you love—there is a life on the line, and we need to get it right for the dog's sake.

Living with a dog who is exhibiting major behavior problems is enormously stressful but with the right tools and the right professional help, you can resolve or reduce many of these conflicts.

This book asks (and answers) the most important questions facing dog owners right now:

- Why are modern dogs so stressed and what does stress look like in a dog?
- Why are so many behavior concerns showing up in modern dogs?
- What are the kindest and most effective methods to help troubled dogs?
- What are the most common behavior problems and how can we best address them?
- What life skills are most important for our dogs and at what age should we teach them?
- What training methods **won't** help the situation?
- What should you consider if behavioral euthanasia is on the table?
- What are our true responsibilities to our dogs and how can we strengthen the canine-human bond?
- Which professionals will help your dog the most and how can you know who to trust?

Over the past 20 years, canine professionals have seen vast increases in troubling behavior in dogs. A large study from the Center for Canine Behavior Studies[1] reported that as many as 85% of dog owners were experiencing a behavior concern with their dog. A Finnish study of more than 13,000 dogs concluded that 72% of the dogs showed problematic behaviors such as aggression or fearfulness. I once assumed that the cushy indoor pet life was healthier for dogs than the street life of a community or village dog, and, while it is true that street dogs face serious dangers (like traffic or a greater risk of disease), they have one vital thing in their lives that house pets lack: autonomy. Street dogs can choose where they go for

Dogs are truly a part of the family, and we show it every day by spending tons of money for the very best in vet care, treats, toys, and more.

the day, what they do or don't do, and where they sleep—and the more control an animal has over its life and experiences, the more content it is. Take away all agency and the resulting stress pops up as unwanted behaviors.

As our fast-paced culture has rapidly changed around us, it has also changed dramatically for our dogs. Until the 1950s, most dogs spent much of the day making their own choices about where they wanted to go, when they wanted to nap, and more. It's much more likely for today's dogs to have limited choices, being confined in the house or crate

1 Ian R. Dinwoodie, et al., "Demographics and Comorbidity of Behavior Problems in Dogs." *Journal of Veterinary Behavior* 32 (July–August 2019): 62–71.

all day and having very little stimulation. While dogs are uniquely adapted to living with humans, they are still animals with their own internal, natural desires and needs. Their new restricted lifestyle is safer in many ways (lower risk of disease or injury, of example), but it can also lead to unwanted behaviors.

> While dogs are uniquely adapted to living with humans, they are still animals with their own internal, natural desires and needs.

Modern life has changed drastically for our dogs, but we can still be their partners and guides as we walk through life together.

Ignoring a dog's mental, environmental, or genetic needs often leads to behavior "problems," which are just expressions of the dog trying to satisfy canine needs.

You are the most important person in your dog's life. Working with the right tools and professionals, you can make a major difference for them.

Dogs are neither stupid nor stubborn, but they can be stressed, and even in humans we can see that unwanted behaviors often follow stress. Because dogs can't tell us where their stress is coming from, it is our responsibility to look at their lives from their perspective and use science-backed, compassionate methods to help them. Canine professionals around the world are constantly seeking better, faster, and fairer methods. They are flipping the script—getting a complete picture of the dog's life before implementing a plan. Rather than asking "why is this bad dog being disobedient," they're wondering "what is causing the dog's stress and what can we do about it?"

Over my 20-year career as a canine behavior consultant, I've learned the most from the thousands of troubled dogs I've met and their dedicated owners, but I've also learned a lot from the incredible professionals I've met along the way—from veterinary behaviorists to neuroscientists to ethologists to very skilled dog trainers. In writing this book, I asked some of them to contribute their unique knowledge and they graciously agreed. It is my honor to share this collective wisdom with the one person who can do the most for your dog—you.

Annie Phenix
Heber City, Utah

1

Why Are Modern Dogs So Troubled?

If there was just one overriding cause of stress in today's dogs, we could focus our efforts on that one cause. How I wish that were the case! Instead, there is a myriad of factors that can contribute to our canines' discomfort. We humans and our fast-paced lifestyles are often at the top of the list, but did you know that stressors can affect puppies negatively even before they are born? In this chapter, we will look at the range of factors that cause a dog stress, affecting their outlook on life and their interactions with people, other animals, and their environment.

OUR DOGS FEEL OUR STRESS

We know from studies that if a dog's guardian is stressed or anxious, the dog can mirror that stress. A 2019 study published in *Scientific Reports*[1] showed that a dog's level of cortisol (a stress-related hormone) mirrors the personality traits of their owner.

---

1   Ann-Sofie Sundman, et al., "Long-Term Stress Levels Are Synchronized in Dogs and Their Owners." *Scientific Reports* 9, 7391 (2019). https://doi.org/10.1038/s41598-019-43851-x.

Many signs of stress in dogs are subtle, like a tightly closed mouth, concern-filled eyes, or a tentative facial expression.

One of the most important gifts we can provide to puppies is ensuring that the mother dog is not stressed before, during, or after delivery. Stress in a mother dog can be passed onto her offspring.

Imagine what our dogs have been dealing with. According to the American Psychological Association, 78% of Americans reported that the coronavirus was a significant source of stress in their life,[2] but Americans and many others in the world had been deeply stressed for a long time before:[3]

+ More than three quarters of adults reported symptoms of stress
+ 284 million people worldwide have an anxiety disorder
+ Job stress costs United States industries more than $300 billion a year

Imagine being a vibrant, curious eight-week-old puppy and landing in a home where stress is rampant. It makes me exhausted just thinking about it. As UK trainer and behaviorist Shay Kelly has noted, "when we see 'bad' behavior in dogs, it is very often an animal's desperate attempt to meet their own needs."

A PREGNANT MOTHER PASSES STRESS TO HER PUPPIES

Puppies can feel the negative effects of stress even before they are born. We know that stress in utero can have life-long effects on humans, and it's the same for dogs—puppies' brains and hormonal and nervous systems develop before birth. If the mother dog is stressed while pregnant, that stress can be shared with her puppies.

When a mother dog's cortisol level is extremely elevated, an enzyme that would normally neutralize cortisol in the placenta becomes overloaded, and

---

2 "Stress in America™ 2020," American Psychological Association, created October 2020, https://www.apa.org/news/press/releases/stress/2020/report-october.

3 See the following article for more relevant statistics and links and references to primary sources: "Stress Statistics 2022: How Common Is Stress and Who's Most Affected?" SingleCare Team, medically reviewed by Scott Dershowitz, LMSW, CMC, updated April 26, 2022, https://www.singlecare.com/blog/news/stress-statistics/.

Providing the necessary support to mother dogs and keeping them stress-free is important in developing healthy, happy puppies.

Pregnant dams can face two types of stress: negative or distress, and positive or eustress. Both types of prenatal stress have long-term effects on puppies. Pups whose dams experience distress during pregnancy are more likely to be reactive, anxious, and irritable as adults, with dysfunctional stress management systems, lower intelligence, and shorter attention spans. Conversely, puppies whose dams have enriched pregnancies are more likely to be calmer and more stable adults, that learn, breed, and digest better.[5]

some of the cortisol is passed to the developing puppies, influencing the type of world their brains will expect to encounter.[4] A healthy puppy's brain can afford to spend energy on healthy growth and exploration, but a frightened, stressed puppy's brain spends most of its energy on fear responses. While behavior experts can help reduce your puppy or adult dog's behavior concerns in many ways, we can't change a brain that was born in a high state of fear using behavior modification alone.

A world of behavior problems can be thwarted if we all appreciate the importance of safe, secure environments for mother dogs. The American Kennel Club (AKC), as well, has called for more prenatal enrichment and less maternal distress:

Breeding dogs is a big business with a lot of money involved. Puppy mills (inhumane mass breeding facilities) can produce more than two million puppies a year. Puppy mills are not set up to ensure the well-being of mother dogs or their puppies. The American Society for the Prevention of Cruelty to Animals (ASPCA) notes that tiny cages, filthy conditions, poor vet care, no grooming, no walks, no playing or petting, non-stop breeding, sudden separation, and stressful transport all make puppy mills massively harmful. If you wanted by design to acquire a puppy that has experienced stress in utero, stress for the first few weeks of life, and stress in transport, get yourself a puppy mill puppy. It is the perfect arrangement for creating dogs with big, serious behavior problems that even the best behaviorists may not be able to help.

The average cost of a purebred puppy is around $1,300 and a show-quality puppy can be 100 times

---

4   Jessica Hekman, "How a Mother's Stress Can Influence Unborn Puppies," *Whole Dog Journal*, published October 20, 2014, updated September 23, 2021, www.whole-dog-journal.com/puppies/puppy-health/how-a-mothers-stress-can-influence-unborn-puppies.

5   Gayle Watkins, PhD, "The Perinatal Period and Puppy Development," *American Kennel Club*, published September 24, 2018, https://www.akc.org/expert-advice/dog-breeding/start-even-younger/.

more expensive than an average dog of the same breed. There are many incredibly responsible dog breeders, and I have shared my life with many well-behaved purebred dogs, but breeding a well-balanced, good tempered, healthy dog is not easy. Just ask the experts who study and breed service dogs—they specialize in creating such dogs yet as many as 50% of puppies do not "make the cut." (Chapter 6 contains information on how to properly breed healthy, resilient dogs and includes an interview with a world-recognized breeder.)

Providing everything a mother dog needs to birth physically and emotionally stable puppies is a hard endeavor that eats into a breeder's profit (because of the testing and veterinary care involved). Think about all the books and advice available for human mothers and how careful most pregnant women are. To create resilient puppies, we need a similarly high level of prenatal care for mother dogs. Dogs in a perfect world would be bred first for temperament and second for conformation to breed standards and performance abilities. Unfortunately, breeders mostly seem to be doing it exactly backward—and dogs and their exasperated guardians pay a high price for it.

Stress reactions and behavior problems in dogs won't change on the large scale until all dog owners refuse to purchase dogs from puppy mills and irresponsible breeders. Updated laws are needed to protect the health and well-being of parent dogs and their puppies. It is not the bad breeders who suffer—it's the dogs and their caring owners that must face the music.

OUR DOGS' BRED-FOR TRAITS DON'T MATCH THEIR ENVIRONMENTS

Years and years ago, when people began keeping dogs, dogs had jobs to do and were selectively bred based on what they were good at: guarding their owners' homes, herding other animals, hunting for food or vermin, and the like. Fast-forward to today, when most dogs are kept as pets: they are still hardwired to do these jobs but find themselves more often on the couch than out in the field or on the farm. What the dog has been bred for matters in terms of their mental and physical needs, and this holds true for mixed breeds as much as for purebreds. (You can get your dog's DNA analysis from several companies; I use Embark: *www.embarkvet.com*.)

In personal discussions about one of her recent studies, Dr. Erin Hecht of Harvard's Department of Human Evolutionary Biology has said that "different breeds of dogs have different brain anatomy." Dr. Hecht and her fellow researchers looked closely at what influences brain anatomy in dogs. They discovered that as we have bred dogs over time, we have actively reshaped their brains.

DNA tests are useful tools for owners of mixed-breed dogs. A simple swab can help you determine what natural drives might be "coded" into your dog's DNA.

The study found huge variations in brain structure depending on the breed of the dog. That Border Collie and that Jack Russell are both family pets, but inside their brains they have the framework to perform the specific jobs for which we bred them (although they'd still need training and early exposure to enhance those traits).

> Only 20–40% of your dog's behavior is genetic. The rest is shaped by the surrounding environment.

Because dogs are individuals, you can come across Border Collies who aren't interested in sheep and Jack Russells who don't dig up the flower beds every day. What you often get, however, are countless dog owners frustrated with family pets that are simply expressing their genes (in ways that don't work with their owners' lifestyles). We don't put Basset Hounds on huge ranches and expect them to round up 2,400-pound bulls. Heelers on the other hand make excellent cattle wranglers but they don't hold a candle to a Basset Hound's single-track, rabbit-hunting brain. When someone adds a toy dog to their home, they shouldn't expect a guard dog (although someone might want to tell that to Chihuahuas). Toy dogs have literally been bred to be "comfort dogs" since 1500 BCE, but you'd be surprised how many calls behavior consultants get from surprised owners whose toy dogs have acute separation anxiety. When we bring a dog into our lives, we give little thought to what the dog's brain was designed to do and expect the same level of obedience and relaxation from every dog. This dynamic sets up a perfect storm for frustrated canines and humans.

Dr. Jessica Hekman (*www.dogzombie.com*) studies the genomics of behavior in pet dogs at

A Border Collie has within its genetic code a drive to work 8–10 hours a day as a hard-working farmhand. Genes matter.

the Karlsson Lab at the Broad Institute of MIT and Harvard. She says that 20–40% of any personality trait in a dog is influenced by genes and the rest is shaped by the environment. "Personality is influenced by both genetics and environment. The two influences work together in very subtle and nuanced ways. The environment is a subtle thing. It can be in utero influences. It can be things that happen when the puppy is tiny, it can be interactions with other puppies in the litter."

While genes *are* vitally important, she points out that a dog's environment is key to whether the genetic programming shows up. "Genes and the environment intersect, and the environment is critical. We know that children who have bad childhoods cannot handle stress as well as those who had cheerful childhoods. Early life stress makes animals less resilient."

The importance of enrichment and environment to animal development has been demonstrated in rats. Studies have proven that when their environments are rich, rats' brain weights, sizes, and even number of neurons increase. Those things do NOT generally increase if an animal is not given enrichment, particularly when it is young. Studies have also repeatedly shown that enrichment creates rats that demonstrate more complex behaviors, improved concentration, memory and attention, superior learning, improved performance, and reduced emotionality.

Resiliency in dogs makes for a much more enjoyable life, not only for the animal but also for those sharing a life with them. Do you want a dog who can bounce back after a stressful event? Or do you want a dog who reacts with teeth bared or tail tucked, trying to bolt at every new thing introduced to its environment?

OUR DOGS NEED BETTER SOCIALIZATION AS PUPPIES

I am thrilled that puppy owners are becoming more aware of the dire need for puppies to receive proper socialization at an early age. There is, however, some confusion about what entails good socialization and how/when it should occur. In this section, we'll look at the key socialization stages for puppies and how owners can make the most of these time periods to raise puppies into happy, confident, and well-adjusted dogs. (Also see the section on canine enrichment in chapter 9 starting on page 207.)

The most critical time to help a puppy feel safe with exploring the new world outside the womb is at the breeder's house. Puppies begin to explore

The most important time for puppies to begin safely exploring their world is around three to four weeks of age. At this point, most puppies will show more curiosity than fear.

their environment around three to four weeks of age. A breeder can make the difference, creating either a resilient, happy dog or a timid, anxiety-ridden dog. At three weeks of age, puppies generally haven't entered what is commonly called the "fear period" or "sensitive period." Something that may scare them at seven weeks old might not even warrant a glance when a puppy is three weeks old.

The fear response in the brain begins to develop between five and eight weeks, and you should be highly aware of what your puppy's brain is doing during this period. You need to ensure that all new experiences are calm, safe, and short. Puppies that are "backyard-bred" dogs miss that all-important sense of safety at the most critical times, as do puppy-mill dogs and purebred dogs who are not raised in the home with quality human interaction. A well-rounded puppy will be one that is lucky enough to be born inside the home and tended to with as

It's important for your puppy's new experiences to be linked with positive feelings and memories, not fear! Make sure they feel safe and secure as they explore.

much care as a human infant. As their young brains continue to grow and make predictions about their world, it is crucial that new experiences be associated with positive feelings rather than fear.

Intensive socialization is most effective up to four months of age, though the dog, of course, will continue to learn throughout its life. We cannot stop biology, no matter how hard we try or how much we may want to, and it is impossible for behavior consultants to take your already-troubled adult dog, reset his brain to "puppy settings," and redo all of his early life experiences. There are no do-overs. We can use force-free methods to help him adjust, but what is done to the brain as it forms is done.

The American Veterinary Society of Animal Behavior (AVSAB) knows that puppy socialization is vital—it has even posted a position statement about this topic on its website (you can view it at *www.avsab.org/wp-content/uploads /2019/01/Puppy-Socialization-Position-Statement-FINAL.pdf*). According to AVSAB, the primary and most important time for puppy socialization is in the first three months of life and it should be the standard of care to safely expose the puppy to as many people, places, stimuli, and environments as possible (without causing overstimulation or fear) even before all vaccinations are complete. There are secure ways to socialize your puppy (which I discuss in chapter 6), but a qualified trainer can be the gift of a lifetime for helping you socialize your new housemate.

OUR DOGS NEED PROPER TRAINING

Currently in the U.S., there are no national (or local) certification requirements or education standards for dog trainers. Anyone can claim to be a dog trainer or even a behavior expert, regardless of their knowledge and experience. Add to this the well-intentioned owners who train their dogs themselves based on outdated methods and ideas, and you can see how dogs are at a disadvantage when it comes to learning about behavior and interacting with the world around them.

Further, there is a longstanding, bitter divide in the dog training profession. Many of us—myself included—commit to training without the use of harmful protocols or tools. Other trainers (they sometimes refer to themselves as "balanced trainers") claim that some dogs "just need a firmer hand" and that aversive tools like shock collars, pinch collars, chains, spray bottles, and more are needed to train a dog.

Science does not agree that harsh training methods are better for dogs. Several recent studies looked at how training methods affect a dog. They showed that it does matter how a dog is trained—it matters a lot. One 2020 study[6] came to this conclusion:

> Our results show that companion dogs trained with aversive-based methods experienced poorer welfare during training sessions than dogs trained with reward-based methods. Additionally, dogs trained with higher proportions of aversive-based methods experienced poorer welfare outside the training context than dogs trained with reward-based methods. Moreover, whereas different proportions of aversive-based methods did not result in differences in dog welfare outside the training context among aversive-based schools, a higher proportion of aversive-based methods resulted in poorer welfare during training. ... Critically, our study points to the fact that the welfare of companion dogs trained with aversive-based methods is at risk, especially if these are used in high proportions.

It makes no moral sense to punish a dog for exhibiting canine behavior, even when we don't like the behavior presented. This is not to say that Rover is entitled to eat out of the trash can or knock down your senior parents. Of course, we should train for polite in-home behavior, but we can effectively guide our dogs without resorting to pain. Pain, fear, and

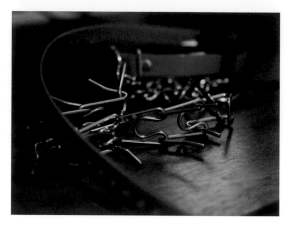

Some trainers use aversive tools like shock or pinch collars, but evidence shows that these methods often cause greater harm.

force most often create new problems or make the existing problems even worse. Many national and international organizations have released position papers regarding the various training methods. For example, the AVSAB has a three-page position paper endorsing reward-based motivational training.[7]

This paper notes that aversive dog training can have acute effects like "stress-related behaviors during training, including tense body, lower body posture, lip licking, tail lowering, lifting front leg, panting, yawning, and yelping" and long-term behavior problems like "aggressive behavior towards people and other dogs, and anxiety-related behaviors such as avoidance and excitability." In other words, if you want to make your dog anxious and miserable, apply force and make your dog fear you. If you want more effective training that results in higher obedience levels and a happier dog, use reward-based training.

---

6   Ana Catarina Vieira de Castro, et al., "Does Training Method Matter? Evidence for the Negative Impact of Aversive-Based Methods on Companion Dog Welfare," *PLOS ONE* 15, No. 12 (December 16, 2020). https://doi.org/10.1371/journal.pone.0225023.

7   You can read this statement at www.vet.osu.edu/vmc/sites/default/files/files/companion/behavior/avsab-humane-dog-training-position-statement-2021.pdf.

Don't Set Unrealistic Expectations for Your Dog

Dogs have been so ubiquitous in our lives that until very recently, we haven't spent much time thinking deeply about them or their specific needs. Yes, we buy them cute doggie coats, cool collars and harnesses, expensive food, chewy treats and toys, and comfy beds, but are those things even on a dog's must-have list? Are we providing the right environment for dogs to safely express their unique and necessary natural behaviors? We know 80% of the world's dogs roam free, so are our in-home pets actually our captives? Zookeepers spend vast amounts of time working hard to ensure that their captive animals have proper enrichment. Shouldn't we do the same for our dogs?

If this book achieves nothing else, I want it to turn the conversation about dogs on its head. We know dogs are amazing creatures who bring incredible joy to our daily lives. One reason we get so upset when unwanted behaviors show up is that we think of our dogs as our best friends and bad behavior shows us that we're failing our friends. We fail dogs in many of the same ways we fail ourselves: we are in too big of a hurry, we want it all and we want it NOW, we are so focused on achieving and acquiring that we have no time left to feel gratitude for what we DO have.

Dogs are frustrated. We expect perfection from our dogs—we want our dogs to be quiet, not chew on things, not jump up to say hi, not run in the house, and not play too roughly. We ask them to join our families and want them to love our friends and only bite bad people that try to hurt

We buy a ton of fancy toys and accessories for our pets, but does all this stuff actually serve to meet their needs and enrich their lives?

us (and we expect the dog to magically know the difference). We also demand that they love all other dogs even without training and adequate early exposure to safe dogs. We spend a great deal of our time with dogs telling them "NO" and "DON'T." We put enormous expectations on them, and they often manage to deliver, at great costs to themselves. But dogs are often set up to fail— we allow puppy mills and backyard breeders, purchase dogs because they're popular, cute, or fit into a "designer" category, and don't prioritize breeding for good health and solid temperaments. We are breeding problems into our dogs and then expecting them not to surface.

Ask an Expert

Trainer and Behavior Expert Helen St. Pierre Discusses Why Dogs Are So Troubled

This interview has been included in its entirety.

Behavior expert Helen St. Pierre has 20 years of experience working with many different dog breeds and operates a senior dog rehome and rescue nonprofit.

▶ **Many dog trainers note anecdotally that they are seeing more troubled dogs than ever before. Are you seeing this in your work as well?**

Yes, I am overwhelmed with how many more difficult dog behavior cases I am seeing on a daily basis. Reactivity, separation issues, aggression, and hyper-arousal are just a few of the main concerns I get called about every day.

▶ **What in your professional experience are some of the top reasons we are seeing so many troubled dogs in our modern world?**

Expectations of our pet dogs have increased dramatically, I think in part due to social media pressure and the images, videos, and reels we now see of dogs doing things that we have decided are the standard of what "good" dogs should be. On top of that, the lack of standardization in the behavior and training industry means that the public has a lot of outdated, misinformed (even if well-meaning), and unregulated information to sift through that is often contradictory. As a result, dogs are often over- or under-socialized, trained with techniques or methods that do more harm than good, and when you couple this with the massive increase of people acquiring dogs, it's not surprising we are seeing what we are seeing.

The other side to this of course is where a lot of dogs are coming from. The demand for certain breeds or mixes has

Reactivity and aggression are the two main issues Helen encounters with her clients. Dog owners have to be willing to put in the time, effort, and patience to work on adjusting these reactions.

created an industry of people capitalizing on the demand and producing animals that are not genetically sound physically or behaviorally. The rescue industry is also in this same boat: though not breeding purposefully, many dogs are not being vetted, evaluated, or regulated properly, so many dogs are going into ill-prepared homes.

▶ What kinds of behavior problems are you seeing the most of?

Reactivity and aggression are my two main complaints from clients, as well as the usual adolescent dog struggles. Although the reality is that the behavior problems I see the most are on the humans' part, not the dogs': lack of understanding of canine development, history, and ethology, not to mention the required patience and time it takes to raise a dog that is nice to live with.

▶ What top three things do you wish potential dog owners knew about how to help a troubled dog?

Management and training go hand in hand. Without adequate management, a dog will continue rehearsing behaviors that the handlers don't like. So, before training can begin, management has to be implemented. Understand that all dogs are individuals. Respecting and listening to your dog's needs and personality, regardless of what the human wants, is the only way to truly start working together as a team. Enrichment is key. Dogs are not made to live sedentary lives. We cannot expect animals that we keep in captivity to conform to our lifestyles because it's what we want. We need to treat them more as a privilege than a right.

▶ How would you describe what a perfect day would look like for a newly adopted dog who is showing signs of anxiety or reactivity?

Bring them home and give them a safe place to observe their new surroundings. Let them settle in and leave them alone. Offer them food, sit beside their space, and read a book to them out loud. Talk quietly and softly, and only interact with them to take them out for the bathroom. Wait until the dog decides to be your friend rather than forcing friendship on the dog. Remember that the dog is the only new thing to the house, but the entire house is new to the dog.

When Stress Is Too Much:
A Look at Thresholds and Exposure to Triggers

Like us, dogs can strongly react when they are pushed over their thresholds. Generally speaking, when dog trainers bring up thresholds, it's in the context of behavior modification work with dogs showing anxiety, stress, fear, or aggression. It can also apply in dog sports, obedience training, and trials, however, as well as in doggie daycares and dog parks.

What is a threshold in this context? It's the distance at which your dog can see, hear, or smell a trigger that is unique to that dog while maintaining emotional control (the dog remains unbothered). A "trigger" is whatever the dog decides is of great concern—something that it feels could be a threat to its well-being. Triggers can be other dogs, cars, loud vehicles, skateboards, children, trash cans, low-flying airplanes—really the sky is the limit.

"Under threshold" is the lovely spot at which your dog can see, hear, or smell something that might regularly trigger a strong reaction, but the dog is able to stay calm, either because of behavior modification work or because the dog perceives the trigger as being at a safe enough distance. "Over threshold" is the point at which the dog's emotional state changes—the dog displays behaviors like barking, lunging, drooling, panting, or attempting to escape the situation.

Many dogs have a self-appointed "dome" of space around them in which they feel safe even if their triggers are in the vicinity (think of a person's "three feet of personal space"—many dogs are in the 10–15-foot range). Every dog is different, however. I have worked with anxious dogs that at first need an American football field

Cats and other small animals are triggers for many dogs (and vice versa). Lunging and barking are a few common signs that your dog may have hit their threshold.

between them and their trigger to even begin behavior modification work. This depends on their life experiences, age, health, and genetic influences, and on how the human handler deals with their over-threshold reactions. Punishing the reactions, for example, often worsens the situation and does nothing to assure the dog that they are safe from the threat. The handler adds fear, and the dog associates the trigger with punishment, making it feel like even more of a danger. The best methods are behavior modification and the other smart, effective, force-free methods discussed in chapter 4.

Oblivious pet owners can also quite easily push an anxious dog over threshold without trying (sometimes it happens to a dog on every walk). Most of us become deeply embarrassed or frustrated by not being able to control our dog, feelings that then affect how we treat our dog. Repeated exposure to triggers also elevates stress hormones, which take hours or even days to come back down. If you are walking your fearful dog every day, and every day a trigger gets too close (such as other dogs being walked nearby), your dog's system never has a chance to come back down from that highly stressed state. The dog may not even demonstrate a dramatic display of stressed behavior. Dogs can be very subtle in their responses and it's usually only the over-the-top responses that make owners pick up the phone and call the professionals for help.

The number one thing an anxious dog needs is to be given a sense of safety in its home and in the world. For this reason, I sometimes suggest an owner stop walking their dog in public for one to six months. I ask them to first focus on increasing their dog's sense of safety at home, then tackling the world at large. Some owners come to learn that their dog is perfectly happy with their well-designed home life and don't want to venture into the outside world. I often suggest taking breaks from dog sports, doggie day cares, and dog parks at first for the same reason—it takes a highly social and well socialized dog to enjoy these types of potential canine chaos.

Another concept dog trainers talk about a lot is "trigger stacking." Trigger stacking is when stressor after stressor after stressor affects a dog throughout the day until the animal

Some dogs are triggered by common things they might experience on their daily walk (including other dogs just walking calmly nearby). This daily exposure can create a constant feeling of anxiety and high stress in the dog.

hits their limit and goes over threshold. Their responses will often be sharp, loud, extreme, and even hysterical (a human example would be experiencing an ugly case of road rage after staying up all night with a sick child, worrying about your mother in the nursing home, then spending your whole day putting out fires at work).

We often don't pay enough attention to the triggers that cause stress to our canine housemates. An over-threshold event can seem to "appear out of nowhere" to the owner, but the dog could have been building up to it for days (maybe a loud thunderstorm on Thursday, a sick infant in the home screaming all day Friday, kids on bikes flying past him on his Saturday walk, and a loose-leash dog barreling into him on Sunday). The dog's nerves could be "shot" after all of these stressful experiences, and when on Monday the owner accidentally drops a glass, the dog might explode into a HUGE reaction. It is crucial for owners to be aware of their dog's threshold levels and be on the lookout for possible trigger stacking.

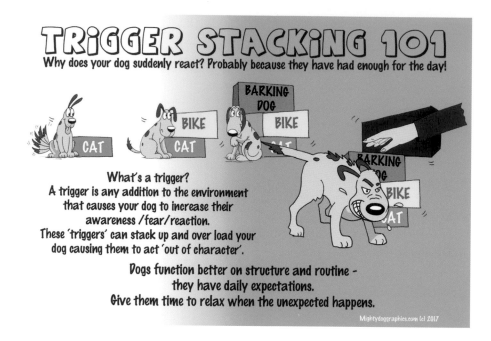

TRIGGER STACKING 101

Why does your dog suddenly react? Probably because they have had enough for the day!

BARKING DOG
BIKE
CAT

What's a trigger?
A trigger is any addition to the environment that causes your dog to increase their awareness/fear/reaction.
These 'triggers' can stack up and over load your dog causing them to act 'out of character'.

Dogs function better on structure and routine - they have daily expectations.
Give them time to relax when the unexpected happens.

Mightydoggraphics.com (c) 2017

OUR DOGS NEED MORE EXERCISE AND STIMULATION

Whether an energetic sporting dog, a more docile companion breed, or any mix in between, all dogs need a certain amount of physical activity and mental stimulation, which will vary from dog to dog. Whatever their background, dogs are meant to expend their energy in constructive (not destructive!) ways. As pet owners, we must provide these opportunities for our dogs for their overall well-being.

> Every single dog needs and deserves mental and physical stimulation every single day.

So, while we tend to have busy lives full of work, appointments, and errands, what do our dogs have to occupy their days? In reality, not that much. It can feel to trainers like people get a dog and expect it to

sleep all day, wait patiently for a single 10-minute walk, then sit quietly the whole rest of the night. How B-O-R-I-N-G. Some dogs may have mind puzzle games or good things to chew on, but how much time do these really fill? Dogs have serious energy requirements. Some active dogs—such as herding dogs and always-ready-to-go Huskies— have a very high need for mental and physical stimulation. Other breeds such as pugs or Maltese may need less stimulation, but they are not stuffed dogs—they still require mental engagement. The amount of stimulation needed changes from dog to dog, but every single dog needs and deserves mental and physical stimulation every single day.

Dogs who do not get enough daily stimulation will seek ways to alleviate their boredom and frustration. The unwanted behaviors caused by a lack of engagement run the gamut from excessive barking to OCD-type behaviors. A lack of stimulation and exercise also raises obesity levels in dogs (something that continues to rise year after year). Just like in

Compared to a human's busy day, our dogs just don't have that much to do. Many bad behaviors can grow out of this boredom.

humans, obesity leads to many health concerns, including heart problems, diabetes, and inflammation.

If you do an internet search to find out how much exercise your dog needs, you'll find a range of thirty minutes to two hours, but, as with everything, it depends on the dog. Some dogs, in fact, get triggered on every single outing and their stress hormones are always elevated, so too much or the wrong type of stimulation can be the cause of their behavior issues. The information on the internet neglects to explain and talk about the merits of different types of stimulation. For example, I am a big "nose work" enthusiast—sniffing makes the dog brain happy and tends to tire out a dog much quicker than a long run. We have an obligation to find the types of activities that engage and stimulate our individual dogs.

I am not here to shame anyone—instead I want to inspire owners to ask probing questions about the quality of their dogs' lives and highlight modern solutions. Dogs need our help—and we *can* help them. Helping begins when we take a hard look at the dog's environment and whether that environment is truly serving the dog. If it isn't, we need to first ask ourselves how we can improve that environment, rather than expecting and demanding that they adapt to an unadaptable landscape.

For the first time in a long time, I feel optimistic that people are asking the right questions to help dogs live alongside us in a way that makes sense for both species. New solutions and insights are being explored every day, and I am so excited to share these new concepts, training protocols, and success stories with you throughout the rest of the book.

It's important to find activities that work with your dog's personality and drives to help keep their minds and bodies active. This could be going for a run or a hike, but it can be as simple as using interactive toys and mats or trick training.

Veterinary Behaviorist Dr. Amy Pike on Common Behavior Problems in Dogs and How to Work with a Veterinary Behaviorist

This interview has been included in its entirety.

Dr. Amy Pike is one of less than 100 board-certified veterinary behaviorists around the globe.

▶ **What are the most common types of troubled behavior you are seeing in dogs?**

Fears or phobias and aggression are the two most common types of behavior problems that I see in canines. If I had to break it down to the two most common diagnoses, it would be fear-based aggression toward unfamiliar people and fear-based aggression toward unfamiliar dogs. A close third would be separation anxiety.

▶ **What in your professional experience are the top reasons we are seeing so many troubled dogs?**

The level of expectations placed on the canine species we share our homes with has evolved over the years I have been in practice. We used to treat dogs like dogs—they did dog things, and we understood this as the dog just being a dog. Now, owners tend to treat dogs more like human children. While this has been good in some respects with owners now investing much more into the care and welfare of their pets, it has come with some unrealistic expectations of their pets, as well. For example, I constantly hear from owners who say that their dog should never growl at or bite someone. I explain how aggression is merely a behavioral strategy, and that while this is an unwanted behavior from our standpoint, it is a very normal behavior for a dog to employ when they are scared or lack control over their body or environment. When the owners understand the emotional underpinnings of aggression, it makes more sense to them why their dog feels certain ways about things (ways that human kids do not).

I also think that the rescue and no-kill sheltering movement has shifted things in our world, as well. When I was first in practice 20 years ago, shelters and rescue organizations would not have adopted out many of the patients that I see get adopted out on a daily basis. If there was any inkling of aggression or behavior problems, either historical or present in the shelter, the animal was euthanized. Again, this is one of

Many modern dog owners treat their dogs like human children, without understanding the important ways a dog's emotions and reactions differ from those of a human child.

those shifts that is really a double-edged sword. Many of the pets that would have previously been euthanized, if placed in the right environment and ensuring their needs were being met, could have easily been adopted out. Unfortunately, the shift, in some cases, has gone too far the other way, and I see animals adopted out that are downright dangerous, impossible to live with, suffering with emotional disorders, or are simply adopted into the wrong family or environment.

▶ **Can owners schedule an appointment directly with a veterinary behaviorist or are most appointments referrals from other veterinarians? What do veterinary behaviorists need most from dog owners before and during an appointment?**

Owners can absolutely schedule an appointment with a veterinary behaviorist directly. However, most of my clients come from referrals from their veterinarian or trainer when it is realized that the problem goes above and beyond something a general practitioner or a qualified trainer can handle.

The biggest thing that I ask of my clients is open, honest communication. I need them to tell me if they may have reacted to their dog in a way that was not ideal (for example, hitting or yelling at the dog, shocking it for performing certain behaviors, etc.) so we can not only discuss how they can modify their own behavior in the future, but also understand why things may have worsened after that response. I also need them to be honest with me about how much time and financial and emotional effort they can put into a treatment plan. If they have already reached their breaking point for rehoming or behavioral euthanasia, it is important that I know this so I can appropriately support them as well. And while I ask that honesty of them, I am also honest with them—if this pet can no longer live in their home or truly needs a better environment to thrive, I will tell them that.

▶ **Are you optimistic or pessimistic about the future well-being of our pet dogs?**

I am highly optimistic about the future well-being of our pet dogs. I think the newest generation of pet owners is more highly committed to their pet's welfare than ever before. Not only that, but they are much more open to seeking care from a veterinary behaviorist and including psychotropic medication as a part of that treatment plan, to the benefit of our anxious canine companions. I am also seeing a big shift away from aversive training techniques in the up-and-coming generations—they may not understand the specifics as to why we want to avoid using those techniques and tools, but their brains, their guts, and their hearts tell them to not use these methods on their beloved family members.

▶ **What do you love most about your work?**

The connections I get with the families. We joke that we often know our clients are pregnant before their own family does because we get involved helping to prepare the pet for the impending change. We hear about kids graduating from college, heading off into the military, or the sister-in-law who won't move out of their basement, etc. To be such an integral part of that pet's life is such an honor that my clients grant me each and every day. It's why I get out of bed every day.

The Most Common Types of Canine Aggression

Dogs present a vast array of behaviors. Trainers will tell owners that "any dog can bite," and that is true (all dogs have teeth!). Any dog can also dig, bark, growl, and exhibit predatory behavior, depending on the circumstances. Aggressive behavior is probably the most troubling to owners, since it is frightening and can be dangerous. In this chapter, I'll discuss common types of canine aggression and how humans contribute to it (in many cases unknowingly), and I'll explain the differences between aggression, fear, and reactivity, which can be difficult to decipher.

We are the judges of what is acceptable behavior for our dogs and what is not, but the question quickly becomes: do we have enough in-depth understanding of canine behavior to judge their actions? Most of us readily agree that biting and harming other dogs or humans is unacceptable. But what about a dog who bites to defend herself from being kicked by a person? Or a dog who gently "mouths" your hand but never bites? How about a terrier who's a "good dog" for ridding the barn of rodents and snakes but also chases and tries to kill chickens? How does the dog know which animals are off-limits? She doesn't—it's our responsibility to teach her the difference.

Further, our behavior changes as our environment changes, and the same thing happens to dogs. In fact, I believe dogs are affected by this even more than humans, because dogs have less control over their circumstances. Imagine moving to a new town: moving is stressful for humans, but all a dog knows is that suddenly he's in a different place and doesn't know why. His home is no longer his home, and everything is new and scary again. Is it so surprising that a dog might show a fearful or aggressive reaction?

In this chapter, learn about common types of aggression and the difference between aggression and fear:

Dogs require time and training to learn how to appropriately act on their instincts. A working terrier, for example, needs to be taught that chickens should be protected, not chased.

This Border Collie might look aggressive to some observers since he is showing his teeth—but body language must be taken in context. He was simply yawning when this photo was taken and not showing any aggression.

According to the *Merck Manual of Veterinary Behavior*, canine aggression accounts for 70% of the caseload for referral practices. It's interesting, but sad, that this is the number one behavior concern and that many owners don't understand it very clearly. So what exactly is—and is not—aggression?

Many "aggressive behaviors" that owners report, such as lunging, barking, or growling at approaching dogs or people often come from a place of fear or frustration. When a dog uses this kind of behavior, she is, in effect, letting us know how uncomfortable she is. Often, before displaying these "big" behaviors, she's already tried to let us know about her discomfort in subtler ways, using canine language. If these "whispers" don't get our attention, the dog raises her hackles and looks threatening.

Such behaviors are often reinforced by how the dog perceives the results. For example, you're out for a walk with your dog. Another dog and owner are walking toward you, your dog starts barking, and the other person and dog cross the street (whether or not because of your dog's barking). Your dog will infer that it was her behavior that made them go away. She will have learned that barking "works" to get rid of the trigger. While we may see this as aggressive behavior, it's simply a "trapped" on-leash dog protecting herself in the way she thinks works best.

Dogs show so many types of aggression because we put them in "unnatural" environments in which they feel the need to protect themselves. Some dogs also get a stronger dose of predatory-response genes, and still others have been selectively bred to be protective. In fact, some American Kennel Club breed standards specify that dogs of these breeds will be "wary of strangers." Now, a dog that is "wary of strangers" does not sound like the ideal family-friendly dog, yet so many of these breeds live with families and are expected by their owners to not show these innate behaviors (unless there is an actual threat to the family).

No matter what type of behavior the dog displays, the owner must realize that they are one of the most critical things affecting a dog's environment and outlook on life—not other dogs, pesky squirrels, or excitable children. The owner. After all, there are two ends of the leash, and both the dog and the human need to adapt and be flexible for training to work. If your dog displays undesired behavior, you won't be able to change it unless you are wise, patient, and educated on the matter. In my work with dogs, I focus on the human's behavior every bit as much as the canine's. We are in this together, for better or for worse, so let's learn to recognize the different types of aggression and our role in it.

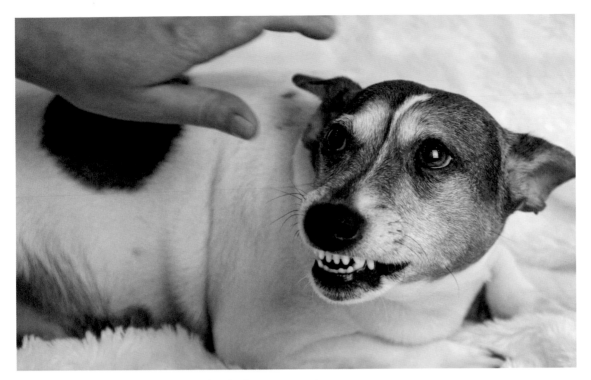
Fear is a common starting point that can develop into an aggressive response.

FEAR-RELATED AGGRESSION

Fear-related aggression is generally considered to be the most common form of aggression seen in modern dogs. Each dog is an individual, so their triggers for displaying over-the-top reactions are unique to each. Most often it is other dogs coming toward them, but it can be children, skateboards, bikes, or anything new the dog is unfamiliar with. I once had a sweet Golden Retriever client dog that I considered to be "bomb proof" look up at the ceiling in a hardware store and suddenly lose her marbles and begin trying to run backward, yelping in fear. I looked up and saw a Halloween witch decoration hanging from the ceiling. Most dogs will seek to avoid seeing, hearing, or smelling their triggers by backing away like this, but they often cannot because they are leashed or confined in some way.

Potential causes include genetic influences, inadequate socialization, reinforcement of the displayed behavior (often unintentional), allowing no means of escaping the threat, and harmful training protocols that cause the dog to associate the trigger with a specific negative outcome (if the reactive dog is punished in some way for their fear reaction).

How Humans Contribute
- Poor breeding practices
- Not offering proper neonatal and early puppy care
- Not offering proper early socialization
- Introducing new stimuli improperly
- Expecting dogs to accept all new stimuli
- Not understanding dogs' fear behavior
- Punishing dogs for fear behavior

Behaviorist Dale McLelland on Working with Troubled Dogs

This interview has been included in its entirety

Scottish behavior expert Dale McLelland with one of her rescue Rottweilers named Theo. She rescued him from an abusive situation and helped him overcome his fear issues. He went on to become one of her training partners and a true gentle giant.

▶ **What piqued your interest initially about working with troubled dogs?**

It wasn't a conscious decision, it just seemed to grow from the desire to understand more about dogs and why their behaviors may be different from what we expect or from what we would consider to be the norm. Before I see them, many of the dogs I work with have been through the usual routes: training classes and using various methods and approaches without success. I always wanted to know what the dog really needed instead of trying to find a magic formula or new method that would "work." The answer is often right in front of us—the dog is always telling us something, we simply need to be much better at listening. The more dogs I saw and worked with, the more questions I had and the more I needed to learn. After all, we have a duty of care and must look for ways to support dogs when they are clearly struggling.

▶ **Are you seeing a sharp increase in your practice of more and more troubled dogs? If yes, what are the most common behavior concerns you are seeing?**

Most of the dogs I saw previously were sensitive dogs that found what we consider to be everyday life to be a challenge. That is still the case, and there are more requests for help than ever before. That may be down to several factors ranging from greater awareness about seeking help, to the greater pressures of life and, of course, greater expectations of appropriate dog behavior. Dogs struggling with novelty is a huge issue, which may be meeting or seeing new dogs, new people, or being put into new situations with which they have no experience to compare. I would say that an increasing trend seems to be more guardians and family members being bitten by their own dogs. That brings with it additional stresses and emotional trauma.

▶ What in your professional experience are some of the most pressing causes of modern-day stress in dogs?

It's so hard to pinpoint. Many factors and variables contribute to stress and trauma in domestic dogs. Living with humans in a human-orientated world isn't always easy. Additionally, there is a greater number of dogs in the population than ever before. The relative ease with which a dog can be purchased, the fact that many start their lives in less-than-ideal situations, the increased stress of owners, and owners' unrealistically high expectations but low understanding of canine behavior all combine to create a life for dogs that can be challenging. Dogs are not perfect little individuals—they do dog things—and their stresses must be unbearable at times. It seems an obvious thing to state that dogs need to be able to simply be dogs but sadly, it does need repeating.

▶ What are the top three things you advise owners to do when they finally understand that they are living with a troubled dog, especially a reactive dog?

There is enormous pressure on guardians to have the perfect dog and realizing that your dog might not fit that picture can cause stress, anxiety, and embarrassment. We know that dogs are often seen as extensions of ourselves, and a dog that bites, fights, or lunges is not the image that any responsible guardian would want to portray; this can lead to even more pressure to "do something about it."

My top three pieces of advice would be:

1. Accept that this does not mean that there is something wrong with your dog and instead look objectively at the situation.
2. Avoid apportioning blame. The behavior is generally not anyone's fault; it is what it is, and the dog is providing you with important information.
3. Recognize that allowances will have to be made. Large-scale change can feel overwhelming, but smaller steps can lead to much better outcomes.

▶ The dog training industry is currently evolving at a fast pace and new ideas about training are being considered all over the world. What changes are you seeing? Do you have some favorite new ways to help troubled dogs?

We are seeing the shift from a traditional model to a more holistic view of dog behavior—nothing happens in isolation after all. So many events and factors contribute to the way a dog may behave in any given situation that only looking at the observable behavior can give a blinkered view of the situation. Simply attempting to change that observable behavior to a more "desirable" one is solely solution-focused and based on partial information. We know that the dog is experiencing the world, interactions, and training methods. These things will generate an emotional reaction; the behavior that we see is not always an indicator of the internal experience of the dog in question. I may smile in response to a question being asked, but that doesn't mean I feel happy. It's important to consider how this situation feels for the dog: are they coping, are they being forced into using certain behaviors to deal with the unknown, and can we help them feel less threatened?

In general, dog training approaches can be too quick to jump in with activities and solutions—dogs need time to process information. If we are constantly interrupting this normal brain activity, we can inflame situations rather than diffusing them. I am a great believer in allowing dogs the time they need to process information, not marking and treating (which can be useful in some situations), but simply enabling them to build up a mental picture of the world in complete safety.

Sometimes what a dog needs most is just time and a safe space from which they can process and learn about the world around them.

Sometimes a puppy's energy is too much for a mature dog and they warn the puppy with teeth exposed. Both dogs here are showing teeth but aren't harming or intending to harm one another.

CANINE-TO-CANINE AGGRESSION

One of the most distressing calls I get from concerned owners involves dogs in the same household fighting with each other. Often it happens when a new dog enters the household, but even more troubling for owners is when two dogs who have gotten along for years suddenly start fighting. These fights are enormously stressful for everyone and often stun the dog owner: how could these two friends attack one another? Why? There are many reasons, including tight spaces, barriers, social maturity, physical pain in one or both dogs, age-related deficiencies, a lack of impulse control, resource guarding, redirected aggression, poor dog-to-dog communication skills, jealousy, bullying, genes, poor early socialization, or dramatic changes in living conditions. Aggression toward unfamiliar dogs can start from a place of fear (or pain) but can also come from these other influences or territorial aggression.

How Humans Contribute

- Poor breeding practices
- Not offering proper neonatal and puppy care
- Not offering proper early socialization
- Not offering safe early introductions to other dogs
- Ignoring health- or age-related issues
- Improperly introducing a new dog into the home
- Expecting friendly behavior toward all other dogs
- Incorrectly interpreting canine communication (on the part of humans and other dogs)

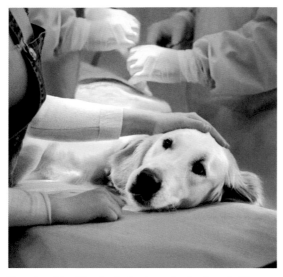

Dogs tend to hide physical pain and a dog in pain (like a human in pain) can be afraid and irritable—potentially causing aggressive responses. The first step in addressing behavior concerns with your dog should always be a visit to the vet.

PAIN AND MEDICAL AGGRESSION

Dogs innately tend to hide their physical pain. It's a leftover trait from being in the wild, as limping animals broadcast that they are easy prey. The first thing trainers ask of our clients is to schedule a vet visit to rule out any pain or health-related causes. This is especially vital if the aggression appears suddenly and is out of the ordinary for that dog. Think about how awful we feel when we have severe back or nerve pain, for example. We can get crabby when we are hurting, and so can dogs. Conditions like arthritis, thyroid disease, hip dysplasia, organ disfunction, cancers, pancreatitis, tumors, menstrual pain, and pregnancy are just a few of the possible contributors to aggression. Dog owners should always train their dogs to be comfortable wearing a muzzle for instances like these, since even the best dog in the world is capable of biting while in deep pain.

How Humans Contribute

- Poor breeding practices
- Not recognizing subtle pain responses
- Not understanding behavior issues that can accompany pain
- Not seeking veterinary attention
- Punishing a dog who is in pain

RESOURCE GUARDING

Resource guarding shows up when a person or another dog tries to remove an object (food, toys, treats, etc.) from a dog who views the object as important and valuable. The dog might hunch over the object, put a paw over it, give a hard stare, growl as a warning, and even bite in exasperation.

Each dog decides which resources are of vital importance to them and which are not. It is more abnormal for a dog to *not* want to protect a juicy

This dog is showing a clear message by hunching over the toy and displaying possessive, warning behaviors: this toy is MINE!

bone than it is to see a dog happily enjoy another dog or person taking the bone out of its mouth (please don't do this—it is terribly rude). Some common items dogs tend to guard include their favorite human, bones, food, toys, dog beds, furniture, and sometimes even seemingly unimportant things like water bowls. (We humans are often the same—one of the first words we learn is "*mine*"!) We can more easily teach cooperation and sharing to human children since they can clearly show us exactly what is important to them, and we can also attempt to reason with them if needed.

Genes and early experiences contribute to resource guarding in dogs. A hungry puppy experiencing a scarcity of resources leads to a world of trouble when the dog grows into an adult. If the owner uses punishment or anger when the dog shows resource guarding behavior, it will escalate the problem.

How Humans Contribute

- Poor breeding practices
- Lack of proper early socialization
- Lack of proper training
- Expecting a dog to willingly give up resources (toys, food, etc.)
- Not trading (giving the dog an item to replace what you took away)
- Not understanding how important resources are to dogs
- Punishing guarding behavior

AROUSAL AGGRESSION

If you've been to a dog park more than once, it's likely you've seen two dogs having a great time running helter-skelter through the park when one of them suddenly turns on the other dog. Dogs and puppies can easily become over-aroused, and because they can't yell out "STOP THIS, I AM UNCOMFORTABLE," they use their canine communication skills to end the situation. I shared my life with a pair of amazing Border Collie siblings who never had a fight and rarely had disagreements. However, every time they went swimming in our pond, they would get the "zoomies" and run and chase one another. Whenever my female had enough of her brother chasing her, she'd air snap at him. Sometimes they would stand on their hind legs and "box" one another (though this was short-lived, and they never hurt each other). Secure and controlled puppy play dates with safe dogs can help to minimize this response.

We've all seen dogs playing with one another, but if one of the dogs becomes "overloaded" and decides they are done with playtime, they may show aggression as a way to stop all the excitement.

How Humans Contribute

- Not noticing dogs' signs of over-arousal
- Expecting dogs to always control their emotions
- Not taking precautions in public places
- Permitting new dogs into your dog's space without precautions
- Letting "dogs be dogs" and work out issues on their own

TERRITORIAL AGGRESSION

Certain breeds have been bred over centuries to guard our bodies, our homes, and our possessions. Some dogs were bred to be warriors on the battlefield. And other dogs may be small in size, but still have the drive to fight when their territory is under threat (even if the threat is all in their own minds). Territorial aggression is not usually based in fear (although fear can be a component). The dog isn't seeking to escape the perceived threat but is instead defending its home turf (including the home, the yard, and even the car).

We humans have historically valued this trait to the extent that we purchase very expensive, highly trained self-protection dogs. My first dog in college was a 95-pound male Rottweiler who I purposefully chose for self-protection as a young woman living alone. Even though I lacked knowledge of how to train him for that role, I was lucky that he naturally fulfilled it—he saved my life from imminent threat twice (including once when he scared away an intruder who had broken into all the surrounding condos). Untrained territorial dogs often have issues, however, especially when they deem everything and everyone near their territory as a threat. Protective guard dogs serve a valuable role, but they do not always make the best family pets.

How Humans Contribute

- Breeding for protective behavior and territorial aggression
- Punishing instead of redirecting/retraining
- Expecting protective behavior with no aggression
- Not understanding the difference between fear and territorial responses

Territorial protection is bred into some breeds. It's often a good thing until it isn't—should the dog bite someone or another dog intruding on its territory.

Maternal Aggression

We've all heard the expression "Mama Bear," and for good reason. Most mother animals (although, for a variety of reasons, including poor health, not all) come hard-wired to protect their offspring, but a feeling of maternal safety is important *WELL* before the puppies are born (since we know, as discussed in chapter 1, that mothers can pass stress hormones to puppies). Giving birth is hard physical labor and it comes with a lot of hormonal activity. Raising your offspring is a lot of work. It is vital to give nursing mothers and their puppies a quiet, safe place to exist.

Note: Sometimes people think of maternal aggression as a mother dog eating her puppies. That is enormously rare, however—imagine how much strain and stress the poor mother dog would have to feel to engage in that extreme behavior.

All mother dogs have a natural instinct to be protective of their puppies. Ensuring that a mother feels safe and secure during her pregnancy and throughout her puppies' early developmental stages will help prevent maternal aggression.

How Humans Contribute

- Poor breeding practices that are stressful or unhealthy for the mother

- Not providing a quiet, safe space for the mother and her puppies

- Not limiting maternal stress

- Not caring for the mother and puppies inside the home

Predatory Aggression

If you have seen online videos of sudden attacks from dogs—whether targeting an animal or a person—you know how scary they can appear. Hunting, like all types of aggression, is a natural canine behavior that presents differently in different dogs. When I lived on a large Texas ranch, my male Border Collie sniffed out a nest of newborn wild rabbits. He nudged them softly with his nose and went on with his walk. My very calm, very sweet, and very large Shiloh Shepherd, however, immediately ran over and ate every baby rabbit before I could reach him. I never saw that behavior in him before or after, but in that instant, nature took over.

Predatory aggression isn't based in an emotional outburst like the other kinds of aggression; it is most often silent since it would do the hunter no good to alert their prey. Dogs are born predators—unlike prey animals such as horses or deer they come prewired to hunt. Humans have tried breeding that instinct out of many of our dogs, however. A working Border Collie follows the instinctual predation sequence, but we have bred out the biting and killing part of the sequence. You can, however, come across a Border Collie who still retains a killer's instinct and acts upon it. In fact, any breed of dog (including mixed-breed dogs) can exhibit predatory aggression—it is not limited to a certain type.

A normal predatory canine sequence includes staring, stalking, chasing, biting, and then killing. It's even more frightening when a dog skips steps. Often there is a genetic component that releases this behavior. Sometimes there is something terribly wrong inside the dog, such as a brain tumor or other health factor. Trainers are sadly seeing more and more "good" dogs seemingly lose their self-control and bite their human companions (sometimes even killing them). Considering the millions of dogs with whom we share our lives, however, this is still very rare.

Sometimes these dogs land in rescues or shelters, and the very best organizations will not rehome dogs that have shown aggression and have serious bite records. However, the problem of well-meaning but gravely misinformed rescues rehoming dangerous dogs is growing, and caring families pay the price. Along with enormous pain and heartbreak, there are legal ramifications involved if you find yourself living with a dog who bites. It is well worth the trouble to ask many questions about any dog you plan to bring into your home, no matter where the dog comes from. If a dog has a "hard" mouth and is willing to chomp down on a person or another animal, that is generally not something that can be reversed with behavior modification or medication.

How Humans Contribute

- Poor breeding practices, including breeding fighting dogs

- Not providing prenatal care

- Not socializing puppies

- Separating puppies from their mother and siblings before learning bite inhibition

- Not using muzzles when needed

- Not understanding dogs' predatory instincts

Any breed of dog can show predatory aggression—they all have a certain level of that innate hunting instinct.

Dogs often show signs of aggression if they are on leash (can't run away) and feel threatened. These extreme reactions often scare other dogs or people, reinforcing the dog's sense that this type of response works.

AGGRESSION VERSUS REACTIVITY AND FEAR BEHAVIOR

Before we look more closely at the types of aggression our dogs can display, we need to differentiate between aggressive behaviors and reactive behaviors.

A reactive dog is one who responds to normal events in her environment with a higher-than-normal level of intensity. Some of these reactions include barking, whining, lunging, hypervigilance, panting, pacing, restlessness, and difficulty responding to her owner (even to well-known cues like "sit"). Reactivity is generally based in a fear or anxiety response. When the brain is faced with fearful or threatening stimulus and the fight-or-flight hormones are flowing, all their training is thrown out the window and the brain and body work overtime to self-protect. In a reactive dog, this

same fight-or-flight reflex kicks in whether there is an actual threat present or not. From the dog's perspective, the threat is very real. It's rather like you coming around a bend on your peaceful mountain hike and coming face-to-face with a grizzly bear. If I asked you to solve a math problem with a grizzly bear in front of you, you probably wouldn't even hear my question—your brain would primarily be seeking a way out of the imminent danger.

Which dog behaviors count as aggressive? I use the definition that Dr. James O'Heare, DLBC, uses in his book, *Aggressive Behavior in Dogs: A Comprehensive Technical Manual for Professionals*: "Aggression is defined as attacks, attempted attacks, or threats of attacks by one individual directed at another individual." Aggression has been described as a forceful pursuit of one's interests that can include violent or hostile behavior toward another

Imagine coming around the corner of a hiking trail and seeing this—a reactive dog feels that same tension and anxiety much of the time.

or a group. Full-throttle aggression in a pet dog is rather rare, but it does occur and is a natural behavior. It's the kind of behavior that makes you gasp when you see it (even in videos). If you have ever been on the receiving end of a hard, aggressive canine stare, you will never forget it. Your body instinctively feels the heat, and the hair on the back of your neck stands on end (*if* you even have enough time to respond before the dog's threat turns to action).

As we examine types of canine aggression and reactivity, it is important to realize that dogs don't wake up on a random Saturday and decide they will exhibit X, Y, or Z aggression. They live in the moment and respond to stimuli in their environments. There's also rarely one clear type of reaction shown—a dog can start off as reactive and fearful, then feel pushed to defend itself to such a degree that it attacks the threat (even if the dog is still terrified).

This German Shepherd is exhibiting signs of fear: hunched body, tail tucked close in, ears back, whites visible around the eyes, and mouth shut tight.

The Healing Power of Three—the Owner, the Veterinarian, and the Professional Trainer

The three most influential people in a troubled dog's life are the owner, the veterinarian, and a well-qualified trainer. This chapter looks at the power of this influential-person trio and breaks down what each person needs from the others to create the best possible outcome for your dog. It's important to find a good veterinarian to discern if the dog has any medical problems that are contributing to behavior issues. The vet's findings, combined with the help of a qualified force-free trainer, can put the dog on a speedy path to healing. It can seem hard to find the right trainer and veterinarian for you and your dog—but it can be done.

THE OWNER

You, the owner, are the most influential and important person in your dog's life. You live with Fido day in and day out while the veterinarian and the trainer might only see your dog a few hours each year. In fact, because of the growing number of available internet consultations, it is entirely possible that these two participants in your dog's life might only see your dog via video conference in a given year.

You also have the emotional bond with your dog. While the professionals have seen and helped thousands of dogs over their careers, you see your dog every day. You are the first person who recognizes behavior changes or possible physical problems. You are your dog's guide, benefactor, guardian, and number one source of love, joy, and engagement. Never devalue your role in your dog's life (and never allow anyone else to do so either).

These days there can be a lot of pressure to be an educated and compassionate dog guardian. Hopefully this book is a stepping stone to help reduce stress for both you and your dog. If you've made it this far, you already have more practical information to help your dog than many dog owners. Remember that you have every right to ask professionals about their education, experience, and how they will treat your dog.

You are the most important person in your dog's life, and you're the first one who will notice behavioral changes or possible physical problems.

Be certain to research professionals you're thinking about hiring to work with your dog (groomers, trainers, etc.). Check their history and certifications and call them to ask questions directly and find out more about their approach

One hurdle facing owners is knowing where to find accurate information. The first step for many is the internet. Search engines are great for some things, but they can become problematic in a hurry if your search requires more detail. Companies can purchase advertisements to appear higher on the results page—which some internet browsers might mistake as a sign of value. A trainer or veterinarian having paid to appear at the top of the page gives you zero information on their experience, education, and methods—you are as likely to see a highly trained veterinary behaviorist as you are someone with no credentials but a good advertising team. (Chapter 10 discusses who you can trust as training partners and what questions to ask potential professional training partners.)

One personal rule I follow is to never leave my dog with another person unsupervised. In the rare cases in which it is required—such as with a groomer—I do tons of homework first—researching their credentials, experience, and philosophy—then I call them and ask a lot of questions. I most often employ a mobile dog groomer who agrees to either allow me to stay in the wash van or come in from time to time. If your dog is going to be more comfortable with you present, stay. I follow these steps with *anyone* who will have contact with my dog (including doggie day cares, dog walkers, and pet sitters). The goal is to communicate how you expect your dog to be handled and to become an expert at evaluating how professionals answer your questions.

It is both good and bad that we humans are the number one source of, well, everything for the dogs who live with us. If we get it wrong, both species can suffer, but if we really, really get it wrong, one of the species faces a dangerous risk of losing their life.

Your vulnerable puppy needs a quality team of professionals as they grow up. Little Finn came to me at just 5½ weeks old and needed months of extra care and time to adjust to his new life.

Depending on your lifestyle, formal obedience training is optional. Quality veterinary care, however, is necessary for the life of your dog.

Many people also claim to be experts simply because they've lived with dogs. Having lived with many dogs is not the same thing as becoming a credentialed behavior expert or veterinarian. Often, they resort to quick-fix solutions like using pain and punishment for unwanted behavior instead of slowing down and evaluating why the dog is behaving a certain way and how to alleviate the dog's stress reactions.

Look for professionals that will truly be members of your team, working toward the health and well-being of your beloved dog. The first professional you find may have more training and experience than you (this is why they are experts, after all) but if they don't show compassionate communication, keep searching until you find the right people to build the right team for you and for your dog.

THE VETERINARIAN

While obedience training might be optional for many dog owners (for example, many can live with a dog who pulls on leash or jumps on visitors), when your dog is injured, sick, or needs vaccinations, you must see a veterinarian.

I admire veterinarians. They have a terribly difficult and stressful job and most veterinarians need a heroic nature to survive. They work with several different species of clients who can't tell them with words what the problem is, and they often have two anxious clients: the human and the pet. The American Veterinary Medical Association (AMVA) estimates that 1 in 6 veterinarians have contemplated suicide and a recent study found that veterinarians are 2.7 times more likely than the public to die by suicide.[1]

---

1   "Merck Animal Health Veterinary Wellbeing Study III," *Merck Animal Health*, January 2022, https://www.merck-animal-health-usa.com/about-us/veterinary-wellbeing-study.

What Trainers and Veterinarians Need from Owners

The following are a few of the most important things trainers and veterinarians need from owners, based on information shared with me by trainers and veterinarians over the past 20 years:

- A lot of the strife between humans and dogs can be reduced if we consider life from our dog's perspective.

- Even though you are the true expert on your dog—that is not the same as being a veterinarian or a trainer, both of whom are trained to play different roles in your dog's life.

- Please be up-front about your ability to stick to any plan set by your trainer or veterinarian.

- **Leash your dog in public places!** Leashes exist for the safety of all of us.

- Have special training and vet visit treats (their favorite meats or cheeses) on hand for appointments.

- Trainers and veterinarians have busy lives, families, and obligations, just like you.

- Please start proper socialization and positive reinforcement with your dog at a young age. Even better, consult with professionals *before* bringing your dog home.

- Understand your whole dog and all their needs. Dogs need proper exercise, enrichment, and fun daily activities.

- Take your dog's breed into account (even mixed breeds). Don't expect a Rottweiler to be a Golden Retriever.

- Know your dog well and be honest about it. If you feel your dog might react with teeth or fear to handling or training, let the person working with them know this.

- Work on building resiliency in your dog through a wide range of experiences so that he will be better able to handle veterinary exams and training protocols.

- Muzzle train and crate train your dog so that if either should ever be necessary, they won't cause undue stress.

- Understand that working with serious behavior issues takes time. There are no magic solutions, despite what you may see on TV.

- We love it when you are dedicated to helping your dog no matter what and are ready to put in the work.

- Know in your bones that you need to be your pet's #1 guardian and strongest defender. Protect your dog and call out anyone who puts their hands on your dog in a potentially harmful way.

- Never let anyone harm your dog and call it training.

What are their stressors? It's important to look at and understand the "why":

- Competition is stiff to get into veterinary school and it's a long, grueling endeavor.
- Many veterinarians graduate with high debt only to face stressful, long days and lots of overtime.
- Veterinarians are often accused of "only being in it for the money." While it is a business, it is one based on caring and veterinarians love animals, too. No one goes to veterinary school dreaming of becoming a millionaire.
- Their expenses are often high: rent for offices, modern equipment costs, and staffing payments and benefits.
- Veterinarians face daily moral dilemmas with human clients who are unable or unwilling to pay for medical treatment that could save their pets' lives.
- They have frustrating interactions with some owners. I know many veterinarians who have been asked to euthanize entire litters of healthy puppies (they've all refused). Often the same owners refuse to spay or neuter their adult dogs—even when the veterinarian or a rescue group offers to cover the cost.
- Veterinarians care about their animal patients and it hurts when they lose one.
- Veterinarians experience a high rate of online bullying—an AVMA survey found that 1 in 5 vets have been cyberbullied.
- Burnout is common.
- There is a serious lack of veterinarians and vet techs nationwide. Some ER clinics closed for good because of understaffing.

A new program created in 2016 by veterinarian Marty Becker ushered in an entirely new approach to veterinary care. His program—Fear Free®—provides training for veterinarians, trainers, and owners to teach cooperative care and reduce the fear animals experience during veterinary visits.

Fear Free's mission is to prevent and alleviate fear, anxiety, and stress in pets by inspiring and educating the people who care for them. In their own words, their courses were "developed and written by the most respected veterinary and pet experts in the world, including boarded veterinary behaviorists, boarded veterinary anesthesiologists, pain experts, boarded veterinary internists, veterinary technicians (behavior), experts in shelter medicine, animal training, grooming, boarding, and more."

Dr. Marty Becker, known as "America's Veterinarian," is the founder of Fear Free. Dr. Becker and his team have certified 80,000 Fear Free professionals from around the world.

Dr. Marty Becker Talks about His Game-Changing Fear Free Program, Which Benefits Veterinarians and Their Canine Clients

This interview has been included in its entirety.

▶ **How many veterinary professionals are now Fear Free Certified? How many are you projecting will join this year (2022)?**

We have more than 80,000 veterinary professionals who are Fear Free Certified, and we are projecting an additional 15,000 this year.

Fear Free is the world's leading organization training cooperative care to veterinarians and staff around the world. This program helps to reduce and even remove anxiety or stress out of a veterinary care visit for both owners and dogs.

▶ **How do you respond when or if a veterinarian feels they will lose income if they go slower with each patient and thus perhaps see fewer patients each day?**

Studies show that doing a Fear Free exam only takes seconds longer (26 seconds) and the actual time and quality of the exam itself is better because less time is spent wrestling with the pet being examined (who commonly thinks they're going to be harmed or even killed). In a Fear Free practice, there is no decrease in the number of pets being seen per doctor, customer satisfaction scores increase, injuries decrease, practice income increases, and the number of employees who leave decreases.

▶ **How do we get veterinarians onboard—what can trainers and owners do to help enroll vets?**

It's been said the only person who likes change is a four-month-old baby with a wet diaper. It's hard enough to change yourself, let alone someone else, and veterinarians are notoriously stubborn. But things ARE changing. Almost ⅔ of all veterinary schools in the United States now require Fear Free certification of students before graduation. Students are learning the nomenclature and protocols in animal handling and are seeing them practiced in the teaching hospitals and then putting them to practice before graduation in community practice rotations. Upon graduation, they want to work in veterinary practices that embrace Fear Free. Increasingly, pet parents are only taking their pets to animal professionals (veterinarians, trainers, groomers, pet sitters, and boarding facilities) who use Fear Free. If you're a trainer or groomer, find a Fear Free practice in your area to refer to.

▶ What feedback are you getting from certified veterinarians in terms of how this program has helped them help animals?

Fear Free is the most significant and successful transformation in small animal medicine since the invention of antibiotics and vaccinations. Simply put, Fear Free benefits every animal visiting a practice by reducing fear, anxiety, and stress and increasing happiness and calm. Pets can remain calm and pet parents can take their pet to the vet's office (or trainer, groomer, boarder, etc.) without feeling like they're hurting their pets by trying to help them. Surveys show veterinarians are seeing six major benefits from using Fear Free in practice:

1. **Oath**—The practice matches up with the oath they took at graduation "to prevent or relieve animal pain and suffering."

2. **Better Medicine**—With Fear Free, vital signs are more normal, physical exams are more normal (pets aren't hiding pain and sensitivity), and blood work and other diagnostics are more accurate.

3. **Fewer Injuries**—Bites, scratches, back injuries, etc., drop precipitously once you rachet down fear, anxiety, and stress and lower fear-based aggression.

4. **Easier to Attract and Retain Team Members**—Nobody wants to work in a place that makes life worse for animals or ignores their emotional well-being. Rather, veterinarians, vet techs, and other team members want to work in a place where you can love animals and they love you back.

5. **Better Economics**—Studies show that all key practice indicators (KPIs) and net income increase when a practice becomes Fear Free certified.

6. **Fun**—When dogs drag their moms and dads into the practice and almost all cats take treats, everyone wins. Pets are happy and calm, pet parents are happy and calm, team members are happy and calm—and practice is just like you dreamed it could be.

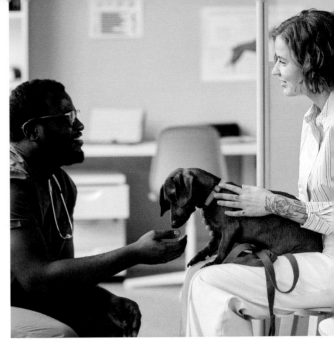

Fear Free is all about making the dog's comfort a priority. It changes the vet's office from a potentially scary place to a place many dogs actually want to go visit.

▶ What are the top three benefits to animals who are seen by Fear Free vets?

1. The pet going into a veterinary practice because they're sick, injured, or need routine or preventive care will not have the anxious feeling in the back of their mind that they are going to be harmed. By maintaining their calm, a negative experience won't get seared into the amygdala, they heal faster, they don't have immunosuppression that can decrease vaccine effectiveness, and there's a decrease in digestive upset.

2. Because the pet wants to go to the vet and pet parents don't mind taking them, the pet is much more likely to receive the medical care it deserves.

3. Because pet parents don't delay regular checkups and are more likely to take the pet to the vet at the first signs of illness, the veterinary healthcare team can catch illnesses and conditions in their earliest phases, which can prevent more serious problems, increase the chances of a successful treatment or cure, and save money.

I can personally speak about this program as a Fear Free Certified Professional—and I absolutely love it! It has been so badly needed. I recently had my first experience working with another Fear Free Certified Veterinary Professional, Dr. Angela West with Park City Mobile Vet in Utah.[2] Her visit was the best veterinary experience I have had in over 50 years of living with animals. I have sensitive cattle-collie dogs who don't care to be overly handled by strangers. She walked into our home with good dog treats and a can of spray cheese—a tool known and beloved by trainers, but I'd never seen a veterinarian using it. She spent 10 minutes getting to know my dogs and putting them at ease. When my dog Finn gave a small growl while we held his head for a front leg blood draw, she immediately released him, gave him time to self-collect, spent a few minutes reassuring him, then quickly and easily drew the blood sample from his back leg instead. I highly recommend the Fear Free program and encourage you to make the good sort of trouble and ask your veterinarian's office about getting Fear Free Certified.

A difficult experience at the vet for you or your dog can leave a mark that is hard to erase, but a positive experience with a modern, kind, forward-thinking veterinarian is the icing on the cake of a well-lived life for your dog.

THE PROFESSIONAL TRAINER

Ah, dog trainers. My messy, complicated, empathetic, compassionate, funny, smart, worn out, and often-warring tribe. I love these people! Most of us become dog trainers (though not all of us) because we have a deep connection with and love of dogs. We see their worth, just as we see how troubled they can be—and we make that trouble our trouble.

There is often a misconception that trainers spend all day playing with cute puppies. Who wouldn't want that as a job? The truth is that those of us who specialize in behavior cases aren't so eager to see puppies as our clients—we work with troubled dogs, and it is upsetting to see anxiety behaviors in puppies (although we applaud owners who bring in troubled puppies since the sooner we can start working with them, the better). More often, we are lending a hand to stressed-out owners or sitting and crying with them as they make difficult decisions.

Trainers are the third (and often undervalued) part of your dog's care team. It's not glamorous to be a dog trainer, nor is it a high-income field. Veterinarians are often given respect the minute they walk in the door because of their white coats

Behavior consultant Mikkel Becker working with a dog using Fear Free training. Establishing a trusting bond is key to any training program.

2   See www.parkcitymobilevet.com/about-us.

and stethoscopes. They also have a standard of care to which they are trained and consequences for not upholding that standard. Anyone anywhere right now can call themselves a dog trainer—there is no formal regulation.

Because of this lack of regulation and training requirements, dog owners never quite know who exactly the trainer in front of them is. It can lead to mental and physical harm for your dog, and even death in the most extreme and negligent cases. It is a blight on our industry, and it should never be the case. There is little in the way of consequences for such a trainer and things will not change until governments catch up and create regulations to protect dogs and their owners from charlatans.

Good dog trainers do what they do because they love dogs and want to give them the opportunity to live their very best doggie lives. Many of us understand canine communication very well and it is impossible for us to miss the signs that a dog is suffering. We work hard to educate ourselves on current training protocols that do not cause pain or fear and our training is based in scientific knowledge and real-world wisdom. We are constantly reading articles, attending conferences, and watching webinars to learn more about our complex four-legged clients. Quality trainers easily can spend $5,000–$10,000 per year on continuing education credits, renewing expensive certifications, and buying new books. The average salary for many dog trainers is between $35,000–$50,000, so the added

Good dog trainers are always learning—researching new techniques and recent studies about the complexities of canine behavior, health, and communication.

expense for this education takes a toll, but most trainers I know gladly spend the money.

The bottom line is this: a well-educated, compassionate, and invested trainer or behavior consultant can be the one person who can reach your dog and alleviate her stress. Good trainers save you time and money and we save your dog from unneeded misery. Be kind and understanding and know that there is often no quick fix for serious behavior concerns. Be gentle with your dog and with us. We are here to help.

Ask an Expert

Trainer and Behavior Consultant Mikkel Becker on Working Closely with Your Veterinarian

This interview has been included in its entirety.

Mikkel Becker spends some time with her dapper dog Indiana Bones.

▶ What do you feel dog owners don't know about working with veterinarians?

The pet's veterinarian and veterinary team can be critical in their work of overseeing and treating areas of concern that directly contribute to the emotional, psychological, and behavioral health of the dog, as physical and emotional health are inextricably linked.

Beyond the pet's own family, the pet's veterinarian is the dog's ultimate total health advocate, with an ability to see beyond the surface to what might be going on underneath and contributing to outward behavior changes or concerns the pet parent may be seeing. It's my firm belief that for a dog to be properly treated for a behavioral issue, it's essential that their care is continually overseen by a trusted vet, as physical health directly impacts emotional health, and vice versa.

Many, many issues—including anxiety, reactivity, or aggression—are linked to underlying health problems, such as chronic pain, that either directly caused or exacerbated the issue in the first place. It's also essential to note that there are veterinary specialists, including those with advanced training in behavior, who have the added ability to guide pet guardians in nutraceutical and pharmaceutical choices that can complement the training, management, and behavior modification changes they're employing. Pharmaceutical and nutraceutical help by no means provides a magic cure-all, but instead, for pets in need who may suffer from conditions that can include compromised serotonin levels in the brain, it can help create a better headspace in which they can better learn and retain the different behaviors and improved emotional states their guardian wants to impart.

Dogs, just like people, have very complex mental and emotional lives, with cognitive and psychological conditions that in many ways resemble those of humans. Just like us, when they're overly panicked and stressed out, it's nearly

Veterinary specialists, especially those with behavioral backgrounds, might be able to provide your dog with medications that even out possible hormone imbalances to help your dog truly benefit from training.

impossible to capture and hold their attention on the things we want them to focus on. Instead, the dog will probably be responding from a survival-based fight-or-flight response. They're not in a rational thinking mode, but instead are in life-or-death autopilot mode—simply seeking to survive. In such a panicked state, it can be difficult for dogs to receive and enjoy the reward we're pairing with the less pleasant event. And, while elements can be adjusted to make things less aversive and overwhelming for the dog, in some cases it's simply too much for the dog or owner. From a welfare standpoint, it's a kindness to our dogs to help them to feel better emotionally and mentally so they can receive and fully enjoy the type of happy, feel-good rewards and experiences we want to impart. Their ability to enjoy positives will help them more readily retain these new behaviors.

We do dogs a disservice when we neglect to provide veterinary intervention and continued oversight into the emotional and behavioral health of dogs, because in many cases there are underlying issues that may be causing or contributing to the problem itself. Further, there are oftentimes different nutraceuticals or pharmaceuticals that can complement and further build upon the ability to directly intervene and help the dog feel and think in different ways.

It's important to remember that for many pet guardians their dog may feel "unreachable" primarily because their dog goes into that tailspin survival mode easily and has a hard

time coping with and recovering from a stressful event. For these dogs, nutraceutical and pharmaceutical medications can make the difference in helping the dog to be more receptive and ready to learn. These additions can help to reduce the speed and intensity with which the animal's brain and body move into stress-based survival responses and can help the dog to recover faster from a stressful event. In addition, when the dog feels good emotionally, they're better able to use the rational, higher-functioning parts of the brain. This allows for voluntary, conscious choice, rather than their body flying uncontrolled into autopilot-like survival responses.

Such veterinary-guided intervention pairs well with reward-based training and behavior modification plans implemented directly by the trainer partners and pet guardians; meaning there's an entire team available to note and address problems of concern; tackling these issues from the inside out.

▶ **What are the top three skills you advise owners to work on with their dogs before they go to a veterinary or training appointment?**

Treatment station training is important. This offers a clear green light signal to the pet's guardian and subsequent handlers that the dog is comfortable and ready to proceed with the interaction, handling, or care task. If the dog starts to lean away or move out of their stationary position on the treatment station this is a clear "red light" to stop the interaction or handling task. Unlike mat training, in which the dog generally reclines in a settled position and is left alone while in the space, treatment station training guides a dog onto a nonslip area where they become accustomed to being interacted with in a positive way. Rather than a resting position, the dog remains in a standing position unless cued otherwise to allow easy access to different parts of the body for the handling and exam. Since slip and scare moments on slick floors in veterinary hospitals are common, the treatment station also offers a more secure place for the dog to stand for their exam and care (much of which may take place where the dog is most comfortable, such as on the floor or bench). In addition, the treatment station also offers an easy way to get the dog onto the scale—you can place their nonslip space indicator on the scale, the weight of which can be zeroed out before the dog is encouraged to step on top.

Teach your dog hand targeting as a way to allow your dog to approach on his own terms. It's a good tool for guiding him to specific spots in the veterinarian's office, too!

Touch/hand targeting is helpful for care as it allows the dog a go-to way to say hi and approach staff at a pace they're comfortable with. This is helpful for allowing the initial touch to occur on the dog's terms, rather than having hands immediately reaching toward the dog. Allowing the dog to complete the approach and rewarding their efforts starts off the interaction on a more positive note. In addition, hand targeting can also be used to move the dog from place to place, such as onto the scale.

Lastly, a lot of angst for dogs comes from the unknown and unpredictable. As such, I really like to give dogs a heads-up on what's going to happen before it takes place. For this reason, **I'm a big fan of communication cues** (also called predictor cues). These are ideally imparted in a positive manner by starting slowly on neutral body parts with people the dog is most comfortable with (this would include immediate family members petting the dog on comfortable places, like their chest, shoulder, or under the neck). Then, as the dog remains relaxed, communication cues can be transitioned to occur with touching other parts

of the body and with less familiar people; continuing to pair the process with ample positives to make it a feel-good experience for the dog and a happily anticipated event. Say the word first, such as a general "pet" cue to indicate the dog will be touched, then the familiar person pets the dog in a comfortable place on the body, followed by a tasty treat reward. This not only reduces the angst of uncertainty about what's going to occur by giving the dog a proper heads-up before handling occurs at places like the vet, but also imparts a form of reassurance, as it's been made into an event the dog is already comfortable with. And, if the dog is stressed and uncomfortable with the interaction or intent of touch, the communication cue provides the dog with the ability to move away and signal their distress before the interaction or handling progresses, reducing the risk of the dog responding defensively.

Then, if I had my wish, I'd strongly encourage pet parents to teach their pooches a chin rest on an inanimate object, like a stool with a rolled towel or Snuggle Puppy® placed on top. This further allows the dog to have a clear way of signaling their guardians and other handlers, like the veterinary team, as to whether they're comfortable and ready to proceed. The people can then do so safely at the pace the dog is comfortable with, allowing for pauses or stopping points if the dog needs a break or if elements of the situation need to be adjusted for the dog to feel more comfortable with what's taking place.

▶ **What are some of the top benefits for dogs seen by Certified Fear Free Professionals?**
Dogs are continually learning, whether it's in a training session or during regular, everyday interactions. One of the places of particular importance for the dog in terms of their learning experience is what they encounter at places of care like the vet. These experiences can make or break the dog's trust and happy responsiveness to different people, places, and types of touch. As such, it's important to work with professionals who are trained and committed to overseeing and protecting the emotional well-being of your dog at the same time they're providing physical care.

Fear Free veterinarians keep emotional medical records for your dog that include notes on their stressors, any sensitive body parts, and how staff can best keep your dog feeling comfortable, happy, and safe.

Fear Free Professionals have extensive training and continuing education requirements that educationally and practically guide the veterinary provider in ways to better approach, interact with, handle, and treat pets during different aspects of their care. Rather than forging through the fear and getting care done regardless, Fear Free professionals make it a priority to watch over both physical and emotional health as one whole. In some cases, this means making the choice to stop and try a different approach or even come back at another time rather than risking a negative experience that can't be taken back. For those situations where veterinary care is urgent, such as in emergency veterinary hospitals, steps are taken to substantially reduce the emotional distress or physical discomfort the animal feels; all while providing creature comforts that can soothe, positively distract, and calmly reassure the dog to reduce the negatives and up the positives of the experience.

Just as veterinarians keep a medical record on pets, Fear Free providers also keep an emotional medical record on the pet with specific information that includes specific stressors for the pet, such as sensitive areas of the body or a particular dislike of certain places or procedures, as well as directly indicating ways the team can help the animal to feel most comfortable, happy, and safe (including favorite ways to be approached or touched, known tricks, favorite treats, and preferred toys). The goal and benefit of a Fear Free approach is reducing the risk of the animal enduring a stressful handling or treatment experience that can have long-lasting or lifelong repercussions. Instead, the Fear Free team is all about preventing and reducing fear, anxiety, and stress and about imparting positive emotional experiences that can boost the pet's emotional experience and enjoyment of visiting the vet to make it an overall less distressing and more pleasant event; meaning the pet is more likely to receive timely, thorough, quality veterinary treatment and care that's less stressful and safer for the pet, their guardians, and the entire veterinary team.

Stress is the top reason pets aren't taken into the vet as often as recommended (the stress to the pet being the top concern and stress to the pet parent just thinking about having to take their pet in being the third-highest concern). As such, Fear Free directly addresses the barrier stress creates to dogs receiving timely, quality medical care by making it a less stressful, more pleasant experience that's enjoyed by both pooches and their people. Just like the treat that being extra spoiled with special goodies and star treatment when visiting a favorite grandma's house can be for a child, so too does the veterinary team do their part in trying to make the veterinary hospital a Disneyland of sorts that has all the magic and feel-good fun of extra tasty treats and positive encounters (ideally resulting in an animal who is reluctant to leave and ready to come back again). And, when certain invasive or unpleasant elements need to be done, the Fear Free team takes a guided, practical approach for ensuring it's as minimally aversive as possible, while providing ample means of comfort to help the animal feel secure. When the animal is less stressed, their quality of care is also improved—not only can a more thorough exam or treatment be achieved, but the animal is more likely to act like their normal selves and will more accurately display issues of concern, like a change in gait, that otherwise may be masked by stress-fueled adrenaline.

4

Top Methods Used by Professional Trainers to Address Aggression and Reactivity

This chapter is the heart of this book for the unlucky owner living with a reactive or aggressive dog. It gives you up-to-date, professional knowledge to help with troubled behaviors. A biting dog faces a very real threat of being euthanized, so these solutions can indeed be lifesaving. The crucial aspect of all the protocols (which go well beyond helping just reactive dogs) is that we work hard to make the dog feel safe. Remember, the first step in any training or behavior program is to get your dog thoroughly checked out by a veterinarian.

This chapter explores professional protocols and tested techniques for ongoing success:

When I wrote my first book on canine behavior (*The Midnight Dog Walkers*), the chapter that seemed to upset owners the most was the one titled "Don't Walk the Dog." In that chapter, I discussed the need to allow stressed canines days, weeks, or even months to settle into their new homes or reorient themselves after a stressful event. When I tell owners in my reactive dog classes to refrain from walking their dog for the first 20 to 30 days, I hear things such as:

- My dog is so hyper and will destroy my house without two long walks a day!
- My dog will be bored!
- It's cruel to not walk the dog!
- But my dog gets so excited to go on a walk!
- But that's how I get my own daily exercise!

Of course, dogs need proper and productive exercise. There is even an old expression in dog training that "a tired dog is a good dog." But there is a big difference between a tired dog and an overwhelmed dog, and that difference is critical. Most of the time, I am begging owners to get their dogs outside more, but that is definitely not the case for any dog showing fear, anxiety, reactivity, or aggression. Instead, I ask these owners to begin

Canine enrichment and indoor play can be more effective for reactive or aggressive dogs—they get all the stimulation without the stress of a potentially trigger-filled walk.

To a person who is afraid of spiders, a black widow would be an extreme trigger—your dog has "black widow" triggers, too.

reinforcing calm behaviors, playing inside with their dog, and using canine enrichment. In fact, I strongly encourage the owners in my class to not expose their dogs to the outside world during the first two weeks (at least) of class.

It is critical to keep the dog under threshold while changing their perspective on triggers and stressful events. You are rebuilding trust and communication between you and the dog. In class, we spend four weeks in training building up that trust, and one scary incident can wipe it out.

Let's look at a human analogy: Say I have an intense fear of black widow spiders. You spend one month showing me a black widow spider from a great distance indoors, moving me closer little by little, and depositing $1 million every time I looked at the spider. I would slowly start to associate black widow spiders with the reward rather than with my fear. You decide it's time to leave the house, but as soon as we go outside, a black widow zooms down and lands on me. In a millisecond, my previous fear level returns, and my trust in you is gone. It was too early in the training process to face my trigger in such an intense way.

If you instead spend six months building up trust, and then I see a black widow in the window

of the house across the street the first time we go outside, it won't bother me. You gave the process more time, and you introduced the perceived threat slowly when we went outside, so I know you can still keep me safe from spiders. Now, while I'd never want spiders crawling all over me, my perspective has changed to the point where I'd be able to handle seeing one without screaming and running from the room. I might even feel a bit of subconscious happiness because of the reward.

When looking at this human analogy, we must remember that adult humans can clearly say "no" and communicate their fears. Our dogs do not have that power. They do their best to say "no" using the communication tools at their disposal, but most of us don't recognize these stress signals. When we repeatedly ignore those signals, they begin to use behavior we can't ignore, like barking, showing teeth, snapping at the air, and sometimes biting.

Thankfully there are newer methods for lowering a dog's anxiety. I advise you to begin working with an experienced, highly trained, force-free behavior consultant. Working with a professional eliminates

Sometimes the immediate solution that will lower a dog's anxiety is to do nothing. Give your dog the space and time they need to rest and recover.

A dog who feels it must respond to a perceived threat with its teeth faces the real threat of being euthanized, so training to curb those responses is really a matter of life and death for the dog.

the risk that the canine student might learn incorrect skills. If hiring a professional is not an option, use the following protocols as a place to begin and explore online resources about the protocol you feel will help your dog the most. Understand that this will take however long it takes; all dogs are individuals and have unique timelines, genetics, and responses to triggers. Also understand that there are times when we are unable to help a dog, and hard choices must be made. I discuss these rare, difficult situations more thoroughly in chapter 11.

SLOW THINKING

Upstate New York resident Dr. Laura Donaldson has a unique biography in the world of dog trainers. She holds a Ph.D. in humanities and is a professor emeritus of Cornell University in Ithaca, New York.

More than 15 years ago, two of her own dogs started fighting in the home, starting her journey down the path toward becoming a full-time behavior counselor. She's achieved an incredible number of professional certifications that include becoming a Certified Dog Behavior Consultant (CDBC), a graduate (with distinction) of the Karen Pryor Academy, and a Control Unleashed Certified Instructor, and completing various mentorship programs with some of the world's foremost experts on canine aggression and master's level academic courses in animal learning and behavior analysis, companion animal nutrition, psychopharmacology for animal scientists, and the exploration of animal behavior.

Dr. Donaldson's keen academic mind and her deep love of dogs informed the development of her behavior program *Slow Thinking is Lifesaving for*

Dr. Laura Donaldson developed *Slow Thinking is Lifesaving for Dogs* to help troubled dogs by first changing their thinking, then working on the problem behaviors.

Dogs. This unique program incorporates cutting-edge canine cognition research and focuses on how changing a dog's thinking patterns can help them find more appropriate ways to respond to triggers. Dr. Donaldson studied several successful programs that worked with aggressive behavior in school-age children, including the Brain Power (Los Angeles) and Becoming a Man (Chicago) programs. These programs focused on changing thinking patterns first, then focused on changing behaviors. The resulting approach is fundamentally opposite to one of the oldest approaches to helping trouble dogs: first changing the behavior and then working to change the dog's thinking. Dog training for decades has instructed us that we can only work with canine behavior we can observe. Now, thanks to modern technology like fMRIs, we can observe thinking in dogs—which is both fascinating and industry-changing!

New ways to help troubled dogs have been developing rapidly over the last 20 years as cognition research on dogs indicated that they have cognitive abilities on par with humans. A dog's thought-processing mechanisms are like our own, although Dr. Donaldson stresses that that does not mean

that humans and dogs think alike. It does mean that we have underestimated dogs' cognition for a very long time, both as trainers and as owners. Dr. Donaldson has pointed out that while dogs do not think linguistically as humans do, dogs (like us) do process and interpret environmental information and make decisions using this information in sophisticated ways.

Dr. Donaldson breaks down two types of thinking. **Fast thinking** involves the well-known fight-or-flight reflex all mammals have. If you have a reactive dog, you know all too well how quickly your calm, sweet Fido can turn into a screaming, lunging maniac upon seeing his trigger. This is fast thinking. Fast thinking can save your life if a bear jumps out in front of you, but it's also difficult to live with

Advances in our understanding of canine cognition have proven that, while dogs don't think linguistically like humans, they are quick learners who process environmental information to make complicated decisions (just like humans do).

Fast thinking is an immediate, subconscious response to stimuli, thus it's often inaccurate. With fast thinking, the dog's perspective is inclined to view new stimuli (including other dogs and people) as threats, prompting a defensive or aggressive response.

(especially when you have the same fear reaction to a stuffed teddy bear that you'd have to a living grizzly). Fast thinking, according to Dr. Donaldson, is necessary, automatic (subconscious and involuntary), and biased (can be highly inaccurate and dysfunctional). She makes an excellent point that fast thinking is an overlooked component of aggressive behavior. Dogs engaged in fast thinking make inaccurate risk assessments and tend to see danger lurking everywhere.

Slow thinking develops your dog's ability to process information more intentionally (which can be lifesaving). Slow thinking is resource and time intensive, deliberate, and requires significant cognitive effort. Dr. Donaldson stresses that slow thinking is a key problem-solving skill that allows for much better risk assessment than fast thinking. Slow thinking gives the dog agency and a path to making functional decisions independent of a human prompting or commanding the dog.

How do we teach a dog slow thinking? The following are some **beginning steps** (as I interpret them) to introduce your dog to slow thinking. This is a very brief overview, so I suggest you check out Dr. Donaldson's webinar, which goes into far more detail and provides more scientific information.[1] She also has an in-depth program for professional trainers and many free interviews online. Her program is trademarked, and I want to thank Dr. Donaldson for allowing me to share her remarkable program with you.

---

1   Dr. Laura Donaldson, Slow Thinking is Lifesaving for Dogs webinar, available at www.fourpawsfourdirections.com/slow-thinking.

BEGINNING STEPS FOR TEACHING SLOW THINKING

Learn to accept and work with your dog's personality and quirks. Wishing for something different won't help you find a solution.

STEP ONE: Begin with No Expectations

Expectations lead to disappointment and frustration. Instead, take a deep breath and see the situation how it really is rather than how you want it to be. Accept your dog's behavior issues and get ready to help her learn a different way of thinking.

OVERVIEW

Beginning Steps for Teaching Slow Thinking

- **Step One:** Begin with No Expectations

- **Step Two:** Let Your Dog Make Decisions

- **Step Three, Part 1:** Reinforce Default Calm Behaviors Indoors

- **Step Three, Part 2:** Reinforce Default Calm Behaviors Outdoors

- **Step Four:** Practice Cognitive Reappraisal

2

Watch what your dog chooses to do if you aren't giving him cues. Does he run straight for the toys? Does he chew on the furniture? You need this information to work with who your dog is.

3

If your dog calmly sits on his own, reward and praise him to reinforce the behavior in everyday life.

STEP TWO: Let Your Dog Make Decisions

Take a step back and review the past week. How many times a day did you command or cue your dog to either do something or (more likely) stop doing something? If we are constantly telling our dogs what to do, we eventually take away their freedom to make decisions on their own. We need them to be able to problem solve through slow thinking, but we muck this up by over-cueing them.

Try to go one day—or one week—without cueing your dog. In other words, let your dog be a dog and make doggie decisions. If one of her decisions is to eat your socks, pick up your socks before she can eat them. Spend the week learning about your dog's preferences. What are her favorite treats? Does she love chasing a ball more than going for a walk? Does she prefer just hanging out with you in the living room over going for a car ride? Does she get enough calm sleeping time throughout her day?

STEP THREE, Part 1: Reinforce Default Calm Behaviors Indoors

Choose a quiet, controlled indoor environment, such as your living room. Reinforce simple, default behaviors like "sit" (or lying quietly on a mat) in a way that will make the default behaviors become a habit. Try cueing a sit every time you stand up or sit down, before giving the dog access to a toy (or other reinforcer). Likewise, reinforce calming behaviors without cueing them whenever the dog displays them.

To paraphrase Dr. Donaldson: *Relaxation is a cognitive act. We emphasize these default calming behaviors so dogs can become independent problem solvers without cues from their owners. Calmness is emphasized so it becomes a habit, giving them a powerful tool to use instead of barking, lunging, and growling.*

Try to reinforce calm activities outdoors. Sit with your dog and read a book or let him wander nearby while you garden. Make sure he knows that calm behavior is the behavior you want.

Zoe practices cognitive reappraisal with the cat next door.

STEP THREE, Part 2: Reinforce Default Calm Behaviors Outdoors

Once you notice a large increase in these default behaviors, take your dog into a secure outdoor space and spend time reading a book or gardening—doing human things—while keeping an eye on your dog. Reinforce default calm behaviors in the outdoor space. Your silence outdoors is even more important—give your dog time to think without having to contend with your voice as well as outdoor triggers.

STEP FOUR: Practice Cognitive Reappraisal

Just as this chapter exists at the heart of the book, **Cognitive Reappraisal** (CR) is at the heart of the Slow Thinking is Lifesaving for Dogs program. CR helps dogs learn the three R's: rethinking, reframing, and reappraising.

Introduce your dog in a calm, safe way (at a distance, for example) to environmental stimuli, to reframe how they see the trigger and lower the intensity of their emotions. CR can help change human neurobiology, and it is no different for dogs. CR changes the meaning of stimuli for the dog, especially those that would normally involve negative emotions or prompt hyper-aroused responses like barking, lunging, growling, and even biting. CR nurtures your dog's ability to think before acting, helping them accomplish "more accurate risk assessment."

Behavior Consultant and Trainer Dr. Laura Donaldson Explains How Slow Thinking Is Lifesaving for Dogs, Plus Cognitive Reappraisal

This interview has been edited for length. Please see https://foxchapelpets.com/positive-training-dogs/ to read the full interview.

Dr. Laura Donaldson is a highly certified trainer and behavior expert who created Slow Thinking is Lifesaving for Dogs. She teaches dogs to slow down their thinking so they can truly assess a situation before reacting (or overreacting).

▶ **You have said in interviews and webinars that a dog's cognition is on par with human cognition. Could you elaborate on how they are similar and how they are different?**

I will try to answer the question from my own perspective as a practitioner, an academic, and a long-time companion to more than a few much beloved, working Border Collies. As background, however, I want to highlight a *New York Times* opinion piece that researcher Gregory Berns wrote entitled "Dogs Are People Too" (2013).[1] In this mini-essay, Berns describes how his use of awake neuroimaging such as fMRIs should become a watershed moment in how societies regard dogs. He particularly waxes eloquent on the similarities between human and canine versions of a brain region situated between the brainstem and the cortex called the caudate nucleus. The caudate nucleus plays a key role in producing those positive emotions we feel when contemplating the things we love like chocolate ice cream, swimming in a cold lake, and cuddling with our dogs. Berns notes that many of the same things that activate the human caudate nucleus also activate the canine caudate. I quote him at length here: "Neuroscientists call this a functional homology, and it may be an indication of canine emotions. The ability to experience positive emotions, like love and

---

1   Gregory Berns, "Dogs Are People, Too," *New York Times*, October 5, 2013, https://www.nytimes.com/2013/10/06/opinion/sunday/dogs-are-people-too.html.

Helping dogs develop slow thinking habits allows them to relax and reframe their thinking so they can more accurately evaluate the world around them.

attachment, would mean that dogs have a level of sentience comparable to that of a human child. And this ability suggests a rethinking of how we treat dogs. Dogs have long been considered property. Though the Animal Welfare Act of 1966 and state laws raised the bar for the treatment of animals, they solidified the view that animals are things—objects that can be disposed of as long as reasonable care is taken to minimize their suffering. *But now, by using the MRI to push away the limitations of behaviorism, we can no longer hide from the evidence. Dogs, and probably many other animals (especially our closest primate relatives), seem to have emotions just like us. And this means we must reconsider their treatment as property* [emphasis mine]." I would argue that this includes reconsidering the use of shock collars and other punitive technologies like prong collars, the use of which has long been justified because dogs allegedly occupied a rung below humans on the "great chain of being." Not any longer—and this is precisely why the issue of cognitive parity between dogs and humans is so profoundly important.

In 2016, Cook, Spivak, and Berns published a study[2] using "awake neuroimaging"[3] to measure and document canine impulsivity. The results of this research enabled the authors to theorize a parity "between human and canine neurobehavioral mechanisms for control and support the dog as a comparative model for better understanding maladaptive behavior in humans." This echoes the conclusions of the caudate nucleus research because it showed (literally, via the fMRI [functional magnetic resonance imaging] scans) that dogs and humans possess remarkably similar neurobiological mechanisms not only for exercising self-control but also for experiencing positive emotions. I should quickly note that talking about *cognitive parity*, or the close cognitive similarity of dogs and humans, does not mean that dogs "think" like humans through the medium of verbal language. The term *parity* instead implies strong parallels between dogs and humans in how they process information from the environment and then use this information to make decisions about their behavior. Several of the most important cognitive parities between dogs and humans—and the ones addressed in my Slow Thinking is Lifesaving for Dogs program—are *slow thinking* as well as what I have described as *fast-twitch thinking* (FTT).

While readers may recognize the term fast thinking, I also call it fast-twitch thinking because this phrase more accurately describes the muscle memory characteristics of fast thinking. The muscles of mammals, including humans and canines, are composed of fast- and slow-twitch fibers. While slow-twitch fibers are associated with long duration, muscle contraction, and endurance, fast-twitch fibers enable quick, powerful contractions, albeit for much shorter periods of time. This is precisely how FTT functions because it is blazing fast, usually involuntary, and requires minimal cognitive effort. While FTT lubricates society as we know it—do you really want to think about which way to twist open a doorknob

---

2   Peter F. Cook, Mark Spivak, and Gregory Berns, "Neurobehavioral Evidence for Individual Differences in Canine Cognitive Control: An Awake fMRI Study." *Animal Cognition*, 19 (2016): 867.

3   Berns and his research group used only positive reinforcement techniques to teach dogs how to enter the fMRI apparatus and then to stay unrestrained within the tube. If dogs chose to leave the apparatus or showed any signs of stress, all measuring stopped.

or which direction to read this paragraph?—it can also be very misleading. "First impressions," otherwise known as fast-twitch thinking, can and do lead to inaccurate conclusions, including social stereotyping. Like humans, dogs also use fast-twitch thinking. For example, dogs on leash who bark and lunge at every dog they encounter are engaging in a form of FTT that many people label as "reactive" behavior. Such behavior is largely automatic and its cognitive distortions ("every other dog I see is dangerous and going to hurt me") function very much like cognitive distortions in human perceptions. When caretakers, handlers, and dog training professionals fail to recognize the cognitive underpinnings of canine "reactive" behavior, they also miss a critical component of helping dogs feel safer, develop more socially appropriate coping skills, and enjoy a better quality of life.

▶ **Your program demonstrates a massive switch from the old-school method of trainers working to change behavior first and change thinking second. Your program teaches that we can indeed change thinking first and that, in turn, changes behavior. I am enthralled with this idea! Do you feel it is a radical change of course? Are you finding this method works faster than traditional methods?**

Apropos of Gregory Berns's insight about how technologies like fMRI dissolve "the limitations of behaviorism," I endorse his conclusion that "we can no longer hide from the evidence." The inner processes of both canines and humans have now become both observable and demonstrable. Far from making a radical change, I'm just following the science! There can be no doubt that changing thinking also permanently and positively changes behavior. Indeed, the documented success of human-centered Cognitive Behavioral Therapy (CBT) testifies to this truth. The American Psychological Association's Division of Clinical Psychology has declared that CBT is as effective—and often

even more effective—than other forms of psychological therapy, including psychiatric medications. Because of the close cognitive parity between humans and canines, I am very confident in believing that these statements also hold for dogs.

There are several basic principles at work in a cognitive approach. First, behavior issues often originate in distorted, unhelpful ways of thinking; second, learned and well-rehearsed patterns of dysfunctional behavior contribute to psychological problems; third, both dogs and people with behavior issues *CAN* learn more adaptive coping mechanisms without resorting to laborious and often difficult to implement desensitization/counterconditioning protocols. That serious behavior issues like aggression frequently result from a subject's misreading of social cues explains why desensitization/counterconditioning sometimes underwhelms as a therapeutic approach, especially in non-human animals. I explore this process intensively in my article, "Behavior Matters: Counterconditioning and the Cognitive Revolution."[4] Rather than counterconditioning's focus on reciprocal inhibition, my Slow Thinking program emphasizes subjects learning the cognitive skills of disengagement and calm, accurate information processing. A wonderful example of this is Cognitive Reappraisal (CR), which is a cornerstone of my Slow Thinking program.

I like to describe CR in terms of the three "Rs": rethinking, revaluing, and reframing. Cognitive reappraisal involves thinking differently about stimuli in a way that diminishes the intensity of negative emotions and changes the meaning of emotionally evocative stimuli. CR has a range of beneficial effects, including reduced emotional intensity, reduced startle responses, reduced behavioral avoidance, and reduced amygdala activation.[5] Both PET (positron emission tomography) and fMRI have supplied hard data that cognitive reappraisal directly influences amygdala circuitry. Studies of healthy human individuals that have

---

4   Laura E. Donaldson, "Behavior Matters: Counterconditioning and the Cognitive Revolution." *APDT Chronicle of the Dog* (Summer 2018): 44–47.

5   Laura Campbell-Sills, Kristen K. Ellard, and David H. Barlow, "Emotion Regulation in Anxiety Disorders," in *Handbook of Emotion Regulation, Second Edition,* ed. J. J. Gross (New York: The Guilford Press, 2014), 393.

15-year-old Gildin has learned successful coping behaviors late in life thanks to Dr. Donaldson's program.

been corroborated and duplicated many times over show that CR reliably decreases amygdala activation when subjects encounter negative emotional stimuli. This finding turns much received wisdom about behavior on its head. Here, thinking alters neurobiology rather than biology determining thinking.[6] This strongly suggests that CR is transformative and highly effective at reducing negative emotions in the context of stress.

I want to end my response by telling the story of Gildin, whose name means "spark of silver" in the elvish language invented by J.R.R. Tolkien in his *Lord of the Rings* books. Gildin is a 15-year-old Jack Russell Terrier who was rescued from Bulgaria by Susanne, a professional dog trainer based in Austria and a student in my online Slow Thinking course. According to Susanne, who gave her full consent to sharing Gildin's story, "there are no words for the suffering he had gone through—over a decade of hiding in a tiny wooden hut, sleeping in his own dirt, living off scraps he collected at night, when the other, bigger dogs at the shelter were resting. From humans, he obviously knew only neglect and

violence. Gildin showed clear signs of severe PTSD when he arrived, completely unable to engage with his environment, except for short outbursts of defensive aggression. He had no communication skills, was impossible to touch, froze at the mere sight of dog or human alike and slipped into learned helplessness on many occasions." Susanne worked hard to help Gildin recover some semblance of confidence in his world. However, shortly after Gildin began to recover, he was diagnosed with cognitive dysfunction. At this point, Susanne wondered if the Slow Thinking is Lifesaving for Dogs program could help Gildin: "How could it work with a dog who might suddenly forget where the garden door is, or simply not know that the tasty stuff in his bowl is for eating and who doesn't know day from night?" Despite these difficulties, Susanne decided to try.

"I had to adapt many things because of his cognitive dysfunction, of course." While Gildin might not remember single training steps or game sequences, with the help of Slow Thinking protocols, an "old, traumatized dog with severe dementia has found his way back into this world— taking part, making decisions, and exploring his environment. If you are ever asked if Slow Thinking works with *ANY* dog—yes, it does." Susanne reports that recently when they were taking a daily walk, Gildin was approached by a big dog who was being overtly confrontational. Rather than running away, Gildin instead "stood and watched. It was so obvious that he was thoroughly considering the situation instead of giving into his first impulse. Then, the most amazing thing happened. He looked at me, and then moved on in our chosen direction in a polite curve through the field next to us. Right past the other dog, who was barking and growling. That was perfect cognitive reappraisal in practice. I was so proud of him." I can only nod and agree with her assessment.

I salute this little dog's bravery and courage as well as the skill and tenacity of his human. It would be hard to find a story that more poignantly illustrates the power of thinking to change not just a subject's behavior, but also their lives.

---

6   FYI, the amygdala is thought to be a central processing region for activating the body's response to fearful or threatening stimuli, including negative arousal as well as fear-related behaviors.

ANIMAL CENTRED EDUCATION AND FREE WORK

Posture and behavior educator Sarah Fisher created ACE as a process to combine observations of the animal's posture, movement, and nervous system responses.

Horse veterinarians approach potential problems by thoroughly observing and evaluating the horse's movements and behavior. Sometimes because of small office spaces, dog veterinarians don't have as much physical space to observe dogs like this.

Animal Centred Education—known as ACE—is an integrated approach to supporting animals that combines an online learning center with practical ACE workshops taught by British trainer Sarah Fisher. Fisher's ACE courses use observations of the animal's posture, movement, and nervous system responses; ACE Free Work; and gentle bodywork. Fisher says:

> Whilst it is not always possible to determine the root of the problem, fear and pain in the body, including digestive discomfort, are the common denominators in the majority of cases that I see. This applies to many behavior struggles, including aggression toward both people and dogs.

Fisher began her career studying human massage, anatomy, and physiology. As a lifelong lover of both dogs and horses, she developed ACE in 2018, expanding on traditionally horse-related therapy and training methods with the goal of improving the lives of all animals. She leads teaching staff workshops all over the world for animal rescue organizations and she is a highly sought-after speaker for animal industry organizations.

Sarah Fisher designed ACE and ACE Free Work to give us a non-intrusive way to observe dogs without having to put hands on them or set up a potential conflict (from a human giving food to a human-nervous dog, for example). It offers dogs the chance to explore movement and a range of sensory experiences at their own pace and provides a foundation on which further learning can be built. ACE Free Work is not tied to any specific goal for the dog the way obedience competitions might be. At her 90-acre property, Tilley Farm, which opened in 2001 to assist rescue organizations and dog owners, Fisher has safe spaces set up with all kinds of interesting things for dogs to see, touch, sniff, observe, and taste. The dog enters the area off leash with the handler close by neither restraining nor touching the dog. ACE teachers quietly observe the dog (and the sessions are filmed) as the dog makes its way through the environment, looking for signs of movement patterns that might indicate skeletal, muscular, or nerve issues. Items for the dog to explore include lick mats, food in a bowl, a yoga or dog mat, a low dog platform, and other items. ACE Free Work influences all the senses, including proprioception (the sense of self-movement and body position) and the vestibular system (which provides a sense of balance and spatial orientation).

Once the dog is comfortable in this environment, Fisher invites interaction with either the guardian or herself, always observing the dog's reactions and responses. If the dog initiates body contact, she introduces touch to the dog in small increments to get a hands-on assessment of bodily reactions and to feel for stiffness, body sensitivity, or changes to the texture of the coat. ACE evaluators learn a lot about a dog's level of willingness to move and explore the Free Work environment.

The entire time, the ACE teacher is laser focused on every part of the dog, making mental notes of body posture or body parts that are unbalanced. "We put food in the room on the floor and on different objects at different heights (such as on a chair) to observe how the dog moves around those items. A dog with elbow dysplasia or a luxating patella would have difficulty leaning forward, for example, to lick a lick mat that is flat on the floor. I want to have food at all different levels and observe the dog. If a dog avoids a soft surface like a thick yoga mat, perhaps the dog has undiagnosed joint pains or has soft tissue damage," Fisher says. "Free Work allows us to begin to study the body parts and … [discover] issues that need further veterinary work or [adjust] how the guardian is interacting with the dog to alleviate the stress or pain."

A dog's nails and paw pads may show uneven wear or other indications of pain, tension, or other gait problems—ACE involves evaluating the whole dog.

Fisher's approach to helping troubled dogs involves trained ACE professionals observing the movement of the dog to look for any indicators of pain, tenderness, stiffness, or inefficient or unnatural movement. She's worked with countless bite cases and has extensive experience and knowledge from working with aggressive and reactive dogs. Fisher writes about her work: "Dogs with a bite history are usually tight in the back, stiff and choppy in the gait, fixed in the neck, hard eyed, and aloof. There are other patterns to look for in the coat texture, body temperature, and color of the gums, eyes, and skin."

Fisher also observes the dog's nails and paw pads to see how they are wearing (gaining valuable information on potential gait problems). No detail is overlooked, from eye movement and blinking rate to whether a dog's ears are level or not. There are over 100 muscles in a dog's head, and tension is a clear indication that something is off. She adds: "Tension in the lower back triggers the flight reflex and dogs that dislike being touched or approached by people or dogs are often carrying tension through the lumbar area and hindquarters. They may have hip problems or be dropped in the pelvis."

Fisher posted this nugget on her ACE Facebook page: "What we saw in some of our sensitive visitors was tension around the shoulders and upper thoracic spine, and an inability to stand in balance with a leg at each corner (for want of a better description). [This posture] is common in dogs who find some aspects of the human world a tad overwhelming [and] can also be linked to underlying pain. This common postural pattern is often accompanied by touch, noise, and sight sensitivity; sensitivity to the sight and sound of something moving in the environment, sensitivity to contact from certain textures, and sensitivity to contact from the human hand."

Scottish behavior expert Dale McLelland had this to say about her experiences with ACE Free Work and a troubled dog she nicknamed Mr. McBitey:

Fisher's observations are amazing—tiny details and nuances that can help to build a picture of what is going on for that individual dog. One of the key moments with Mr. McBitey was the idea of his nervous system "learning" that touch wasn't the predictor of something negative. We could see that, over time, instead of standing rigid and fixed, he slowly blinked and relaxed his ribcage and stomach and from then on it was a case of building on those little moments. Free Work and observations for me are not about pairing good things to build positive associations in a mechanical way—it's about the dog leading and genuinely participating, providing time to process information as well as highlighting issues in body posture and patterns.

Some dogs can be nervous around humans even when it comes to taking food or treats. They may want the treat, but they don't want the contact. ACE Free Work helps us avoid creating this sort of conflict for our furry friends.

Fisher explains that one of the core components of Free Work is to ask "why" when behavior is observed. Some questions that might arise include:

- Why does the dog avoid food? Is there a gastric issue? Is there an arthritis issue stopping the dog from being able to access the food?
- If a dog always presents only his head to be petted by the handler, could there be pain in another part of the body?
- If a dog is tired after a short Free Work session rather than relaxed, what could be contributing to that?
- What if the dog is really hyper after Free Work and has the "zoomies"—why?
- Is the dog's tail held out to one side to help with balance? Why?
- Does the dog always walk counterclockwise (or to the left) versus changing directions freely?

The ACE methods were developed by Sarah Fisher, shown here with a furry friend and partner Anthony Head, at Tilley Farm, near Bath, England.

Fisher can also help a people-shy or people-wary dog in the Free Work setting. Once the dog is comfortable in the space and is actively seeking and exploring the room, Fisher brings a new person into the area while the dog is busy in the room. The dog has the power to choose whether to ignore the person or meet them at the dog's own pace. If the dog is highly concerned, Fisher will start with an article of clothing from the new person. As a dog's comfort level increases, Fisher switches slowly from having a lot of food placed around the room to having food coming directly from her. She always leaves food in the room for easy access, however, to avoid creating conflict—always giving the dog the ability to choose.

Fisher also notes that just because we think food is rewarding, it may not be for the dog. If she is working with a resource guarder, she switches from using food items to using more items that affect the

- ♦ Why does the dog have abnormal coat patterns?
- ♦ Does the dog love the ball it carries around obsessively or does he need it to self-calm or for other reasons?
- ♦ Is a resource guarding response a guarding behavior or a pain response?
- ♦ Does the dog have a busy brain or pain?

Keep questioning everything and remember: the dog is always right!

Free Work first aims to find any underlying pain issue through trained observation, but it goes beyond that. After the dog has been assessed and any health issues have been treated or medicated, Fisher continues to use Free Work to begin learning exercises that specifically work to help the dog learn new movements. If the dog's issue is found to be behavior based, she uses Free Work to introduce the dog (in a calm setting) to new stimuli like large coats, different object shapes, unfamiliar items like skateboards or wheelbarrows, etc.

Free Work helps dogs whose issues are behavior-based by introducing them to new objects and stimuli (including items like wheelbarrows or winter coats that humans take for granted as being safe) in a secure, calm environment.

dog's sense of smell (such as horse blankets and bags of leaves). As Fisher points out, the beauty of Free Work is that the dog can always choose to disengage at any point. She also notes that the great majority of the time the dogs she observes in Free Work do not act the way their owners predicted, begging the question: why?

I love Free Work and think it is one of the most important advances I've learned about in the world of dog training. I like to imagine a day in the near future when dog owners will set up space for free work in their homes (similar to the playrooms parents provide for their children). The room will include various dog-appropriate objects, toys, and treats. In this fantasy, every time the doorbell rings, the dog is asked to go to his Free Work playroom, and he willingly runs in because it's such a delight for him to be in there. The dog explores his room while the guests come in and the humans enjoy their human activities. This scenario would be so much more freeing and enriching for dogs versus what most households do now (asking a dog to sit still on a mat during the whole visit, for example). Would you have your child stand in a corner and be still while you had guests over? And, if you think my idea is farfetched, you should know that home builders are often asked to build homes that accommodate dogs' needs—why not include a Free Work room?

Dog L.E.G.S.®

Applied ethologist and expert dog mediator Kim Brophey burst onto the national dog training scene with her popular TED talk in 2018, titled "The Problem with Treating a Dog Like a Pet,"[1] which turned the dog industry on its head. Her vision and her life's work has been to facilitate a critical paradigm shift in our relationships with dogs—building bridges and inspiring others with comprehensive, practical science to redefine how we perceive, talk about, and treat our canine companions as a society. Dogs are complex—our methods of living with them and helping them cannot be one-dimensional.

Although Brophey's talk debuted in 2018, she had already worked with dogs and owners in Asheville, North Carolina, for more than 20 years. She is the owner of a training center there called The Dog Door. She earned a BA in applied ethology, which is the study of the applied relationship between human and animal behavior. Her unique degree and background gave her the training and knowledge to speak about the natural laws dogs follow and the fact that human interference (and our rapidly changing world) is a direct cause of most stress, anxiety, and behavior problems being expressed in modern dogs.

Brophey's book, *Meet Your Dog: The Game-Changing Guide to Understanding Your Dog's Behavior* was published by Chronicle Books in 2018. In this fascinating book, she lays out the program she created back in 2009 to help owners navigate life with their dogs: Dog L.E.G.S. Brophey says in her book that these problems may actually be a matter of miscommunication. She created the L.E.G.S. model to represent the four "legs" that prop up a dog, inside and outside. L.E.G.S. stands for Learning, Environment, Genetics, and Self. She created this unique program to organize insights from dozens of scientific disciplines into something understandable for the modern dog owner. It's a framework and blueprint for understanding the huge range of factors that affect our dogs' behavior. Let's take a look at each part:

---

1   Kim Brophey, "The Problem with Treating a Dog Like a Pet," filmed April 2018 at TEDxUNCAsheville, https://www.youtube.com/watch?v=46ND3suK1y8

L = Learning

Learning involves your dog's lifelong experience and education. Brophey notes that while humans tend to neatly categorize a dog's learning as puppy socialization, obedience work, and classes, dogs are actually learning all the time. Dogs are always watching and what the dog learns about the consequences of his choices will affect his behavior in the future. This fact can make a compassionate human squirm when we consider how little control we allow modern dogs and how that might affect their ability to think, learn, adapt, and change their behavior. I've already written about the importance of creating resilient dogs and one way dogs become resilient is having enough autonomy to think and choose how to react to what they encounter in their lives. Behavior problems erupt in our dogs when the instinctual, natural actions they know don't work to alleviate their stress, anxiety, or frustration.

E = Environment

Environment matters for every species—as Brophey notes, we don't put hamsters in fish tanks for a reason. She zeroes in on the inaccurate and even harmful lie we have been told for decades about dogs: "it's all how you raise them." Brophey instead writes that "[a] wild animal lives in a certain ecosystem and has an ecological niche. He is perfectly suited to be exactly the way he is. This is because his design, physically and behaviorally, "worked" in prior generations that adapted to (learned from) a specific environment."

Think of all the ways we restrict our dogs' environments. Like Brophey, when I grew up in the suburbs my unneutered dog jumped our fence and took himself on daily adventures. He didn't fight other dogs and he had the ability to do what he wanted all day—which sometimes included following my bus to school (crossing a four-lane highway). Yes, there were dangers in that and for

Dogs and puppies are complex, thoughtful beings who deserve our commitment to understanding their unique needs.

Many dogs in the past had more freedoms—jumping the fence, adventuring through the neighborhood, etc. There were risks involved that we don't want to bring back, but there are still ways we can restore some of that autonomy to our dogs.

sure he sired puppies in the neighborhood, but he also had agency. We have stripped modern dogs of much of that agency and their troubling behavior shows that they are maladapted to the choices we've made for them. My dog Cricket made life decisions and learned what worked and what did not work (including how to evade cars). In great part I wrote this book to give you tools to help your dog navigate the world we've chosen for them. Being aware of their environmental needs is crucial.

G = Genetics

Brophey writes that genes are the instructions for life and survival, passed down from one generation to the next. "Genes determine the reasonable scope of what an animal can and can't do," Brophey says. "The shape of a dog—his size, body, ears, nose, fur, tail, and even behavior is the product of selected genes intended to promote specific behaviors within specific environments."

Brophey shares a moving story in her first chapter about the time she was called to help a highly stressed Wheaton Terrier who had been obsessively climbing and scratching the walls of the remote cabin in which he lived with his owner. The owner had tried working with other trainers to no avail—trainers who attempted traditional training methods aimed at changing the dog's behavior without asking the "why" behind the behavior. The terrier was about to be put on anxiety medications and if that didn't work, his future was bleak—it is difficult to live with dog behavior that looks to us like it's "crazy." Brophey observed the dog's behavior and told her client she didn't believe the dog was crazy at all. Instead, she thought the cabin had a mouse infestation and the terrier was doing exactly what his genes told him to do: get the mice. It turns out the cabin did have a mouse infestation—once that issue was fixed, the terrier calmed down and life returned to normal.

In her book, Brophey breaks down the historical roles of various types of dogs, including natural dogs, sight hounds, guardians, toy dogs, scent hounds, gun dogs, terriers, bull dogs, herding dogs, or world dogs (which Brophey defines as breeds that were not developed through closed gene pools, artificial selection, or other human intervention). Knowing the background and genetic code of your purebred or mixed-breed dog can make a huge difference in living a conflict-free life with your dog.

The "crazy" terrier story hurts my heart because similar stories happen to dogs over and over again. A family with kids gets a cattle dog with genes programmed to herd and bite the heels of huge cows and the parents can't understand why their bored, highly energetic dog nips at their children's heels trying to herd them. A well-intentioned young student gets a Beagle because she likes how they look but is exasperated on walks since the dog is obsessed with sniffing and won't listen to her. A man gets a German Shepherd because he knows they are great guard dogs but is angry when the dog tries to guard against his mother's visits. I could go on and on. The behavior changes we demand from dogs who are merely doing what they were bred (by us) to do can be cruel. We label our dogs as "stupid" or "lazy" or "disobedient" when they simply never got the memo that we expect them to override thousands of years of genetic programming.

S = Self

Do you think of your dog as having a "self"? You should. Brophey writes that self describes the internal factors unique to each dog such as age, health, disease, disability, nutrition, stress levels, and personal quirks. The self also lies at the heart of our own deep connection to our dogs. Brophey writes: "Like us, your dog is ultimately a one-in-a-million individual creature filled with likes and dislikes that make her unique and special." Brophey lists six "big" internal conditions of dogs that influence behavior: personality/psyche, age/ontogeny, sex/hormones, nutrition/condition, disability/physical injury, and health/physiology.

I've thought deeply about my heartfelt connection with my departed Border Collie named Echo (to whom this book is dedicated). Why did I love her above everything else, even though I've had countless deep connections with many animals and people? For me, it was her darling, sweet face, her epically soft fur, and the fact that she had the heart of a lion despite her small size. It was her shadowing me everywhere, walking just behind me but leaping out to defend me if she felt I needed it. I loved her so deeply in part because she chose me as her highest love, too—I even outranked sheep! I often joked that we were codependent and perhaps we were. It was a dependency I never minded (and feel lost without). It was Echo's self that I fell in love with—her uniqueness.

Humans have spent thousands of years breeding dogs to excel at specific tasks. Many problems arise from us not realizing a certain behavior is a logical response to their genetic programming (like the Wheaten Terrier destroying his home to catch mice the owner didn't even realize were there).

Ask an Expert

Applied Ethologist Kim Brophey Discusses Trauma in Dogs, Ethology, and Why Dogs Need to Have Agency

This interview has been edited for length. Please see https://foxchapelpets.com/positive-training-dogs/ to read the full interview.

Kim Brophey always enjoys any chance to spend quality time with her family dogs.

▶ **At what age did you know you wanted to work with animals? How did you settle on applied ethology? It feels as though most people don't even know what ethology studies.**

When I was tiny, I was obsessed with understanding nature. As soon as I was able to be out in the yard, I wanted to be outside with the snakes, the salamanders, the spiders, and the earthworms. In Atlanta at the time, the dogs were still loose, too, so I had all these interesting relationships with the dogs in the city that just lived in my neighborhood

and would just show up and come around and hang out on their own, like floating relationships and experiences. And I felt a connection with nature that I didn't feel with the kind of modern urban reality and lifestyle. I didn't understand a lot of cultural social norms and expectations and I felt frustrated by a lot of conventions. Everything about nature just made sense to me, and I felt at home with it. I was a little ethologist in the making, boundlessly curious about observing and understanding an animal's behavior in their natural environment and all things in the world. And I think dogs probably circumstantially became the kind of emphasis of my interest because I did grow up in a city. I had limited access to nature in other ways. If I could find a bird that had a broken wing in my front yard then it became my object of obsession, but it just didn't happen very much. But I had always had dogs and so they became kind of the bridge for me, which is why I ultimately ended up naming my company the Dog Door. I ended up wanting to really focus on that relationship between human and animal behavior. My degree in the Applied Relationship Between Human & Animal Behavior brought in that ecological piece, the evolution of animals, and also the relationship between humans and animals historically. It's studying specifically the intersection of the relationship between human and animal behavior in those species with which we have that level of intimacy, whether for good or for bad, including in laboratories, zoos, farms, and as companion animals—basically situations of captivity and domestication only. But there are such unique challenges and opportunities in those kinds of relationships. And it's just fascinating how things can build or completely fall apart at that crossroads.

▶ **You write in your book about how we humans have taken away agency for dogs, even to the extent of harming their genes as we took away their choice of a mating partner. What is the most important way we can give independence and agency to dogs?**

The number one answer for me, for all dogs, is providing true nature therapy without our intervention. What if that could literally be someone setting up a lawn chair in their fenced backyard and allowing the dog to do whatever they want to do in that space. We tend to have this idea that when we go out with our dog, we should be training them, or we should be throwing the ball or making sure they

Helping your dog regain a sense of agency can be as simple as giving your dog a safe space to "be" and do what they want to do.

don't do this or that. We don't give them opportunities to just be and find where their own instincts and interaction with the signals in the environment take them. This is such a simple thing that is so undervalued. I think we do give dogs choices in the wrong way because we don't understand the nuances of what kinds of choices they can handle. I completely agree with the need to up the choice and agency quotient for our dogs overall, but I also think that people's well-intentioned idea of this is to simply follow their dogs on walks in active urban neighborhoods giving them agency to do whatever they want. Dogs can actually become very stressed and overwhelmed by that. I think continuing the discussion on when to give them that agency, and how to create it is important.

▶ **In our interview, you talked about trauma, both in humans and in dogs. You began your TEDx Talk referencing your own personal trauma that you experienced as a young person. How does trauma relate to dogs and how we work with them?**

I think a lot of our judgments on trauma are kind of erroneous, that it must be acute and physically devastating or in some way violent. And the truth is, there's so much psychological and emotional trauma that happens on a micro level that's very real. There's been this kind of dismissal. I think it's a kind of chronic conditioning of "less than"—mistreatment and abuse of power, manipulation, emotional blackmailing, and gaslighting. Gaslighting is one of those things that we are uncomfortable applying to our relationships with dogs. But we gaslight dogs all the time. "What do you mean? Why are you scared at the vet? He has cookies. He's your friend. Right?" Meanwhile, we're tricking them to take their temperature or administer vaccines in potentially traumatic ways. We just make ourselves untrustworthy, not because we mean to, but because we've been taught that dogs couldn't possibly be cognizant or sentient enough for it to matter. And that's so weird.

Even in the best, most caring shelter, a relinquished or abandoned dog is still going to have trauma from the experience.

We also see trauma with rescued dogs. I started my whole career in rescue, and I actually believe—this is a horrifically difficult pill to swallow—but I think over 90% of dogs that end up in shelters in the first place have PTSD. I think the process of relinquishment, abandonment, and rehoming is, in itself, for most dogs as traumatic as it would be for a small child.

▶ **Are you optimistic or pessimistic about the fate of modern dogs over the next 20 years? Why?**

I feel like there is an actual paradigm shift that's happening and the atmosphere within the dog world is qualitatively shifting toward this collaborative spirit, this interdisciplinary, supportive, curious, passionate, nonjudgmental sphere that I would have said wasn't possible, because frankly, it's a 180 from what my experience has been for most of my time. I do think the conversation can change and is changing. We have to kind of continue to hold ourselves accountable to doing better and being respectful and ethical in how we proceed with each other in our dialogues and our collaboration, and hopefully, things will continue to move forward in that direction. There are a million connections that I've made that I know I wouldn't have made if it hadn't been for COVID. It opened everything up and gave us comfort that we all then developed with video chats and online interactions, having online conversations because we couldn't have in-person conversations. Having the rug pulled out from under us made us reevaluate some things that needed to be reevaluated.

What do you love most about your dog? These qualities are the unique elements that make up your dog's "self."

What do you love most about your dog—the one sitting quietly right now at your feet as you read this book (or the hyper fuzzball bugging you nonstop)? Your dog is who your dog is and most of the time we love them just for being exactly who they are. We run into a communication problem when their unique L.E.G.S. needs are not being met, and we must make sure each of these four legs is understood and supported. Don't you think dogs would do the same for us if they could?

I love that Brophey's book and program account for the entire dog, not just the behavior we can observe. I encourage you to sit with the concept of L.E.G.S. for a while. Consider it in relation to your own dog and answer as many questions as you can about your dog's Learning, Environment, Genetics, and Self. What you discover may surprise you and become the beginning of the end for any communication problems. For a deeper dive into this game-changing program, check out Brophey's

websites for seminars, articles, and webinars (see her biography on page 247).

MANAGEMENT

Management is a preventative measure rather than a training technique. Management uses doors, crates, baby gates, leashes, muzzles, etc., to prevent the dog from making decisions or taking actions that would likely harm the dog or permit the dog to cause harm. Management is a valuable tool for dog owners for sure, although trainers will always remind you that management is never 100% foolproof. Muzzles and leashes can break, kids can forget to shut doors, gates can be left ajar, etc. I use management sparingly because it doesn't solve the problem for the owner or the dog—it only (if used correctly and continually with no lapses) prevents unwanted things from happening. Sometimes it comes down to a matter of safety, however, and management is often the fastest tool to use.

Gates, crates, and dog play pens are a few options available to manage your dog's access to certain places or people in your house. They're not a solution to your dog's behavior problem, but they help control the situation so you can protect and more calmly work with your dog over time.

Before you consider using management, read back through this critical chapter and consider whether any of the above-mentioned ideas will work better for you and your dog. Let's say you have that mouse-chasing terrier Kim Brophey wrote about in her book. You decide to employ management to "solve" the problem: you put the dog in a crate eight hours a day to prevent the activity. At first glance you'd think you'd stopped the behavior, but you also imprisoned a dog who was bred to display that behavior. You stop the unwanted behavior, but by crating the dog and keeping him from acting on his natural drives (all while he can still smell and hear the mice) you are likely creating 10 more unwanted behaviors. Imagine releasing this highly frustrated dog from his crate. If he predicts he will be crated most of the day, he will have a HUGE focus on getting those mice when he is free. He could even begin to lash out and bite (especially when you try

to put him in the crate). Not addressing your dog's genetic coding and natural drives is a terrific way to make your dog crazy.

Here are a few ways I would use management in the short term while figuring out how to better resolve the situation from the dog's point of view:

Time-related problems: If I have a new dog who hasn't fully acclimated to my home and a big environmental change is occurring—such as a move, a family member in the hospital, etc.—teaching the dog to be calm and content for a short time in his crate could be helpful to keep him separated from any chaos. A crate is only a good option if he can truly relax and chew on a high-value treat or toy at the same time—otherwise I would use a larger ex pen or a quiet room. If the dog hates the crate and I shove him in there, I am only making a small problem much larger. It's better to not bring a new dog into the home with large changes on the horizon, but sometimes life happens despite our best laid plans.

Another common time-related situation in which management can be useful is the

Since management uses tools (like baby gates and muzzles) to prevent your dog from acting in a harmful way, it is helpful for introducing dogs to new family members!

introduction of new children. If a new human baby will be joining the family, have your introduction well planned (and view this introduction as a process, not a one-time event). Always ensure there is a quiet, safe place for your dog to spend time relaxing or playing away from the new kiddo.

Dangerous food/outdoor problems: There's a dog trainer in Oregon I admire who has a very determined dog named Astrid who loves to gobble up anything and everything she finds on walks. There are a lot of disgusting and harmful things a dog can gulp down quickly in the public sphere. After her dog ate a discarded joint and became violently ill, she trained Astrid to wear a muzzle willingly and happily on public walks. I am a huge advocate of muzzles for managing all sorts of dog concerns (as long as the dog is acclimated to wearing one). It's not fair to throw one on without slowly introducing the dog to wearing a muzzle, but many dogs can acclimate quite nicely. Astrid's owner can't guarantee there won't be something awful (but enticing to Astrid) on the ground while they're out walking, so the muzzle allows freedom and safety on daily walks. Muzzles can also be helpful to manage introducing an adult rescue dog or shelter dog with an unknown background to your adult dog. You can use a strong baby gate as well until you are certain the dogs will get along.

Some dogs have a medical condition called pica that causes them to eat bizarre things such as rocks or animal stool. This is a case for veterinarian help as the muzzle will not stop that medical condition's symptoms—it will just create enormous stress and frustration.

Leashes are another form of management, and they can stop a lot of problems from ever happening.

A muzzle is an effective management tool, as long as time is taken to slowly introduce and acclimate the dog to wearing one.

Note: I wrote extensively in chapters 7 and 8 of my first book, *The Midnight Dog Walkers*, about using counterconditioning (CC) and desensitizing (DS) to help reactive dogs. I still use and value CC and DS, but I most often begin helping dogs with the newer protocols and ideas shared in this chapter. Additionally, there are many other excellent programs in the world of force-free training. This chapter focuses only on the newest and most groundbreaking of these ideas.

Leashes can prevent dog fights and car chasing and they can protect dogs in dangerous outdoor areas near cliffs, fast-moving water, etc.

Sight or sound reactivity: While you will hopefully be working with an educated force-free behavior professional to help with your dog's reactivity (or other behavior concerns), there might be a time in which stopping your dog from seeing or hearing its triggers is helpful for the dog. For dogs who live in a house with a window or glass door that allows them to see all their triggers passing by, investing in inexpensive film to cover the glass can help resolve unwanted behavior. Turn on white noise or soft music to help dim the outside world's noises.

My two cattle-collie brothers think it is grand fun to chase delivery trucks (safely on their side of our wood and wire fence). Our dogs can see through our fence, so stopping them from seeing the trucks isn't an option unless we take the expensive route of tearing down the current fence to put up a solid one. Instead, we have learned the times when these trucks are likely to be in our neighborhood and we shut the dog door—we deny the dogs access to the triggers. They still look through the window,

If your dog is triggered by seeing the world pass by their favorite window, try applying a film to limit how much of those triggers they actually see.

but they don't have the same reaction. If they did, I would need to try other changes, such as shutting the blinds, if I planned to stick with management as the only solution.

5

Other Behavior Concerns and Real-World Solutions

There are a range of common behaviors beyond aggression and reactivity that cause stress for dogs and owners. If your dog displays any of these behaviors, you should first visit the veterinarian to rule out any contributing pain or medical factors. If the behavior issue is not related to a medical issue, we can often address behavior concerns with behavior modification. Remember, working to change an unwanted behavior is different from teaching obedience skills, so behavior issues require a deeper look.

Please be aware that entire books have been written about some of these disorders and the advice here is meant to be a starting point. When excessive behavior shows up and the owner can't quickly help their dogs, it's time to call in a qualified behavior consultant sooner rather than later. We don't want the dog to spend years rehearsing undesirable behaviors, nor do we want them to have to suffer when there is help available.

These step-by-step training protocols are ones I have successfully used for thousands of dogs (as have many other force-free behavior consultants). Having said that, please keep in mind that there are countless ways to fairly train dogs that do not involve pain, force, or fear. There is no "Great Rulebook of Dog Training" that says, "You Must

Note: Some dog behaviors might not concern one owner while they'd drive another owner bonkers. If the behavior you observe in your dog isn't the result of a medical issue and the behavior isn't overly stressful for the dog, consider whether mild versions of the behavior might be something you can adjust to.

A dog chasing its tail might sound completely normal, but if it occurs often or is extreme or disruptive, this compulsive behavior requires intervention. There's some evidence that it might even be related to a seizure disorder.

Train This Way." Who knows? You may come up with something entirely brand new that works for you and your bestie (without harming your dog). It is important to trust your bond with your dog and be open to trying alternative techniques you might find or devise while researching advice from other professional, ethical, and certified trainers.

OBSESSIVE COMPULSIVE DISORDER (OCD)

Watching a dog repeatedly display OCD-type behavior can be heartbreaking. The animal is in an obvious state of distress and his brain is directing him to self-harm over and over again. I once heard veterinary behaviorist Dr. Soraya Juarbe-Diaz at an industry convention say, "Know the normal, treat the abnormal." Troublesome OCD behaviors are definitely not in the "normal" category of canine behavior. To paraphrase veterinarian and dog trainer Dr. Jennifer Summerfield,[1] studies have shown that abnormal, repetitive behaviors are associated with abnormalities in a particular area of the brain called the cortico-striatal-thalamic-cortical (CSTC) loop.

OCD behaviors are repetitive movements or activities that have no obvious purpose or function. These behaviors interfere with normal behavior and can be severe. The most common types include tail-chasing, hallucinating (biting invisible flies), self-mutilation, flank sucking, spinning, circling, staring, pacing, vocalizing, fence-running, and pica. Inventive dogs display their own unique forms, as well. To make this behavior even more tragic, it tends to intensify over time, and can become difficult to stop. It also tends to increase with age. Sometimes a dog can display an OCD behavior when faced with disappointment or frustration, but just as often there is no observable cause.

There are countless positive ways to work with dogs. Food is a primary reinforcer and one that most dogs love. It is not a bribe to reinforce desired behavior with tasty treats.

The causes of OCD behaviors are varied. Containment in a tight kennel for hours (or permanently in the case of puppy mill breeding dogs) can contribute. Chronic stress can bring out these behaviors. Physical causes include an abnormal nervous system, allergies, skin infections, pinched nerves, spinal problems, abnormal chemical activity, neurological disease, or physical pain that increases the dog's anxiety. There is some evidence that compulsive tail chasing could even be a type of seizure disorder. Additionally, these behaviors sometimes start off innocently enough—the owner thinks it's amusing, rewards the dog over and over, and the dog continues. Some larger dogs can be more prone to these issues, including Doberman Pinchers, German Shepherds, Great Danes, Labrador Retrievers, and Irish Setters. Some Bull Terriers can become obsessed with spinning.

---

1   Mardi Richmond, "Understanding Canine Compulsive Disorder," *Whole Dog Journal*, January 2019.

HOW TO HELP YOUR DOG WITH OCD BEHAVIORS

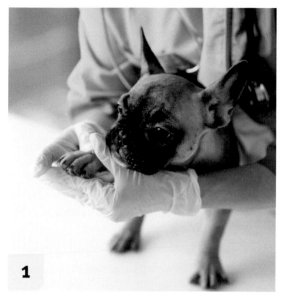

Step one for any excess canine behavior is to get a veterinarian health check to rule in or out any health issues that could be contributing to the behavior.

▪ ▪ ▪ ▪ ▪ ▪ ▪ ▪ ▪ ▪ ▪ OVERVIEW

How to Help Your Dog with OCD Behaviors

- **Step One:** Rule Out Any Medical Causes
- **Step Two:** Make Sure Your Dog's Emotional and Physical Needs Are Being Met
- **Step Three:** Provide a Predictable, Calm Home
- **Step Four:** Interrupt and Redirect the Behavior

Evaluate what your dog truly needs and make sure those needs are being met.

STEP ONE: Rule Out Any Medical Causes

If you think your dog's behavior is compulsive—meaning the dog cannot stop doing it—or it is causing physical or emotional problems for your dog, the first step is to take your dog to your veterinarian to rule out any medical contributors. OCD behavior has nothing to do with your dog "being naughty."

I highly recommend meeting with a veterinary behaviorist online or in person if you can.[2] Medical therapies can include antibiotics, anti-inflammatory medications, seizure medications, anxiety medications, psychotropic drugs, or simple bandages or head collars. Training or behavior modification alone cannot solve a brain, hormone, or nerve issue.

STEP TWO: Make Sure Your Dog's Emotional and Physical Needs Are Being Met

Conflict and stressful environments can cause anxiety and increase the dog's stress reactions, including OCD behaviors. The same is true if the dog isn't getting adequate physical exercise. Take a step back and look at your dog's life to see where you can make any improvements in her lifestyle. If you are not seeing results, hire a qualified behavior consultant sooner rather than later (see Resources for Owners on page 233 for more resources).

---

2   Search for veterinary behaviorists through the American College of Veterinary Behaviorist's directory, available at www.dacvb.org/search/custom.asp?id=4709.

3

Providing a quiet, restful home for dogs can help several different behavior concerns. Dogs need quality down time as much as humans do.

4

Encourage and redirect your dog toward calm behaviors like relaxing on a mat.

STEP THREE: Provide a Predictable, Calm Home

Ensure that your dog's day is predictable and calm. Ensure your dog has down time and quiet, restful parts of her day. Always use reward-based training—it is cruel to punish OCD behaviors. There are some tools, such as head halters, that may help with dogs who spin, but I advise working with a qualified trainer to introduce such tools.

STEP FOUR: Interrupt and Redirect the Behavior

Try interrupting and redirecting your dog's behavior. This can be tricky—the interruption shouldn't be dramatic, but instead as neutral as possible. For example, if your dog begins to spin, try tossing a delicious raw, meaty bone into the dog's crate and inviting the dog to go in for a chew. Asking for or encouraging calm behaviors throughout the day (like relaxing on a mat, deep breathing, or even giving the dog a massage) can ease some milder OCD-type behaviors.

If, after trying all these steps in consultation with professionals, there is no change and you conclude that the behavior is not causing the dog mental or physical harm, you will need to learn to accept the behavior. Sometimes using the tools available to help the dog (medications, etc.) can cause more stress than not using them. And some dogs unfortunately do not get better.

EXCESSIVE BARKING

Our house is on a corner lot in a very quiet, older neighborhood and all of us here enjoy the peace and quiet ... until someone's dog begins barking and barking and barking, sometimes for hours at a time. I can't stand endless barking, not only because it is terrible to listen to, but also because the dog doing it is telling me they have a problem.

Whenever our two cattle-collie dogs bark, my husband or I get up to see what they are barking at. Most of the time it is delivery trucks, sometimes it is a child who had the nerve to ride by on a bike, etc. My dogs either bark at things they have fun chasing (from the safety of their side of the fence) or at things they see as potential threats. They don't bark without reason (even if that reason only makes sense in their canine minds). They were born on a working cattle ranch from working stock parents—their genes tell them to chase and herd moving objects.

Even though my dogs exhibit what I consider to be "purposeful barking," we still interrupt the behavior. If left to their own devices, they would stay outside all day barking at everything, staying amped-up and never relaxing. Instead, we redirect them into playing fun, richly rewarded recall games. We've also become experts at restricting their access to the yard during busy times—that management technique has made the most difference.

A few barks a day is *not* excessive barking. Dogs bark! It is their primary method of communication, just as our voice is ours. When a dog barks for hours at a time, that dog is communicating that something in its world is not right. It depends on the dog and the circumstances, but often nuisance barking dogs are incredibly bored from being on their own all day. They could also have anxiety—the barking could be the result of startling noises, or it could help to self-soothe. Pain can also always be a contributor. Regardless of the cause, excessive barking creates rifts between neighbors and some cities and towns are cracking down. Owners in these places can be fined or eventually have their dog taken away from them.

Barking is a dog's primary method of communication—his voice. When barking becomes excessive, however, we need to intervene and make sure our furry friends are okay.

HOW TO HELP YOUR DOG WITH EXCESSIVE BARKING

Your dog's veterinarian should always be a first stop if you notice any troubling behaviors—pain or other medical concerns can contribute to behavior problems.

Yelling at a dog is not helping the dog understand what you want him to do, and it causes anxiety and stress. Find positive ways of resolving conflict.

STEP ONE: Rule Out Any Medical Causes

Have your dog checked out by a veterinarian to rule out pain or other medical contributors.

OVERVIEW

How to Help Your Dog with Excessive Barking

- **Step One:** Rule Out Any Medical Causes
- **Step Two:** Do Not Punish Your Dog for Barking
- **Step Three:** Identify and Address the "Why"

STEP TWO: Do Not Punish or Harm Your Dog for Barking

Don't yell at your dog, hit your dog, or otherwise harm your dog for barking. It doesn't help and can even encourage MORE barking. Do not put a painful collar on your dog—you are hurting your dog and it fails to solve the underlying problem anyway. Using pain to train or stop behaviors harms the human-canine bond and does not set your dog up to feel like they are in a safe space.

Absolutely do not de-bark your dog. Most veterinarians consider it to be cruel and I agree. Again, it's a drastic, harmful step that doesn't address the underlying "why" of the behavior. The pitiful sounds de-barked dogs make will break your heart.

Step back and look hard at your dog's daily life. Release the idea that your barking dog is doing it to be "bad" or to annoy you. See the barking for what it is: the natural way this non-speaking animal communicates. I know excessive barking can be stressful and annoying, but it is imperative that we get to the bottom of "why" your dog is barking—punishing and harming your dog does not help us do that.

3

Barking is a natural canine activity. It becomes problematic for all when there is excessive barking. It's our job to get to the "why" of excessive barking.

This dog is demonstrating territorial barking, something that is natural for certain protective breeds. When it becomes excessive, there are a number of soothing products and techniques available to try.

STEP THREE: Identify and Address the "Why"

Loneliness and Boredom: Often people with lonely or bored dogs will try adding a second dog, but they're just adding a chorus member. You first have to address the underlying loneliness or boredom. First, don't leave dogs outside alone while you are gone (in some states it's against the law). Curb the loneliness! Take your dog for a longer walk in the mornings before work. Bring your dog to work with you if allowed and if your dog would enjoy it or come home for lunch and entertain your dog with their favorite activity. Make sure your dog has safe toys and especially chewing objects while you are away.

You can hire a qualified dog walker if your dog loves going for walks (thoroughly review the walker's skill set and professionalism). If your dog shows leash reactivity, hire the dog walker to instead spend an hour a day with your dog doing fun indoor activities. We must learn to meet our dogs' needs.

Territorial Barking: If your dog is barking to protect its property or territory, first remember it's a response we've bred into many breeds. Territorial barking is a useful skill to alert you that someone is on or near your property—but excessive territorial barking needs to be addressed. Always start by keeping your dog safely inside when you are not at home. Block your dog's view of outdoor motion—removable film for your windows or glass doors is a simple solution that can make a big difference. Leave on box fans and soothing, calming music. Tiring your dog out before you head off to work can also help induce a nice, long nap. If you want to try calming products like Rescue Remedy®, the ThunderShirt®, or CBD dog treats, I suggest trying one at a time for a few weeks each and taking notes to see if you notice a difference in your dog. If one seems to help your dog, use it.

You can also readjust how your dog views someone walking past your property. Start in a controlled, quiet learning environment—indoors with your dog on the leash at a safe, comfortable distance from a window (you don't want the dog to go over threshold if you can prevent it). Have high-value treats (such as meat or cheese cut into small pieces), and have a human helper make noise outside the window. BEFORE the dog can bark, move the high-value treat to just above the dog's head and nose. If the dog feels safe enough to eat the treat, give them small pieces for as long as the human helper outside the window is in the dog's sight. The instant the person is out of sight, remove the food. If your dog goes over threshold and is uninterested in the treats, move the dog farther away from the window. Have the outside helper begin making small movements and speaking gently. If the dog responds positively, the outside helper should work their way up to making faster, louder movements. The goal is to create an expectation within your dog that a person moving and making noise outside equals treats. Timing and repetition are important here, so don't hesitate to reach out to a positive reinforcement trainer for help and practice often.

Demand Barking: If your dog's issue is one of demand barking, consider yourself a bit on the lucky side as this is one of the easiest behaviors to reduce or stop. Demand barking is just what it sounds like—your dog stands there and barks at you over and over until you give her food or engage with her in some way—for some dogs that engagement might even be you yelling at her to "shut up."

Simple solution: do not respond to unwanted behavior! Turn your back to the dog, cross your arms, and stay silent. You can also leave the room if the dog is demand barking and reenter it once the dog is quiet. The instant your dog stops barking (if the

This dog is demonstrating demand barking and is clearly seeking some sort of food or engagement.

behavior has been reinforced by you or others in the home, this could take some time), turn around and give affection, treats, or a toy (whatever your dog loves the most). If the barking begins anew, stand up and turn away again. The dog will learn that barking makes you shut down while quiet brings your attention back (and fun toys and treats).

Sometimes dogs engage in this unwanted behavior in predictable situations—when you sit down at the end of a long day to watch a movie and relax or when you are on the phone. Be prepared! Have yummy treats ready and do some fun obedience or nose work for 10 minutes before you turn on the TV or pick up the phone. If you are talented, you can continue the obedience work while you start your show. Or give the dog a wonderful

Older dogs may demonstrate excessive barking—schedule an appointment with your dog's vet and create comfortable, quiet spaces for your friend.

chew toy or treat just prior to situations in which you know he is likely to start demand barking. In other words, set your furry friend up to succeed, not fail.

Senior Dogs: Excessive barking can also occur in senior dogs. If you suspect your dog's age is a cause, it's extremely important to follow through on step one and make that appointment with your veterinarian. Sometimes medications can help in this situation. Be sure to have a comfy, quiet place your senior best friend can retreat to when needed.

Separation Anxiety or Noise Phobia: If your dog is experiencing separation anxiety or noise phobias, you will need to hire a behavior consultant and work closely with your veterinarian. These issues can be complex—I've supplied a few starting solutions for them beginning on page 110.

Separation anxiety is a serious and complicated problem to address. You'll need to team up with a great veterinarian and behavior consultant to ensure the best outcome for your furry friend.

EXCESSIVE DIGGING

Digging is a natural dog behavior. It's important to provide an appropriate place and outlet for your dog's digging behaviors.

Behaviorist Lisa Hird found the ideal digging solution for her dog, Jack—he loves his hippo sandbox! This is a great example of working with your dog's natural behaviors versus trying to shut them down.

Dogs dig! Some dogs love to dig more than others—plucky terriers come to mind. Digging can be a lot of fun if you are a dog with four strong legs, a tremendous nose, and natural curiosity. After all, there are a lot of little scurrying critters that live underneath that dirt.

Your big, fluffy dog (such as a Husky, Malamute, or mixed-breed dog with a dual or heavy coat), might dig up just the right amount of grass and dirt, walk a few circles around the spot, and lie down with great satisfaction. This nicely crafted spot provides coolness on a hot day. Other diggers seek to hide their favorite bones or toys to save them for another day or keep them away from "bratty" dog siblings.

Some dogs are left alone all day long and night in their boring backyards with nothing to do, so they start to dig—can we blame them? Bored dogs, lonely dogs, and dogs with separation anxiety can dig and dig and dig. Sometimes it is an attempt to self-soothe and sometimes they are literally trying to escape the situation in which they find themselves.

For those of you who live with diggers, how I wish your dog had come to you with a plastic kiddie swimming pool filled with sand or dirt and puppy toys hidden at the bottom to help alleviate the dog's need to dig. Dogs do not arrive in our lives understanding our weird love of green grass lawns and lovely flowers. We have to teach them about human preferences. I admire cat lovers who create cat sanctuaries and safe cat spots inside and outside their homes. Why don't we do the same for our dogs? Imagine a safe backyard built for a dog's enrichment instead of just an empty lawn. Some of my clients create sandboxes and train their dog to dig to their heart's desire in that spot. I highly recommend this approach. Digging is a natural and common dog behavior and like the other over-the-top behaviors, it only becomes a problem when the digging becomes excessive or destroys your yard or home.

■ ■ ■ ■ ■ ■ ■ ■ ■ ■ OVERVIEW

How to Help Your Dog with Excessive Digging

- **Step One:** Prepare Your Home and Yard
- **Step Two:** Figure Out Why Your Dog Is Digging
- **Step Three:** Do Not Punish or Harm Your Dog for Digging

HOW TO HELP YOUR DOG WITH EXCESSIVE DIGGING

Create a designated digging spot and hide treats in the sand or dirt to encourage your dog to dig in one spot. Some owners put sand or dirt in a plastic kiddie pool and hide their dog's favorite toys and treats in the pool.

Use your dog's strong sense of smell and hide toys and treats—sniffing them out lights up a dog's brain and helps tire the dog in a good way.

STEP ONE: Prepare Your Home and Yard

Recognize that digging is a natural canine behavior and prepare your home and yard for the possibility that your dog might want to dig. Purchase a plastic kiddie swimming pool and fill it with sand or dirt. Then hide toys (including some stuffed with edible, good-smelling treats) deep in the sand or dirt. Emphasize that this is THE digging spot by having your dog nearby on leash while you clearly hide the toys in front of them. Release the dog with great fanfare and encourage her to "go find." This win-win solution accepts that some dogs love to dig and provides them with a place to do so.

Also try hiding yummy treats throughout your yard while your dog waits on leash nearby. Then release your dog to "go find" and encourage this type of nose work over digging. You can fight your dog's genes and become highly aggravated, or you can use solutions that meet your dog's needs.

STEP TWO: Figure Out Why Your Dog Is Digging

Boredom: If your dog is bored, it's easy to correct. Add nose work inside and outside the home—it's a fantastic way to tire your dog out in 10 minutes or less. Increase the number of walks or activities away from home if your dog likes going out in public. Consider hiring a qualified dog walker to visit with your dog and play for an hour or take a long walk if that can be done safely. Ensure you have quality mind puzzles and daily enrichment (I provide some enrichment ideas in chapter 9). Use your dog's mighty brain in all sorts of creative ways.

Many dogs like to hide special items like bones and toys by digging holes. Don't let your dog take these items outside—it won't fix the behavior, but it will help protect your lawn while you work on other solutions.

Anxious Digging: If your dog shows signs of anxiety (such as panting, hiding under furniture, OCD-type behaviors, cowering, or shaking) and uses digging as on outlet, make an appointment with your veterinarian. If your dog does need anti-anxiety medicine, it is better to get them started sooner rather than later. If the excessive digging seems to stem from separation anxiety, you will need to hire a behavior consultant and work closely with your veterinarian. Separation anxiety can be complex—I've supplied a few starting solutions beginning on page 110.

Hiding Bones and Toys: If your dog is digging holes all over your once beautiful lawn to hide bones and toys, use management to curb this behavior. Simply don't let your dog take toys and bones outside. She will still try to hide these items under your couch pillows since management doesn't change the underlying "why" of the behavior, but your lawn will be safe.

You can also give your dog quickly consumed soft bones and treats (and fewer of them), so she'll consume them on the spot rather than trying to hide them for later. Add larger puzzles and toys (available in many pet stores and online) that will engage your dog's mind and attention and won't be easy to hide. Finally, add an indoor "safe spot," such as a crate full of blankets with the door left open, in which she can hide her things.

If this could very well be a photo of your dog, try coming up with cooling solutions that don't involve the need for a bath afterward. Cooling pads and kiddie pools are great options.

Punishing your dog often just confuses him and heightens his anxiety.

Seeking a Cool Spot: If your dog digs to create cooling spots for himself, either dedicate an area of your yard to this (even add extra dirt) or find another way for your dog to cool down, such as cooling pads. A plastic kiddie pool used for its original purpose works, too—put in a few inches of cold, fresh water every day for your dog to lie down in. The easiest solution is to keep your dog inside your nice, air-conditioned home on hot days and any time you're not home.

STEP THREE: Do Not Punish or Harm Your Dog for Digging

Don't come home from work, drag your dog outside to the new holes he dug in your yard during the day, and punish him. He won't make the connection between what he did that morning and your punishment in the afternoon. Punishment doesn't tell your dog what you do want him to do and won't stop this innate behavior.

Don't use painful or frightening tools like shock collars, spray bottles, or thrown objects like chains—which all create unwanted consequences. These harm the human-canine bond. If the tips above don't resolve or reduce your excessive digging concerns, bring in a qualified behavior specialist.

CHASING

For many dogs, chasing is one of the most exciting activities they can do. Their powerful nose lets them know that a deer is around the bend, or their excellent hearing tells them that a distant delivery truck is coming their way. Then their innate desire to chase (and for some, to catch and kill) a fast-moving object kicks in. In other words, to chase something is to be a dog. Their ancestors relied on their ability to chase, capture, and kill for their meals.

Even though chasing is a natural behavior, it can be a seriously dangerous one in our modern world. Obviously chasing cars or motorcycles is a huge no-no, since the dog will likely lose that battle eventually. Humans on bikes are exciting—the rider will definitely react to the dog and there's a lot of motion and speed to light up the dog's brain and body. But, you, the owner, could find yourself in legal or financial trouble if the dog harms someone. The same is true for loose dogs permitted to chase horses or livestock. In many states, people are legally allowed to shoot to kill any dogs chasing livestock or wildlife. It is a serious problem for both the chasing dog and its target.

HOW TO HELP YOUR DOG WITH CHASING BEHAVIOR

▪ ▪ ▪ ▪ ▪ ▪ ▪ ▪ ▪ OVERVIEW

How to Help Your Dog with Chasing Behavior

- **Step One:** Understand and Accept Your Dog's Natural Thrill for the Chase

- **Step Two:** Use Your Leash and Highly Reward Recalls

- **Step Three:** Don't Rely on Harmful Methods, Reset How They View the Trigger

1

Squirrels elicit the "chase" behavior that lives inside almost every dog.

STEP ONE: Understand and Accept Your Dog's Natural Thrill for the Chase

Most dogs are born with an innate thrill for the chase. Once you have accepted that the chase motivation lives deep inside the canine brain, you begin working on ways to redirect or alter that behavior. King is not being a very bad boy when he forgets everything you've taught him when a deer jumps out in front of him on your off-leash hike. He is answering the "call of the wild." Seek out safe ways to let your dog chase, such as the sport of lure chasing. Throwing a ball or a frisbee will meet this need to some degree, although trainers advise being careful with how long you play fetch. Also be careful to not engage the dog in such a way that it could cause injuries or arthritis later in life.

2

A leash is a simple management tool that helps you teach your dog not to chase objects. We want to work to teach the dog different behaviors from pulling but should still allow him to sniff on walks to meet his needs.

STEP TWO: Use Your Leash and Highly Reward Recalls

One tool we've had for decades stops chase behavior before it begins: a well-made leash. Even the most highly trained dog might run off on a chase. A leash cancels that chance. I love to hike off leash with my dogs, but they never go off leash until we have practiced a reliable recall over and over and over again. Successfully calling a dog in full chase mode back to you is Ph.D.-level training. I practice off leash at home and in our yard and on leash out in the world, working my way up to off-leash recalls. Please never punish your dog for the act of coming back to you—that is not the message you want them to receive.

I do not advocate the use of shock collars for recalls. It is painful for the dog and using a recall command and then harming the dog creates confusion. When I attended a Schutzhund school (training for a dog obedience and protection sport), huge, powerful dogs often ran right through the highest shock to get to what was of interest to them. A shock collar is no guarantee that you will get 100% recall. A loving bond between you and the dog AND tons of highly rewarded recall training increases the odds that your dog will return to you.

A recall should be one of the most highly rewarded things a dog can do. A dog must be trained to come back when called and almost all dogs should be on leashes in public. You can buy 30-foot-long lines that give your dog more freedom (*not* retractable leashes—they have too much potential to cause injuries to you or the dog). If you find yourself in a truly secluded location and you have worked diligently to teach a reliable recall, there is something beautiful in being in nature with your off-leash dog running along the trail. The second you unhook that leash, however, you are responsible for what the dog does with the freedom (and there is always the risk of injury to your dog or other people or animals).

3

It's only fair to create a connection with your dog first inside the home and then outside. Having a dog who is able to sit even when faced with stimuli that engages his chase desires solves the problem of chasing. It's important we train this fairly and with a lot of encouragement for the behavior we prefer since the dog will have to override a natural behavior.

STEP THREE: Don't Rely on Harmful Methods, Reset How They View the Trigger

A common dog concern is when your dog's chase behavior shows up on neighborhood walks and he nearly pulls you over trying to chase joggers, bicyclists, and cars. This is dangerous not only because a large dog can pull owners down, but also because they can pull hard enough to break free from the handler. There are several ways to reduce or stop this behavior.

One method I never recommend is using a shock collar. It hurts the dog and your relationship with the dog (yes, even if done "correctly" and even if you are "just" using the beep function). As I said in step two, a dog in full-on chase mode might very well run right through even the highest shock. You might find yourself rushing your dog to see a vet because your shock collar gave you a false sense of security.

One of the most important opportunities we have is to intervene before the dog sees, hears, or smells the trigger to train a different behavior or avoid the chase scenario. You as the handler must be extremely aware of your surroundings so you can put a visual barrier between the dog and any potential triggers. The dog still might smell or hear it, but you've removed the most important trigger for the chase sequence—sight.

Once you've interrupted their view of the trigger, try a fun game of "find it," quickly throwing high-value treats on the ground until the trigger passes by. Or move far enough away from the trigger, drop the treats in front of the dog the whole time the trigger is in view, then stop giving the treats as soon as the trigger moves out of sight (counterconditioning them to reframe how the dog views the trigger). If the dog refuses the treats, you are still too close to the trigger and the dog needs more space.

Try the "find it" game and counterconditioning at home first. Start with a hungry dog on leash in front of a window. As soon as the dog detects a trigger, give her treats. As soon as the trigger leaves, stop giving her treats. The dog begins to connect the trigger with the treats. It is a process, and the timing here is important. Please consult with a qualified behavior expert if you need professional help.

Should We Consider Learning Theory?

Learning Theory—how dogs learn—is an older perspective on behavior that is controversial in some training circles. Remember that there are other influences, such as age, genetics, health, and how they relate to their environment, that must be taken into account. I am thankful to the trainers who consider all of these aspects.

Learning Theory suggests there is a sequence of events commonly referred to as ABC: antecedent, behavior, consequence. An antecedent can be many things, such as cues, the environment, triggers unique to the dog, or training methods. Behavior is the visible behavior the dog exhibits after exposure to the antecedent. Consequences come in four forms, which I'll explain with the following example of a dog chasing:

Antecedent: The dog sees, hears, or smells a trigger that puts her into chase mode.

Behavior: The dog chases the trigger, which is unwanted behavior from a human perspective and natural behavior from the dog's perspective.

Consequences: Based on Learning Theory, there are four possible consequences:

- If the dog catches what she was chasing and isn't harmed, or if the trigger gets away but the dog enjoyed the chase, the dog gets **positive reinforcement**—good stuff happened, so the chasing behavior will increase.
- If the owner zaps the dog with a shock collar until the dog stops chasing, the dog receives **negative reinforcement**—the bad stuff (the shock collar) stopped when the chasing stopped, so the "not chasing" behavior will increase.

   (**NOTE:** I do not recommend using shock collars. Research clearly shows that using aversion in training increases fear and aggression.)

- If the owner delivers hard leash snaps when the dog attempts to chase, the dog gets **positive punishment**—bad stuff happened, so the behavior will decrease. It's not "positive" at all—it only "works" with perfect timing, and it is traumatizing to the dog, even if the dog understands why it's happening.
- **Negative punishment** is a little more complicated. Let's say the dog loves to chase the cat in the home, and it's stressing the cat out. The owner puts the cat in a safe carrier, out of the dog's reach. Whenever the dog shows interest in the cat, the owner puts high-value treats right in front of the dog's nose and may even lure the dog away from the cat with the treats. When the owner leaves the room, the dog will likely head back to the cat. The owner then returns with the treats. If the dog continues to fixate on the cat, the owner takes the treats away—when the good stuff (the treats) stops, the behavior will decrease.

Knowing how learning happens is a strong weapon in your training arsenal. I use primarily **positive reinforcement** to increase desired behaviors. Every now and again, I will use negative punishment (the good stuff stops/the behavior decreases) such as walking out of the room and closing the door behind me to address an avid jumper. Luckily, we can train effectively without the use of pain or fear.

According to Learning Theory, *consequence drives future behavior.* When you observe your dog's behavior, consider the antecedent that may have caused it and the type of consequences your dog experienced as a result.

JUMPING ON PEOPLE

If I could teach dogs one secret to successfully living with humans, it would be this: we do not appreciate you joyfully jumping up to lick us or sniff us in the face to say hello. If I could tell humans one secret to successfully stop this behavior, it would be this: quit lifting your knee up into the jumping dog. I cannot tell you how often I've seen this knee raising turn into a cue for the dog to continue jumping. The dog wants interaction, and he will see the physical reaction of the knee lift and any verbal commands as fulfilling that need for attention. He'll jump again and again and will be gleeful that his owner is as engaged as he is.

Dogs jump on us for a variety of reasons. Dogs have powerful noses, and they learn a lot about their environment by using them. They sniff other dogs to learn about them, so of course dogs want to get their noses up to our faces to say hello and find out more about us. Dogs will also jump if they are nervous or excited about the new person standing in their territory (on the doorstep).

The core of the jumping problem is that one species wants to get a good face sniff in and the other prefers a handshake. This equals conflict from the "jump."

■ ■ ■ ■ ■ ■ ■ ■ ■ **OVERVIEW**

How to Help Your Dog with Jumping on People

- **Step One:** Understand Why Your Dog Jumps

- **Step Two:** Reinforce or Redirect to Desired Behaviors

- **Step Three:** Don't Rely on Impossible Expectations, Try Management

HOW TO HELP YOUR DOG WITH JUMPING ON PEOPLE

We don't like dogs to jump on us (and it can be potentially dangerous)—it's up to us to teach them a better method of saying hello.

STEP ONE: Understand Why Your Dog Jumps

A dog jumps on people for a specific reason, most often to greet the person and get information about them. Unlike other dogs, our faces aren't at nose level—dogs must jump if they want to reach them. Understanding this, we know it's not true that the dog "knows he shouldn't jump" or "is just being bad." In fact, he is being what he is: a dog. Remember that your response might seem like a punishment (yelling, kneeing, etc.), but the dog may very well enjoy it, reinforcing the jumping behavior.

STEP TWO: Reinforce or Redirect to Desired Behaviors

One of my favorite tools is training an incompatible behavior—the dog cannot jump and sit at the same time. Sometimes, however, the command to "sit" can become a cue for the dog to jump. Instead, always highly reinforce the dog every time he offers a sit. I begin reinforcing sit behavior as soon as a dog enters my life. I want to give the dog's brain a chance in a calm setting to realize that if he sits, I'll feed him. Reinforced behavior increases.

As you work on rewarding sit behavior, slowly add more exciting stimuli to the environment, such as new people or favorite toys. I often have new people come in calmly, ignoring the dog. When the dog offers a sit, the new person delivers the reward.

It is also crucial to check the behavior of your human visitors as well. If they squeal, lean down, and pet the dog enthusiastically as a greeting, they will inadvertently excite the dog into jumping up. Remaining calm is important.

Another way to redirect a jumping dog is to use the "find it" game. In this case, teach the "find it" game in a quiet environment first with just you and your dog. Use yummy treats and ask for your dog's attention by saying her name. If she looks at you, mark it with a "yes" (or use a clicker if you're clicker training). Then toss a treat away from yourself and tell her to "find it!"

Once your dog understands the "find it" game, you can prepare yourself for those situations in which she'll want to jump. Have your treats ready and toss them quickly as you enter, or as a guest enters—before your dog even has the thought to jump. To be effective, you need to play this game with high-value treats and have good timing.

Reinforcing the behavior we do want—such as a "sit"— helps that behavior take the place of behaviors we don't want, such as a dog jumping up on a person.

STEP THREE: Don't Rely on Impossible Expectations, Try Management

Some trainers recommend teaching the dog to run to a mat and lie down when the doorbell rings. You can certainly try that. It's somewhat unrealistic and bordering on cruel, however, to expect a dog to lie perfectly still and not allow the dog to greet guests (if for no other reason than that we have bred dogs to be a social species). You also won't fix jumping behaviors that way.

If your dog is a committed jumper and you don't want to train another behavior or have tried and it isn't working for your dog, you can use management. Put your dog in a back room with a great chew toy and then answer the door. This removes the immediate problems but doesn't solve the jumping problem. Your dog will continue to jump on people in other situations.

A Jumping Case Study

I'll never forget this lovely shelter rescue dog I had the opportunity to work with a few years ago—and not just because of her super cute ears. She was a lovely companion except for one bad habit: she was the most committed jumper I have ever met. We first worked on teaching "sit" and she got it quickly enough but could only focus on sitting for a micro-second before jumping up again. She was 45 pounds, so it wasn't a fun game for most people. She was also a frantic jumper, and the treats only made her jumping more excessive. I think this frantic jumping provided her an outlet for internal conflicts—she wanted to greet people but also had anxiety about them.

She jumped on her senior owner repeatedly throughout the day. Trainers who aren't committed to training without harming the dog often recommend using a water bottle mixed with vinegar or something similar to squirt the dog in the face to stop the jumping (do not do this—it's cruel and doesn't work). Her owner had tried this before I arrived, and the water/vinegar spray only increased the dog's anxiety. She simply jumped higher and harder—a true four-legged pogo stick.

I did solve this case, however! I walked over to a nearby open laundry room door and the owner and dog followed me. I stood close to the door. The second the dog jumped up toward me, I didn't say a word. I simply stepped back into the laundry

This cute dog was the most committed jumper I've met in all my years of training. We were able to work out a win-win solution for her and her owner.

room and shut the door—I removed myself. (I wasn't trying to get her to jump into the door—she jumped straight up into the air and did not hit the door.) The most amazing thing happened, and we nearly broke out into tears because it was so dramatic and clear—thanks to her big ears!

This lovely dog was so surprised I'd left. She flattened her ears as the door was closing and had the saddest expression I have ever seen on a dog. She looked heartbroken. When I opened the door a few seconds later she was wiggly and happy and she did NOT jump. In leaving right as she jumped, I made it clear to her at last that I didn't want her to jump on me. The owner practiced this a few times and the behavior stopped. (Note: one could argue that removing myself did punish the dog and wasn't 100% positive. I agree. In the overall training picture, however, the emotional pain she felt for the two seconds I was behind the door, unlike a shock collar, effectively communicated what I wanted from her and didn't cause trauma.)

We've all seen enthusiastic dogs pulling their reluctant owners along hiking paths or down the sidewalk. Pulling is potentially dangerous to both dog and owner, but luckily, it's a fun-to-fix problem for both, as well!

PULLING ON LEASH

While a dog yanking its handler down the street is something we've all seen (or experienced) and while this behavior drives dog owners nuts, it is one of my favorite things to fix. Why? Because there are so many creative ways to go about changing it!

Dogs pull on leash for a variety of reasons. For one thing, they have four-wheel drive, and we slow humans only have two-wheel drive. Dogs have a highly evolved sense of smell that we do not have—we have a puny 6 million olfactory receptors, whereas the almighty dog nose has 300 million receptors. Clients probably get tired of hearing me say that if we could smell as well as a dog, we'd probably never leave our homes since we'd be too overwhelmed by smells. It is actually remarkable that good training techniques are still effective when our dogs are outside.

Have you had the opportunity to observe your dog moving outside unleashed and choosing her own path? They cut left, cut right, back up, go forward, etc. Dogs rarely walk in a straight line because scents generally don't stay still or present in a straight line. We should honor our dogs' incredible noses on daily walks instead of harshly insisting they walk right next to us the whole time at a strict heel. That's not fun for anyone—save a strict heel for obedience competitions and let your dog enjoy sniffing during walks.

OVERVIEW

How to Stop Your Dog Pulling on Leash—Overview

- **Step One:** Let Your Dog Sniff
- **Step Two:** Use a Longer Lead and Reinforce the Behaviors You Want
- **Step Three:** Use the Premack Principle

HOW TO STOP YOUR DOG PULLING ON LEASH

Allowing your dog to sniff while on walks is crucial to their enjoyment and engagement. The drive to sniff is hard-wired into them, and a lot of leash pulling stems from that.

A longer leash is a safe way to give your dog a bit more control while on walks.

STEP ONE: Let Your Dog Sniff

Take a step back and look anew at why your dog is pulling. She goes through life nose first and that nose is a powerful, intense tool (dog noses are used to sniff out cancer and explosives, find missing people or criminals, and even to find bed bugs and rare forest truffles). We need to understand that dogs have a hard-wired need to sniff everything. We need to find a way to balance this need with our need to not have our arms jerked out of their sockets on walks.

The crucial thing is to *let them sniff*. Many owners believe walks are only for exercise. Yes, that is a part of it, but only a small part—the sniffing stimulates their brains and releases "happy" hormones more than that actual walking does. Letting a dog sniff not only helps tire out the dog, but it also allows the dog to engage in one of his favorite genetically-influenced behaviors.

STEP TWO: Use a Longer Lead and Reinforce the Behaviors You Want

First, use a 6-foot to 10-foot leash and follow your dog for the first half of every walk (allowing him to sniff to his heart's content). Note that following a sniffing dog is different from being dragged down the street by one.

Begin training at home without a leash. A leash gives an illusion of control, so getting off-leash compliance lets you know your dog truly understands the behavior you want. Remember that reinforced behavior increases. Whenever you "catch" your dog walking beside you or even behind you, mark it with a "yes" (or click if you're using clicker training), then drop a treat behind you as you continue walking forward. (You drop the treat behind you so the dog gets used to going back rather than forward to get it.)

Continually reinforce your dog with petting, toys, or treats whenever he looks up at you and visually connects (this is a "check in"—see page 142 for more details). Perfect the behavior of your dog wanting to be near you in the quiet, controllable environment of the house, then reinforce these behaviors in the backyard (start on leash and work up to off leash). Then try walking up and down the street many times on leash, rewarding every time the dog is next to you. After a few minutes of this, relax the leash, tell your dog to "go sniff," and let the dog sniff.

Whenever your dog hits the end of the leash and pulls, immediately stop moving and stay silent. You want the dog to turn and look at you. As soon as they do, mark it with a "yes" or a click. Then happily say "let's go" and turn around and go the opposite way. This puts the dog behind you, giving you another opportunity to treat the dog when they come up beside you. If the dog pulls again, repeat the whole process, even if you have to wait several minutes for your dog to turn and look at you. The ultimate goal here is for the dog to learn to stop or slow down to avoid feeling the tightness on the leash.

If you have a second person to help, try walking with two handlers. One handler has the dog on leash and the other walks a few feet behind. Whenever the dog checks in and goes back to the second person, that person marks and treats that behavior. The handler with the leash treats whenever the dog comes back to her side. If the dog is intent on surging ahead, ask the person behind to whistle, clap, or stomp their feet to get the dog's attention. You'll have to work hard to build up this behavior but keep at it and eventually the dog will enthusiastically run back to the second person. The goal is to communicate to the dog that going behind the owner or staying by the owner's side is richly rewarded.

Teach your dog that as soon as she looks back to you (the behavior she's less likely to want to do), she can go investigate and sniff (the behavior she's most likely to want to do).

STEP THREE: Use the Premack Principle

The Premack Principle is best explained through an analogy—it's like a negotiation. Think about what many parents tell their picky eaters at dinner: if they eat their vegetables (something there is a low probability of them choosing to do on their own), they can have dessert (something there is a high probability of them choosing to do on their own). High-probability behaviors (eating dessert) will reinforce low-probability behaviors (eating vegetables).

Techniques based in the Premack Principle demonstrate to the dog that she can do or have what she wants only once she gives you the behavior you want first and works in a wide variety of dog-training situations. I don't recommend it in highly stressful situations (such as reactivity) or where strong genetic factors or emotions are in play (such as predatory behavior), but it works well for teaching loose-leash walking.

When a dog is pulling hard on the leash, she wants to get to something that has excited her sense of smell (or sight or hearing). To use the Premack Principle to communicate that the pulling is undesired, request your dog's attention (the check in—looking back at you and putting some slack in the leash). Once she gives it to you (even though she'd prefer going to sniff something in front of her), immediately thank her for the attention and tell her to "go sniff." Her desire to sniff the thing in the distance is the high-probability behavior. Stopping the pulling movement and looking or stepping back to you is the low-probability behavior. You're using her strong desire to sniff to teach her that if she eats her vegetables first (checks in with you), then she can have her dessert (sniff the exciting thing up ahead).

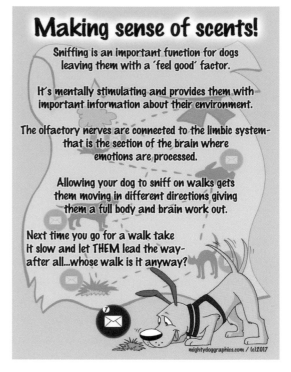

The Best Equipment for Walks

Use equipment on walks that will not harm your dog:

- Use flat collars for ID tags only (I prefer breakaway collars that come apart if twisted). Your dog's neck is a very sensitive spot, and you don't want to cause any damage.

- Attach the leash to a harness (a variety of different types are available) rather than attaching the leash to your dog's collar.

- Use a leather or nylon 6–10-foot leash (depending on where you are walking). Do not use retractable flexi leashes, as they can cause injuries to dogs and owners.

Don't use retractable leashes—they can injure dogs and owners alike (I've even heard of owners losing fingers).

- Longer leashes/lines require greater handling skills so take your take time—get used to using them in a secure place first.

A Premack Principle Case Study

I used the Premack Principle once on a clever hound dog who was obsessed with groundhogs and any holes in the ground that might contain a groundhog. Everything in her breeding and brain screamed at her: FIND THE GROUNDHOG. Every hole had to be checked, then every other inch of dirt. Her constant seeking behavior made walks impossible and certainly not enjoyable.

I said above that I don't recommend using the Premack Principle in highly emotional or genetically programmed situations as it might not work and could do more harm than good, but it proved to be a good fit for this dog. I put her in a harness and on leash and stood 100 yards from a field full of groundhog holes. She could easily smell them from that distance, but we were far enough away that she could still focus on and hear me and respond. Little by little we slowly made our way closer to the field. When she started to pull, I'd stop and say nothing. When she looked back at me or took a few steps toward me, I'd mark it with "yes" and we'd move forward again.

By the time we got to the first hole, she understood that pulling made me stop and looking or stepping back and giving me her attention got her closer to the holes. At the first hole I gave her a long time to sniff to her heart's content (because she had done such hard work getting there).

Depending on your dog, you can use the Premack Principle to reinforce the idea that when your dog behaves how you'd like (not pulling, checking in with you, etc.), she'll get what she wants—time to stop and sniff all the interesting things on her walk.

For a different dog, this might not work—the drive might be too great. Her interest in groundhogs was intense but she was able to successfully learn to listen to her handler even if one was nearby. It was a fair solution to let her do what her brain instructed her to do within the limits of a negotiated settlement (a term first used by Dr. Karen Overall).

SEPARATION ANXIETY— BEHAVIORAL EMERGENCY

Separation anxiety (SA) is when a dog becomes extremely distressed when left alone. They may howl, bark, chew, dig, pant, pace, defecate, or attempt to escape. These dogs are not being naughty, nor are they attempting to punish you for leaving. They have severe anxiety when left alone. It is similar to a panic attack in humans. The anxiety element is important to acknowledge. It can be deeply frustrating (and expensive) to have a dog who has so much anxiety while alone that she'll destroy your furniture or belongings in a desperate attempt to self-soothe or escape. Some dogs literally chew through walls.

Far too often it seems that owners resent their dogs for this behavior. After all, you've tried to make the home comfortable for your dog with new bedding, toys, and treats. What are you missing? Well, the one thing the dog needs most in this case is *you*.

I have a confession and I suspect it is one many other trainers can relate to: in year's past I would have gladly taken a dog with severe reactivity over a dog exhibiting SA or noise phobia. Why? Because for many years, there wasn't a satisfactory method to truly help most dogs with this type of anxiety. I have seen many dog owners completely rearrange their lifestyles to accommodate this kind of behavior issue, never leaving their dog alone, hiring daily pet sitters, changing jobs, or even moving to accommodate the dog. What we do for love! Luckily for us all, we continue to get a better understanding of SA every day and several smart trainers and veterinarians have created new ways to help dogs with SA.

Signs of SA are far-ranging and aren't expressed the same way in every dog. Some dogs show a wide variety of behavior concerns while others might just show one behavior. No matter the behavior(s), the anxiety is still present. The most common signs include excessive barking, whining, howling, crying, defecating or urinating, trying to escape,

Separation anxiety is dangerous for dogs in many ways and often expensive and stressful for owners.

or destroying things. SA seems to be a bit more common in shelter dogs and rescue dogs who have been abandoned or lost their homes than in purebred dogs who often live their entire lives with the same family (though we do see SA in purebreds as well).

SA behavior generally happens within the first 30 minutes of the owner leaving the home. A quality set of cameras set up inside your home will give you the information you need to know whether your dog is showing signs of SA. The panicked behavior escalates over time as the dog desperately searches for relief—relief that she is not capable of giving to herself (only your return will provide relief). Some dogs are explosive in this state and exhibit their concern the entire time the owner is away. Other dogs cycle throughout the day and may experience what look like moments of calm (almost as though they have worn themselves out), although their stress hormones will be elevated the entire time. When dogs are exposed to this level of terror and anxiety long term, it can do irreversible damage to their brains.

HOW TO HELP SEPARATION ANXIETY

1

It is critical to first and foremost consult with a veterinarian to help a dog with separation anxiety—there are quality medications your dog might benefit from.

STEP ONE: Visit a Veterinarian Trained in SA and General Anxiety

Not all veterinarians have training with SA or general anxiety in dogs, so check with your vet to make sure they have experience with this issue. With anxiety, medication can be the difference between success and failure. While there are other medical choices to discuss with your vet, currently there are three medications approved by the FDA: Reconcile (Prozac), Clomicalm, and Pexion (approved for noise aversion). Because all dogs are different, there will probably be some trial and error before you find the medication that works best with your dog's chemistry.

Sometimes clients are hesitant to even discuss medication. Some want to try an "all-natural" route and others feel like they've failed in some way. I can

■ ■ ■ ■ ■ ■ ■ ■ ■ ■ ■ ■ OVERVIEW

How to Help Separation Anxiety

- **Step One:** Visit a Veterinarian Trained in SA and General Anxiety

- **Step Two:** Use Management to Help Your Dog Feel Secure

- **Step Three:** Follow a Quality Behavior Modification Protocol and Work with a Professional

assure you that products like CBD oil alone do not help with severe anxiety—they are only short-term solutions that leave your dog suffering. I can also assure you that there's no reason to be ashamed. You didn't cause your dog's SA and you can't fix it alone. SA is a serious concern and the sooner you discuss the use of medications with your veterinarian, the sooner your dog can move toward healing.

2

A quality set of in-home cameras will help you monitor your dog while you're away—letting you know if he's showing any signs of SA. Some in-home pet cameras even come with audio and treat dispensers so you can interact with your pet throughout the day!

STEP TWO: Use Management to Help Your Dog Feel Secure

Management is a necessary part of helping your dog with SA. As you are working on healing the issue, you must stop leaving your dog alone. The road to curing SA involves desensitizing the dog to being alone little by little. If you work with a trainer and use small steps to help your dog, then the next day leave the dog alone for eight hours, you've plunged the dog back into the very situation that causes the panic. The dog never gets to feel safe, and their stress hormones are always elevated.

It is imperative to create a sense of safety for your dog as you work on fixing the anxiety. Dogs with SA are most comfortable and least panicked when a human is present, particularly a human with whom they feel safe. If you have the option to take your dog to work with you and that works for the dog as well, do so. You can hire a qualified individual or ask a friend or neighbor to stay with your dog while you are not at home. Some dogs do well in doggie day care. A smaller space can help your dog feel more secure, so try keeping him in a large X pen or closed-off part of your home (NOT a small, closed crate, which will increase panic).

3

It is imperative that a dog suffering with separation anxiety not be left home alone. They will not outgrow this condition and leaving them alone increases their panic.

STEP THREE: Follow a Quality Behavior Modification Protocol and Work with a Professional

You can get to a place of healing much faster if you team up with a good veterinarian and an experienced behavior consultant. One option is to work with a veterinary behaviorist, although there are less than 100 board-certified veterinary behaviorists in the world. They are often booked out for months and their expert services are not inexpensive but thankfully you can now hire certified SA trainers, who can work remotely and are trained through a program created by Malena DeMartini-Price (see page 113).

SA is such a complex issue—I encourage you to work with a professional who is highly trained to assist you and your dog. DeMartini-Price's well-thought-out and successful program does not use food (dogs with SA are too anxious to eat) and instead uses a system of desensitizing to help your dog learn how to relax and feel safe while alone.

Ask an Expert

Trainer and Behavior Consultant Malena DeMartini-Price Discusses How to Help Dogs with Separation Anxiety

This interview has been edited for length. Please see https://foxchapelpets.com/positive-training-dogs/ to read the full interview.

Separation Anxiety Expert Malena DeMartini with her dog, Tini, enjoying some quality time together at home in Sonoma County, California.

▶ **What first drew you to study dogs with SA and then create a program to help these dogs?**

Very early on in my career, I was contacted by a client who had a dog with separation anxiety, and I immediately thought, oh, gosh, I'm too green of a trainer. I shouldn't work with this. But she was quite desperate, and no one really was willing to help her, so I said, "full transparency, we're going to kind of do some trial and error." The case was very successful. And because I live in the San Francisco Bay area, a tight-knit community, as soon as people found out that I was successful with a separation anxiety case, the floodgates opened, and I started to receive a lot more of them. As a result, I realized that this was something that needed further investigation and greater understanding on how to work with the problem most efficiently and effectively—there

was just not enough solid information out there at the time. So that's what I embarked on.

▶ **What are some of the most common behaviors you see in dogs with SA? What are some unexpected behaviors?**

One of the things that we really need to do in order to determine whether the dog is having separation-related challenges is observe the dog when left alone. And I want to add a caveat by saying, this doesn't mean you have to leave your dog alone for four hours and watch them the entire time. We can discern the level of panic, whether it's present or not, fairly quickly—usually within the first 10 minutes. I think people really need to understand that this is a phobia, and a phobia by definition is extremely irrational to those that are not experiencing it. But it is very real for the dog. They are terrified to be left alone. For people to discern whether their dog has separation anxiety, using standalone cameras or some other means of viewing and recording your dog when left alone is really crucial.

There are very important differences in behavior. When you see a video of a dog who is barking at the squirrels and the people walking past side-by-side with a video of a dog displaying true separation anxiety, the difference is obvious. These symptoms may not come from separation anxiety but rather from over-arousal or boredom. But when we see the dogs panicking, that is a very different situation. These behaviors include everything from salivation, vocalization, howling, whining, and tearing things up.

▶ **You describe SA as a welfare issue and a behavioral emergency where the dog can go into full-blown panic mode. Why is this condition considered to be an emergency?**

One of the things that's so important is that we realize that this is not just psychological. We have to acknowledge the physiological impacts that continued levels of stress over time can have on the animal. I say it's a welfare issue and I'm mostly referring to the dog welfare, but it's a welfare issue for the pet parents as well. Having a dog that is destroying your house or getting complaints from the neighbors and the landlord—all of these things are very, very stressful. I really feel that we have to treat this as a behavioral emergency. It is not something that's just going to go away if we look the other way for weeks or months or more.

▶ **What are some of the known causes of SA?**

The majority of dogs who have separation anxiety–related behaviors are experiencing it for so many different reasons, including genetics, environment, or issues that have happened in the dog's past. But the new cute puppy with a sound beginning could also have separation anxiety. Separation anxiety has been the number one most researched dog behavior issue for the past four decades in peer-reviewed studies of applied behavior analysis and veterinary medicine. We've got a lot of good information on it. But interestingly, the area that we have the least amount of information on is what causes separation anxiety. We do know that evolutionarily separation anxiety is appropriate as there is an evolutionary purpose of helping to reunite young pups with mom or the other littermates. If we still see it after the dog has matured, we can kind of consider it to be maladaptive, and it needs to be addressed.

▶ **What are some of the first steps an owner should take if they suspect their dog has SA?**

Anything that our dogs rehearse they become professionals at. As a dog, you might be a little panicked when mom runs to the grocery store. And then the next day, she goes to a doctor's appointment and then Monday comes around and she has to go to work, and you are perpetually experiencing and rehearsing panic. I feel strongly that we need to manage the dog in such a way that we are not leaving them alone for longer than they can handle. Owners will say to me "people have to work and have go to doctor's appointments, etc." The reality is that there are so many creative resources available to help you. We have everything from low-cost to no-cost help in friends, family, neighbors, pet sitters, etc. There are more expensive types of care available—you can hire someone to either bring the dog to their home or stay with the dog in your home. As a matter of fact, over 80% of the clients that contact us tell us that they are already not leaving the dog alone.

We just need to stop that panic from going into overdrive because chronic stress will change the dog's brain chemistry. It will crowd out happy feelings and just get bigger and bigger and become more profound. I think it's so important for people to hear that we are not saying you can never leave your house for the rest of your life, there's just a certain amount of time at the beginning of the process when we do need the dog to not be left alone.

▶ **Is there a general time frame for how long it may take to help a dog with SA? Every dog is unique of course, but is there a certain amount of time in terms of days, weeks, months, or longer for which you advise owners to be prepared to work on this issue?**

This is the most common question that I get asked and I understand and genuinely empathize with it, but it really is very dependent on the dog. I do say "don't think in terms of weeks, think in terms of months. Don't stress out that it might be in terms of years." When we think about the life expectancy of the dog being at least 15 years, then those months are well worth it to ensure not only the dog's well-being physically and emotionally but also our own well-being. Spending some time to address the problem early on is important.

Hire a qualified professional force-free trainer to help with your dog's separation anxiety. The Resources for Owners section beginning on page 233 provides references for schools and organizations that certify trainers you can trust to be knowledgeable and to never harm your dog. When working with a client's dog, I always use force-free techniques.

NEVER punish anxiety in your dog. It is extremely unfair and harmful to do so. It can be enormously stressful to share your life with an SA dog—I get that. Understand that the dog cannot help how she feels. She is not being naughty, stubborn, or disobedient. She is terrified. Punishment is guaranteed to cause your dog more stress and will not solve the problem.

NEVER confine a dog with SA to a crate. This is akin to trapping someone with arachnophobia in a room filled with spiders.

NOISE PHOBIA—
BEHAVIORAL EMERGENCY

Noise phobia, in which specific noises like thunder or fireworks cause panic attacks, is similar to separation anxiety, but is a distinct issue. A dog's response to noise phobia can be similar to SA, including drooling, panting, hiding, dilated eyes, jumping, defecating, urinating, barking, or escaping. The busiest days for United States shelters come after Independence Day and New Year's Eve when terrified dogs try to escape frightening fireworks.

According to veterinary behaviorist Dr. Karen Overall, "[f]ear is the worst thing a social species can experience, and it causes permanent damage to the brain."[1] We know that long or repeated exposure to a trigger will cause distress earlier and earlier as the dog learns to fear the precursors to the trigger (a dog becoming afraid of wind because wind is a precursor to thunder, for example). Confinement also makes these undesired reactions stronger and causes even more panic. **Never lock a dog in a crate if they have anxiety issues.**

Noise sensitivity is thought to occur in conjunction with SA. Both conditions probably have a genetic factor and medical issues such as ear or brain anomalies might contribute, but the exact causes are currently unknown. What we do know is that if the dog is unable to stop the noise, the stress behavior increases, and the dog (and owner) will be increasingly miserable. These conditions are serious (those of us who've worked with dogs experiencing SA or noise phobia have at least one horror story). **They do not improve with time. It is crucial to get help immediately.**

---

1   Danielle S. Tepper, "Q&A: Why Fear Free?," *HumanePro Magazine*, https://humanepro.org/magazine/articles/qa-why-fear-free.

HOW TO REDUCE NOISE PHOBIA

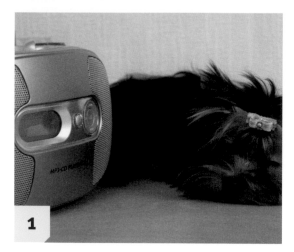

Your veterinarian can suggest many solutions to help your dog's noise phobia, some as simple as using white noise or calming music created just for dogs!

■ ■ ■ ■ ■ ■ ■ ■ ■ ■ ■ ■ OVERVIEW

How to Reduce Noise Phobia

- **Step One:** Visit a Veterinarian Trained to Treat Anxiety

- **Step Two:** Learn Exactly What Triggers Your Dog's Noise Phobia

- **Step Three:** Use Management to Help Your Dog Feel Secure

- **Step Four:** Follow a Quality Behavior Modification Protocol

STEP ONE: Visit a Veterinarian Trained to Treat Anxiety

Take your dog to the veterinarian to rule out any physical contributors to the issue. Pain and even some conditions like hypothyroidism can play a role. Remember your dog is suffering and needs professional veterinary care first and foremost. The primary focus for general veterinarians is physical health and most veterinarians are not usually given in-depth behavior training unless they go on to become veterinary behaviorists. Make sure your veterinarian has experience with anxiety issues from both a veterinary and a behavior perspective. Quality animal professionals (veterinarians and trainers alike) will not take on behavior issues they are not prepared to assist with.

Some medications, such as FDA-approved Pexion™, can help strengthen your dog's panic threshold and calm your dog's anxiety and fear enough to give you time and space to work on changing behavior. Your veterinarian can recommend non-medical solutions, as well, such the ThunderShirt, doggie earmuffs, CBD products, Through a Dog's Ear music, massage, Bach™ Rescue Remedy, Nature's Farmacy Calm Caps, Springtime Stress Free Calmplex, melatonin, Ester-C®, and bromelain. Try one solution at a time and for at least 10 days to determine if it actually helps your dog.

STEP TWO: Learn Exactly What Triggers Your Dog's Noise Phobia

Your dog probably shows early warning signs (displacement signals) if she is concerned about a noise including yawning, stretching, lip licking, doing a "shake off," or being overly alert. Connect the dots to figure out exactly what sounds cause your dog's panicked reaction. Sounds that can bother a dog include thunderstorms, fireworks, trash pick-up day, construction work, motorcycles, babies or children screaming or crying, and sirens. Knowing what upsets your dog will help you create a game plan for avoiding and muffling that particular sound.

Creating a safe space is paramount. If your nervous dog isn't comfortable in a crate (please never shut in a scared dog), try more open containment products like X pens.

Dogs will often try to hide from loud noises like thunder or fireworks. The anxiety they're experiencing is a type of panic attack.

STEP THREE: Use Management to Help Your Dog Feel Secure

It's vital to create a safety bubble to which your dog can go whenever the scary noises start. While it is impossible to completely block out all noise, you can make a difference using things like white noise machines, soft music, and fans. Shut the blinds and shades since some dogs learn to associate lighting or fireworks displays with the threat.

If your dog is crate-trained and likes their crate, make it as comfortable as possible with soft blankets (draped over the top of the crate as well) and good, safe things to chew on. But remember, leave the crate open—never lock a scared dog in a crate.

Please comfort your dog if she indicates that it's needed. Such comforting will not reinforce their fear—fear is simply not something that can be reinforced. Trainers who tell you this are gravely mistaken. It's best if you stay in the same room with the dog while they are experiencing their anxiety. Never punish fear or anxiety—it is cruel and will only make the situation worse for you and your dog.

STEP FOUR: Follow a Quality Behavior Modification Protocol

After you've thoroughly explored the first three steps and created a greater sense of calm and safety for your dog, you can introduce behavior modification protocols to the situation. I most often use desensitization and counterconditioning in these situations.

Begin any training sessions at home in a quiet space. The goal is to keep your dog under threshold. Find recordings of the sounds that scare your dog. Have extra-tasty treats on hand that your dog only gets during these sessions. Slowly turn the sound up to a low volume. While the sound is on, give your dog one treat at time in quick succession. As soon as you turn the sound off, stop giving your dog the treats.

Keep these training sessions very short—two to three minutes at most and only once or twice a day at the same volume level. After a few days, slowly turn the volume up during the training, increasing it every few days. The goal is to desensitize the dog to the scary sounds and help her connect the trigger noise with the extra-tasty treats.

If your dog is over threshold and cannot eat, don't attempt any more training or behavior modification. The volume of the trigger was probably too loud and should be lowered before you try again. Be sure these sessions are only focused on noise issues. Don't include any other skill training (such as sit or down).

6

Raising a Well-Rounded Puppy

Quality prenatal, neonatal, and puppy care will stave off so many potential behavior problems. What a puppy experiences affects the dog throughout its whole life, and we only have one chance to get it right. While of course we can still teach and help adult dogs, the puppy months are the most critical growth and learning period in a dog's life. This chapter looks at how we can set our puppies up to be healthy, resilient, and well adjusted, and how we can continue this good work as the puppy grows up. We will also discuss understanding the needs of a rescue puppy or adult dog, who may not have had the best start in life.

PROVIDE PRENATAL AND NEONATAL CARE

In a perfect world, we would spend as much time learning about the needs of mother dogs as we do the needs of pregnant humans. The experiences of the mother dog before she gives birth can have a lifelong effect on her litter. It's soul-crushing to both know how vital this period is and know just how many stress-filled mother dogs are alone giving birth with no human support. It's even more soul-crushing to think of the countless litters puppy mill dogs are forced to birth in abysmal conditions. As I've said before, puppy mills are the perfect place for creating puppies that suffer physically and developmentally as they age.

So, what does a mother dog need and how can we best support her? First, create the most beneficial space possible to set the mother dog and puppies up for resiliency and confidence. We know that stress during a dog's development negatively influences how the brain develops. To set dogs up for a non-reactionary, fear-free life, it's crucial to de-stress life for the mother dog and her puppies.

Note: This section is not meant to replace the advice of your veterinarian—it is supplemental information focusing on the emotional and behavioral components of having puppies. Your veterinarian should always be closely involved in the pregnancy, birth, and puppy development stages.

It is of vital importance that the mother dog's health and emotional well-being is cared for to improve the chances that her puppies will be resilient.

PROVIDE PRENATAL AND NEONATAL CARE

1

Potential breeding candidates should be evaluated by a veterinarian for physical health and good temperament.

Like all expecting mothers, dogs deserve proper rest, nutrition, and a safe place to have their babies.

STEP ONE: Take Potential Parent Dogs for Veterinary Evaluations

Both potential parent dogs need to be checked out by a veterinarian before either is considered as a breeding candidate. Physical health and good temperament are equally important. A quality breeder will be happy to provide the results of parental health tests, including heart tests, thyroid tests, hearing tests, eye tests, elbow grading, hip scoring, and DNA testing. There isn't a standard for temperament testing, but the ideal characteristics to look for in BOTH parents are resiliency, friendliness, curiosity, optimism, and a lack of fear, anxiety, and aggression.

If you're considering purchasing a puppy from a breeder, insist on meeting both parents and take an opportunity to observe their behavior whenever possible. It's also important to remember that even if both parents get high checkmarks on every test (including temperament), some puppies can still arrive with a genetic predisposition for anxiety or fear.

OVERVIEW

How to Provide Prenatal and Neonatal Care

- **Step One:** Take Potential Parent Dogs for Veterinary Evaluations

- **Step Two:** Provide the Mother Dog with Stability and Enrichment

- **Step Three:** Create a Quiet, Safe Place for the Puppies to Be Born

- **Step Four:** Help the Mother Care for Her Puppies and Gently Introduce Human Contact

Pregnant dogs need stability, safety, and enrichment. Stress on the mother dog will transfer to her puppies.

One option for creating a safe birthing location is a whelping box built specifically for this purpose.

STEP TWO: Provide the Mother Dog with Stability and Enrichment

Dog pregnancies last around 56–68 days. Ensure that during this whole time the mother dog has a stable home in which she feels safe. Pregnant dogs also still need to receive enrichment and physical exercise, but it's best to limit strenuous exercise during the first two weeks of gestation and the last few weeks of gestation.

This is not the ideal time to move to a new home or host large parties. Keep the routine as normal as you possibly can. Your pregnant dog will probably eat and drink more than usual and will need easy access to go outside to eliminate.

A pregnant dog can tire more easily, will have an increased appetite, and might be irritable. Proper nutrition is important, and there are many conflicting opinions about what that proper nutrition should look like. Do your research to determine which food is best for you and healthiest for your dog.

STEP THREE: Create a Quiet, Safe Place for the Puppies to Be Born

As the due date approaches, it becomes increasingly important for the mother dog to have a quiet, safe place she can retreat to and relax in. Preparing for birth includes setting up a whelping box that is safe, warm, and easy to clean. You can purchase whelping boxes made specifically for this purpose, although many dog owners use plastic swimming pools made comfortable with blankets and towels.

You will also need to keep an assortment of supplies on hand, including paper towels and clean bath towels, a bulb syringe to clean puppy noses and mouths, a heat lamp, clean scissors to cut the umbilical cords (in case the dog doesn't bite them), iodine to clean puppy abdomens, and a thermometer to check the mother dog's temperature prior to birth. I highly recommend going over the birthing process with your veterinarian, so you know exactly what to expect.

4

Ensure that the mother dog and her puppies have a clean, safe, quiet indoor space. What happens at the breeder's home will have a lifelong impact on the puppies.

It is imperative for breeders to begin safely handling the newborns with care.

STEP FOUR: Help the Mother Care for Her Puppies and Gently Introduce Human Contact

Assuming the mother dog is actively engaged, and she and the puppies are healthy, she will take care of the newborns for the first three weeks. The puppies and the mother dog still need to have a quiet, safe space after the birth.

It's crucial during this time that the puppies stay warm, as low body temperature puts stress on their sensitive immune systems. Be sure to gently handle them briefly each day or every other day (this will help foster their development). Be mindful as you interact with the pups that you are not upsetting the mother. Track their weight regularly with a puppy scale to ensure they are steadily gaining.

It is critical to engage in handling the puppies in short intervals. Work hard to avoid scaring them and don't allow stimuli, such as loud noises or raised voices, to frighten them. This is where humans can do the most to help create a confident, resilient, well-adjusted dog. By the fourth week, the puppies should be able to walk and move on to new learning adventures.

Breeder and Trainer Jane Ardern Shares What to Look for in a Quality Breeder and What to Avoid

This interview has been included in its entirety.

Trainer, behaviorist, and expert breeder Jane Ardern with her dog Pickles at her graduation with a BSc, Honors in canine behavior and training from Hill University at Beverly Minister.

▶ **What do you recommend dog owners look for in a quality breeder?**

A quality breeder is someone who has a good reason to breed, wants to improve the breed, and looks at the long-term future of the whole breed, not just the two dogs in front of them. They should provide health testing for both parents and, in the case of working dogs, should have evidence that the dog has achieved something to demonstrate its capability for the work intended. Quality breeders will make time and invest in the rearing of the pups, providing them with as much experience and early neurological stimulation as possible. They'll match the puppies' needs and the owners' needs rather than just letting you pick the pink one because it's your favorite color. No one rehomes because they don't like the color of the dog.

▶ **What are red flags in a breeder?**

A few red flags would be not being given access to both parents, not seeing all of the litter, not seeing where the pups are raised and living, and not seeing mum with the puppies. It would also be a red flag for them to not health test or to only health test the father without bothering to test the health of the mother. Others would be not creating contracts or not being prepared to take the pup back if there is a problem.

Responsible breeders will ensure puppies are taught to love being handled by humans and will safely introduce them to many new experiences before they leave for their new homes.

▶ **How can we best support the mother before and after she gives birth in such a way that we are setting the puppies up to be resilient and not stressed the first few weeks of life?**

Make sure the mother is in excellent health throughout, with low stress but still plenty of enrichment and good-quality rest. Provide regular veterinary checks and support throughout and a safe, quiet place in which to give birth and raise the puppies. Owner support is important if the dog is a people-oriented dog and normally seeks support and social comfort from humans.

▶ **What do you wish dog owners knew about choosing a new puppy?**

I wish they knew about the differences between responsible breeders and puppy farmers. Puppies have both stable and flexible behaviors, but puppies can't be molded into something they are not through training.

▶ **What are the most important things breeders can do to properly socialize newborn and young puppies in their care?**

Breeders must teach them to recover from startle responses, desensitization is only part of the life skills required to cope with life. Life is full of surprises, and some will be scary. They should expose puppies to plenty of vehicle travel before they leave and should allow them to interact with socially competent adult dogs. It's important to teach them to love human hands, handling, and restraint and to feel comfortable and safe around humans who have possession of "things of value." Breeders should make sure puppies' first entertainment and reinforcement experiences match their new home, for example, playing with dog toys or chewing dog chews. Creating a set sleep and wake routine is also important.

SOCIALIZE AND TRAIN EARLY

The socialization period is a development stage that begins at about three weeks of age and continues until about sixteen weeks of age. I say "about" because dogs are individuals and, in theory, this stage can begin slightly earlier or extend slightly longer. The crucial thing to know about this all-important time in a dog's life is that the puppy's brain, body, chemical systems, and hormonal systems are developing rapidly.

The lessons learned during this all-important phase will stick with the dog for the rest of her life and shape how she sees the world. Does she feel safe or is there danger lurking around every corner? It's crucial to gently expose the puppy to novel stimuli during this time. The goal is to create positive experiences as you introduce the dog to the world and the world to the dog. The overriding goal is to foster a sense of safety for the young puppy.

Like us, dogs continue learning throughout their lives, but this early period is the most crucial stage in which they begin to figure out their world.

The puppy socialization period isn't just about socializing with other dogs and people, it's also about introducing your puppy to new experiences and letting them know they can look to you for security and guidance.

This is also a critical time to build resiliency in your dog. One way to teach resiliency is to allow the dog to choose when she is ready to sniff or explore something new. Never force a puppy to approach something—if you wait and let her approach on her own once she feels secure enough, you help her build lifelong confidence and resiliency. Some things will scare her, of course (that's only natural), but the goal is to show her she is safe with you and that you are there to provide comfort and guidance.

Sometimes owners and breeders do everything exactly right, but a gene-based fear or anxiety issue overrides even the best socialization. The best socialization in the world cannot by itself fix chemical imbalances or other physical problems. If you see an abnormal amount of fear from your puppy during this time or worrying signs of aggression or resource guarding behavior, immediately begin work with your veterinarian and a qualified, force-free professional. (See the list of professionals you can trust with your puppy in the Resources for Owners section beginning on page 233.)

Proper early puppy socialization and enrichment is a MUST for all dogs.

Make sure to gently introduce your puppy to other safe puppies and dogs of all ages. This helps lessen the likelihood of future leash reactivity or aggression toward other dogs.

Calm, older dogs who enjoy playing with puppies can teach the puppy vital dog communication skills that we humans cannot teach them, or at least can't teach as effectively as another dog.

Socializing with Other Puppies and Dogs

One of the most important things we must do during this time is introduce our puppies to **safe dogs of all ages**. One of the top reasons a behavior expert gets called in for adolescent or adult dogs is leash reactivity, including loud barking and lunging at passing dogs. The puppy socialization period is the best time to arrange for safe, fun, and limited-duration puppy-to-puppy meetings. When my cattle collie siblings were young, I hosted free puppy play dates in my fenced-in front yard. I was sure to get a feel for any puppy who was coming to play before they were approved. Puppies can show aggression to other puppies, although sometimes a snarl or a growl is an entirely normal and effective dog tool for telling another puppy to back off.

These meetings are most effective when done off leash in controlled safe environments (such as a single room or a small yard) with safe puppies meeting safe dogs. This allows the puppies to learn on their own

how to interact with other dogs. I also encourage my clients to interrupt and redirect if any puppies in the group get overstimulated. It's a great idea to remove the puppies from the situation several times during the play date to allow them to rest. Keep these play dates between 30 minutes to an hour.

Many veterinary organizations agree that it is too late to begin socialization after all the puppy shots have been completed, so you'll need to use safe venues like your own yard or a neighbor's. Do not take puppies to dog parks—they are not controlled environments and there is too much risk of scary or even dangerous confrontations occurring. I also don't advocate taking puppies under six months to doggie day care for the same reason.

The Importance of Rewards-Based Puppy Training and Going Slow

A 2021 study conducted by the Center for Canine Behavior Studies[1] put a spotlight on the importance

---

1   Ian R. Dinwoodie, et al., "An Investigation into the Impact of Pre-adolescent Training on Canine Behavior," *Animals* 11, no. 5 (2021): 1298. https://doi.org/10.3390/ani11051298.

of fear-free, rewards-based puppy training. The founder of the Center for Canine Behavior Studies, Dr. Nicholas Dodman, said in the Fall 2021 newsletter that "[t]aking a puppy for reward-based puppy training and socialization in the first six months of its life is as important as having a child attend elementary school." Some of the study's key findings include:

- Undesired behaviors like aggression, compulsive behaviors, destructive behaviors, and excessive barking were ALL reduced in dogs that went to puppy training before six months of age.
- Rewards-based puppy training substantially reduced the odds of aggression in adult dogs.
- Punishment-based training increased the odds of aggression.
- The use of punishment in training is related to an increase of both fear and aggression in dogs.

Before working with a trainer, be sure to check them out thoroughly to ensure they have solid credentials and experience and that they use rewards-based methods (see chapter 10 for more help with

Many puppies will be overstimulated in a shared classroom setting. If this is the case, arrange to have one-on-one instruction.

choosing a trainer). Additionally, if you notice your little one is overwhelmed in a classroom setting (for example, won't take treats), arrange for private, one-on-one instruction. A group learning setting is not always the best situation for many puppies.

It is also crucial to not over-socialize your puppy. Go slowly—especially when the puppy first comes home. Gradually increase their exposure to people, places, environments, and new things as they grow. Consider going on only one public outing a day when the puppy is very young. This gives them the time they need time to reflect on what they have experienced and rest up for the next day. If something scares your little one, take a day or so off. Allow recovery time and make sure your pup feels comfortable and safe. The next time you show her new stimuli, including visits to the veterinarian or groomer, be extra careful to make sure she has a positive experience. If your young puppy is overly frightened by new stimuli during this vulnerable time in their lives, it can create life-long trauma.

My two cattle-collie brothers had a scary early experience with harnesses when they were puppies and to this day they briefly shut down when the harnesses come out—but they recover in a few seconds, and they love to go on walks.

Puppy Expert Christine Young Shares Critical Training and Socialization Tips for Puppy Care

This interview has been edited for length. Please see
https://foxchapelpets.com/positive-training-dogs/ to read the full interview.

Trainer Christine Young with a client's dogs. The Frenchie on the left is Babbett and the Golden Retriever on the right is Baron. Both dogs benefitted from early training with Young.

▶ **What are the first things you advise new puppy parents to do for their new family member when the puppy comes home?**

Every situation and every pup is different, but if you're looking to get started on the right paw, here are three fundamentals that will give you a good foundation:

1. **Create a calm environment**—Start shopping and setting things up before your pup comes home. Prepare a zen-like environment with safe containment areas. Schedule down time. When your adorable fur baby arrives, try to let go of have expectations or agendas.

   During the first few days, let them explore on their terms (not yours). Invite friends and family over AFTER your puppy has a few days of settling in. Let your pup slowly absorb their new world at their own pace. This builds trust.

   Be aware of:
   • too much touching
   • too many new toys
   • too many people
   • too many socializing opportunities too fast

   If you have a multipet household, take time to have your puppy settle in before making introductions, and be sure you know how to introduce each pet safely.

2. **Learn the often-neglected art of dog management—** Expect some of your puppy's antics to test your patience as they grow, often these are your dog's natural coping mechanisms. Before you focus on training to change the "bad" behavior, it is important to develop a solid management strategy.

   When you invest in and learn how to use tools like baby gates, long lines, crates, privacy window film, and more, things will be calmer, cleaner, and more organized. When you need a break, hire a pro pet sitter or dog walker if you have the budget or call up a friend or family member to come hang out with your little one, then run some errands or get some work finished. Restorative efforts like this go a long way.

   Make sure everyone knows how to interact with your new buddy, so they don't mess up your training efforts. Teaching others is a great way to reinforce your own knowledge and skills.

3. **Communication and body language**—Dogs learn our body language much faster than we learn theirs. As you learn how to pay attention to details and read their signals, you will be able to communicate more effectively.

Be a keen observer. Notice what your new pup does when you or others touch them. Do they get loose and wiggly and seem to move toward you to ask for more? Great, you can continue! If not, the subtle changes in their body language (lip licking, stiffening up, or pulling away) are telling us that they are not thrilled about being touched, at least not in this way at this time.

If we ignore these signs and force attention on a young puppy, it can create a dog who avoids snuggling or touch in general. If we respect their boundaries and our dogs believe their communication will be respected, they often settle in beside us asking for a closer relationship.

▶ What is the most important skill you advise new puppy parents to teach their pup?

I help them understand what socialization actually is. It's not just about playing with other dogs and meeting new people (although that's definitely important, too). The sensitive period for socialization is approximately from 4 to 16 weeks. These first couple of months are a time for your new family member to learn that new people, animals, places, events, sounds, scents, surfaces, and so much more are interesting to observe and get used to in their own time. The sometimes-shy pups can learn that they will always have choice and control and the enthusiastic pups learn that being polite and focusing on you will get them access to what they want.

Puppies don't have the ability to fully recover from too many negative interactions during this sensitive period. It's easy for an untrained pet parent to unknowingly make mistakes that can have lifelong consequences.

Keep a few top tips in mind:

- Puppies don't need to approach until and unless they are ready. (Let them come to you.)
- Distance is your friend when putting your puppy in new situations.
- Take time to relax, watch the world go by, and enjoy their silly antics. HAVE FUN!

Yes, socializing at a young age is most beneficial, but it's important to remember that it's never too late. Some new or scary situations will take more scheduled exposures with more involved training, and not all dogs will be able to handle these situations.

▶ What are your favorite ways to teach resilience and confidence in puppies?

Besides the choice and control that we touched on, **canine enrichment** can make a big difference. If you're new to enrichment, think of it like a doggy amusement park that also stimulates their mind and body. By providing your pup with puzzle-like challenges and engaging activities, you encourage them to use their natural instincts and behaviors. Enrichment activities can range from food puzzles to more complex games.

A **predictable** routine builds resilience. Dogs, like us, appreciate having a sense of predictability in their lives. Make a novel safe chew treat to give them in a specific place to help them decompress. At this young age, create that association exactly where you want them to relax. A routine also helps your little one adapt to new environments and situations. When you gradually incorporate unexpected elements into familiar patterns, your dog's trust and confidence will grow.

Puppyhood goes by fast, so **be patient**, take deep breaths, and practice kindness. Setting unrealistic goals can lead to disappointment and often hinders the progress when learning new behaviors. PATIENCE, consistency, and positive reinforcement are necessary. Take things one step at a time and seek guidance from experienced, professional, and reliable resources.

It might feel like your adolescent dog is unlearning everything you taught him as a puppy but remember to be patient and continue to provide him with many options for safe socialization and enrichment.

CONTINUE WORKING WITH ADOLESCENT DOGS

Like humans, dogs also go through adolescence, and you'll certainly see some wild swings in behavior during this stage of growth. The adolescent stage starts around 6 months and lasts to around 18 months (but can extend to 24 months in some dogs). This phase involves sexual and social maturing. Behavior consultants are often called in to help during adolescence—owners who once had the world's most perfect puppy now have an out-of-control teenage dog they no longer recognize. Sadly, these teenage hooligans are the dogs most likely to be taken to shelters. Their brains, hormones, and bodies are changing as they barrel toward full maturity.

I ask my clients with teenage dogs to gather their strength and employ all the patience they can muster. This phase will pass … eventually. Some of the personality changes we see during this time include a lack of attention, appearing

OVERVIEW

Working with Adolescent Dogs

- **Step One:** Recognize Adolescence as a Necessary Stage of Growth
- **Step Two:** Focus on Frequent, Short Training Sessions
- **Step Three:** Schedule Monitored Play Dates with Other Safe Dogs
- **Step Four:** Use Enrichment and Management

to have forgotten all puppy training, a lack of impulse control, an increase in energy, behavior that humans tend to label as "stubbornness," and more worrisome behavior problems like aggression, reactivity, resource guarding, etc. Behavior consultants have a lot of adolescent dogs on our training rosters.

WORKING WITH ADOLESCENT DOGS

Understanding that adolescence and its challenges are a bona fide stage of growth in dogs will hopefully help you dig deep and find patience.

Understand that your dog's focus will be elsewhere a lot of the time during this stage of development. Keep training fresh and fun by breaking it into smaller five-minute segments.

STEP ONE: Recognize Adolescence as a Necessary Stage of Growth

Dogs age much more quickly than we do, so owners often don't realize their dogs are in the adolescent growth stage. They just assume that their once-angelic puppy is now a "brat" (and it certainly can look that way). Internal growth changes are actually working overtime to push the dog from the puppy stage to maturity.

In adolescence, your dog will start exploring the outside world with the additional confidence his new growth and experience bring. This might lead him to learn, for example, that hightailing it after a squirrel is way more fun than listening to a recall from his boring owner. Understanding that adolescence and its accompanying challenges are just part of a necessary growth stage will help you maintain your patience.

STEP TWO: Focus on Frequent, Short Training Sessions

The basic manners your adorable little pup excelled at might go out the window during adolescence. His hormones will cause him to be much more engaged and interested in the outside world, especially in other dogs. Other dogs everywhere are suddenly way more compelling than your bothersome demand to sit. The kitchen trashcan might be so tempting that he starts turning it over every day.

The owner's role during this time—besides having buckets of patience—is to work through these changes. Focus on more frequent training sessions throughout the day that are five minutes long or less. Don't expect an adult dog's level of focus, compliance, or precision. Instead, try to build on all the great puppy socialization and training your dog has already accomplished. Your dog's focus will be elsewhere most of the time, but with continued understanding and quality training, your very good boy will come back.

Ensure that your dog has SAFE canine friends so she can learn how to play nicely.

Your adolescent dog has tons of energy—if he's bored, he'll likely create his own activities, like getting into the garbage can or tearing up your pillows. Use management to stop these types of problems before they show up.

STEP THREE: Schedule Monitored Play Dates with Other Safe Dogs

It's important that your teenage dog still be allowed to meet friendly people and **safe dogs** during this growth stage, but your dog will be more excitable than she was as a puppy. Routine adolescent play dates are invaluable for dogs. They are best organized with the same group your dog had puppy play dates with. Also make sure the dogs will be unable to mate (are all the same gender or spayed/neutered).

As with puppy play dates, adolescent play dates should be monitored to make sure no dogs get out of control. Take breaks and let the dogs rest away from one another. You'll probably see more growling, snapping, humping, or louder responses to play during this period. If the dogs are all being safe with one another, your dog will learn how to read other dogs and to back off when snapped at. If your dog begins truly fighting, however, call in a behavior counselor. There is a myth that dogs "will just work it out on their own." Letting dogs fight it out is just not a good idea—the dogs could get injured or become reactive.

STEP FOUR: Use Enrichment and Management

Continue to provide your dog with daily exercise and mental stimulation. I love KONG® Company products and similar toys. Their magnificent hollow rubber chew toys are an adolescent-dog owner's best friend. Try stuffing them full of delicious snack foods like peanut butter or cheese and freezing them overnight to create a long-lasting treat that will effectively hold your dog's attention. You cannot have too many of these indestructible toys.

Encourage calmness during adolescence whenever and wherever you can. Place chew toys on a dog mat. The dog will go to the mat, probably lie down, and begin chewing. If she gets up from the mat, pick up the toy and put it back on the mat. In other words, show her that if she stays on the mat, she gets the chew toy. If you have more than one dog, give each of them a safe, solitary place in which to chew. I have doggie mats for each of my dogs and separate them with a baby gate.

KONGs and chew toys are fairly safe, but I do not advise leaving dogs home alone with anything that could be a choking hazard (including popular bully sticks). If things like your kitchen trashcan become daily targets, use management instead—put the trashcan in a place where the dog cannot access it. Management is a great solution during this period, so pick up any tempting items like socks, shoes, or loose pieces of clothing.

TAKE IT SLOW WITH RESCUE PUPPIES AND DOGS

I began my career with dogs working with a popular Austin nonprofit rescue group. My job was to visit the shelters in and around Austin and pull dogs and puppies that met our criteria. We weren't a breed-specific rescue—we focused exclusively on temperament. I honed my canine behavior observation skills over a 10-year period picking "solid" dogs from incredibly stressful situations and fostering over 400 dogs with my husband on our Texas ranch.

One of the most important things I learned from these shelter dogs is that we must give them time to adapt to change. **When bringing a dog home from a shelter or rescue, take everything slowly—very slowly.** Many shelter dogs came from loving homes. One day the dog is in a warm, stable home and the next they are in a loud shelter feeling only worry and fear. Other dogs come into the shelter with already deep levels of uncertainty and fear. Most shelters do good work to reduce stress for their dogs, but there is no way to completely remove the anxiety they feel.

Dogs can and do suffer from PTSD, as evidenced in military dogs returning from combat zones. The American Kennel Club notes that PTSD presents

Many rescue dogs will show signs of trauma like fearfulness and timidity, especially when adjusting to new things (including their new home).

in dogs as panic, fearfulness, pacing, being timid, clinging to people, aggressive reactions, and hypervigilance.[1] Of course, not every shelter or rescue dog will develop PTSD. A few dogs don't seem to be bothered at all, but those dogs are rare. In a stable environment, some dogs can unwind and de-stress in three or four days. Others are so traumatized by their experiences that it can take six months to a year before they feel safe enough to open up. Let your dog take as much time as he needs.

If you have a new dog who is fearful of people, slow everything way down. Allow him to settle in—for however long he needs—with just you. This can be difficult if you have a partner in the house or kids the dog might be afraid of, but you still have to protect your dog's space as he adjusts to his new life. You might even realize that your busy family isn't the best place for a dog that is terrified of people, and he might need to go back to the rescue or shelter. A good rescue will search for the right home for each dog.

Once you know your dog is adjusting to his new home (by seeing that he loves to eat his meals,

---

1   AKC Staff, "Dogs and Post-Traumatic Stress Disorder (PTSD)," American Kennel Club, March 25, 2013, https://www.akc.org/expert-advice/lifestyle/dogs-post-traumatic-stress-disorder/.

is sleeping well, and isn't exhibiting any anxious behaviors), slowly and carefully introduce him to new people in a safe, enclosed yard where he can approach or leave at will. Sit with the new person and ignore your dog, just chatting to each other. Watch your dog come and go. If he cries out or tries to escape, you'll know you moved too quickly. Back it up and perhaps let him see new people at a distance first, from the safety of the car or a house window. Give your dog the time he needs. The best chance for success is to bring in a qualified, force-free trainer with a solid understanding of canine body language.

BRINGING HOME YOUR RESCUE DOG

1

Ensure that your new friend has a quiet, safe place all his own. He needs time to adjust and to learn the house rules.

STEP ONE: Prepare Your Home and Create Space for Your New Dog to Learn

Prepare your home. Ensure you have a small, quiet place set aside just for your new dog. This can be an open-door crate filled with comfortable bedding, a larger X pen, or a dedicated smaller room like a laundry room. Have safe chew toys available since chewing reduces stress for many dogs.

Your new dog may not be potty trained and will be unfamiliar with your home's layout at first. A change in diet can also bring on stomach upset. Don't punish your new dog for indoor accidents (when a creature has to go, it goes). Instead take him outside more frequently and use high-value food and an abundance of praise every time he does his business outside to reinforce the behavior.

Your dog may or may not have experienced living inside a home before. Show him around on leash and limit his interactions with others in the home. Give him time to explore and rest in his own space. Introduce him to new people slowly—this is not the time to invite the neighborhood over to meet the new, cute dog. Please also go very slowly when introducing small children to the dog since you're unlikely to know his background or experience with kids. Never allow children to sit on your dog or pull on his ears or tail, and always supervise their time together.

OVERVIEW

Bringing Home Your Rescue Dog

- **Step One:** Prepare Your Home and Create Space for Your New Dog to Learn

- **Step Two:** Slowly Introduce New Experiences and Follow Your Dog's Lead on Timing

- **Step Three:** Seek Professional Guidance

Protect your new family member's space and allow them plenty of time to settle into their new life. It takes as long as it takes, and each dog is an individual and has an individual schedule for how long it will take for them to feel comfortable in their new home.

STEP TWO: Slowly Introduce New Experiences and Follow Your Dog's Lead on Timing

Assume your dog needs at least a week to a month to learn his new routine and the behaviors you want from him. There will be plenty of time to take your dog to visit your relatives and meet the neighbors. Once your dog seems to be settling in well and isn't exhibiting signs of stress, slowly start to add one outing a day, such as a walk in the neighborhood or a short car ride.

It's crucial to keenly observe your dog during these outings and continually communicate to your dog that he is safe with you and your family. If you see signs of stress, pull back on the activity and allow your dog more down time to adjust to your home. Signs of stress will include panting, drooling, not eating, trying to escape, sudden scratching, whining, excessive barking, or excessive chewing.

If your dog begins to show troubling behavior or emotional distress after being in your home for six to eight weeks, immediately schedule an appointment with your veterinarian and contact a canine behavior professional.

STEP THREE: Seek Professional Guidance

If after six to eight weeks in your home your rescue or shelter dog begins to exhibit troubling behavior, immediately get professional help. Visit the veterinarian to rule out physical concerns like undetected pain. If your dog has emotional distress, the sooner you bring in a trained and qualified canine behavior expert, the sooner your dog will be headed down the road to recovery.

Ask an Expert

Behavior Consultant Denise O'Moore Explains How to Survive and Thrive with Adolescent Dogs

This interview has been included in its entirety.

Behavior consultant Denise O'Moore spends her time helping dogs through their various life stages, including the difficult adolescent stage.

▶ **What are the most common behavior concerns owners having during the adolescent phase?**

There are some gender-based changes we see, such as male dogs suddenly lifting their leg to urinate or an increase in sniffing outdoors. Also, their mates are suddenly way more interesting to them. They are going to challenge you. Most owners have gotten that look from their dog in the park when they ask for a recall and the dog stares at them with what looks like a smirk that says: "make me." It's reminiscent of human teens rolling their eyes at their parents. It's not intentional—they are just growing up. Suddenly jumping up on new people tends to show up as well, even if they were angelic little ones who loved to show off a sit whenever you asked for one.

▶ How do you recommend owners train an adolescent dog?

For every action there is a reaction. The key is to find what motivates your dog. We often must increase our reinforcers during this period. Dry, boring dog biscuits aren't going to mean much. Once owners are aware that this is a phase, they can be prepared with extra patience and a plan, such as having the dog on leash when new people come over. I teach almost everything through play. I keep their creative minds engaged. You don't want these guys to get bored because you don't know what you are going to come back to. Strive to be more creative than they are. I love to use tools like brain games, snuffle mats, and activity mats that are readily available online and in pet stores. I can't recommend K9Connectables enough! These toys are like canine Lego®—engaging and stimulating for the brain.

▶ What do you advise dog owners do to help their teenage dogs with the abundance of energy that tends to show up in adolescence?

Choose your battles! Sometimes owners increase the length or intensity of their walks thinking that will help calm the young dog down. Often, however, that just increases the dog's strength and stamina. You are building an athlete you won't be able to handle. This is the period in which the dog is going to try everything and anything, including behaviors she hasn't tried before. I encourage the use of management—such as picking up any tempting shoes and socks left around the house, removing items that look tempting to the dog, etc. Sometimes we need to remove the dog from a situation where bad behavior, such as "counter surfing," might appear and redirect that energy into politely chewing on something wonderful in another room. You can also give them a "safe mat" in the same room—one they are rewarded for going to and staying on (choosing to do this instead of jumping on

You don't want an adolescent dog to get bored. Use brain games, puzzles, snuffle mats, and other exciting toys and products to keep their creative minds engaged.

the counter). Experiment and see what works for your dog and make it as fun and rewarding as possible. This is the time to slow down and really observe your dog to find out the things she loves, and then you can use those things in your training. Strengthening your bond will help smooth out this period of potential tension. Ignoring these new behaviors will not help the dog and these undesired behaviors will get worse. Also, the one thing people often miss is in the few moments after returning from a walk—they tend to remove the leash, harness, collar, and then disappear! Stay a bit and spend some down time with your dog—it's all about bonding and it's important to enjoy time with them as much as they do with you!

Must-Have Skills for Your Dog

This chapter explores the most important life skills a dog can have, and it shows you how to teach them to your dog safely and fairly. Over the years, there have been many shifts in our understanding of what makes a happy life for a pet dog and what training is essential. Many trainers are even shifting our vocabulary, too. Instead of giving the dog a "command" (the dog's behavior stems from a demand), we give him a "cue" (the dog's behavior is based on a history of rewards and a bond with the owner). Trainers want to set dogs up for success and allow them to be dogs, permitting them to safely express all their natural, unique doggie behaviors. In other words, trainers and owners must be guides rather than taskmasters.

A FEELING OF SAFETY

There is one thing you can do for Fido that is perhaps more important than anything else: ensure that your dog feels safe. The outside world can scare all of us at times, so it is critical that the dog view the home as her safe place.

The security in feeling safe can fend off so many of the common behavior problems we see in dogs. It's not a cure-all, of course, but a sense of security increases the chances that these behavior issues won't show up and if destructive behaviors do occur, they won't be as severe. Lacking this sense of safety increases a dog's stress, causing problematic reactions as they try on their own to eliminate or reduce this stress. Chronic stress affects every part of the body, even changing the brain. Our homes are our castles, and this should be true for our four-legged housemates as well.

Training is about rewarding your dog's good behaviors and strengthening your bond with the dog so they feel safe and certain of what you need from them.

It's easy to recognize when a dog feels safe and happy—their posture, ears, and mouth will all be relaxed.

It's easy to tell if your dog feels safe—her body posture, ears, and mouth will all be relaxed, she'll give big, sweeping tail wags, her sleeping patterns, appetite, and play behaviors will all be regular and normal, and she won't show excessive destructive or unwanted behaviors. (**Note:** you can do everything right to create this sense of safety and still face unwanted behavior influenced by genetic factors or early trauma, although creating a sense of safety will help your troubled dog enormously.)

The signs that your dog doesn't feel secure can be more subtle, including stiffness in the body, a lack of tail wagging or a stiff or tucked tail, a tightly closed mouth, "whale eyes" (when a dog's eyes widen and the whites are visible), pinned-back ears, shaking, pacing, excessive vocalizing, running away from you in the house, hiding, yawning, drooling, excessive licking, or a lack of appetite.

Having a safe space where your dog can enjoy an appropriate chew toy is a must. This darling dog, happy, secure, and enjoying her dog toy is named Bonnie. She shares her life with behaviorist Lisa Hird in Britain.

The Top Five Ways to Help Your Dog Feel Safe at Home

It is essential for humans to feel that our home is our safe place—dogs need to feel the same security.

1. **Provide a comfortable, small space that is solely for your dog.** If your dog is crate trained and enjoys the crate, leave the door open so she can come and go at will. Or use a small, low-traffic room such as a laundry room. Provide comfortable bedding, water, and safe chew toys or treats. Don't let kids enter and always ensure that children give your dog space. **Always supervise** them when they are together. It is up to the parents to ensure safety for both the child and the dog.

2. **Provide a stable daily routine so your dog can predict her day.** The routine doesn't have to be, nor should it be, exactly the same every day, but the dog needs to know she'll get fed twice a day and that she will get human attention, exercise, potty breaks, enrichment, and mental stimulation.

3. **Allow your dog to make some decisions for her own life.** An animal with control over her own life is far more confident than an animal who lacks any control. Instead of telling your dog what she can't do, look for ways to tell her what she can do and give her choices within that framework. This might look like allowing her to choose to spend time in her space alone or acknowledging and respecting her wishes when she doesn't want to be petted.

4. **Understand that human stress in the home filters down to your dog.** During stressful situations, try to address and reduce the stress, seek solutions, and don't forget to check on your dog during these times. Provide calming activites for your dog such as quiet, early morning or late-night walks, safe chew toys and treats, and downtime. Ordinary life events for humans—such as a new baby or a move—can cause anxiety for non-speaking family members.

5. **Do not use aversive training or tools with your dog.** If you would not do it to a toddler, do not do it to your dog. Aversive training harms your bond and breaks your dog's trust in you. It creates anxiety, fear, and pain, and removes your dog's sense of safety. Dogs learn more effectively and faster using rewards-based training. If the techniques you're trying don't seem to be solving your dog's behavior problems, call an accredited industry professional as soon as possible to help.

Use high-value treats to reward your dog for giving you her attention—you want to reinforce for your dog that she should look to you for guidance.

THE "CHECK IN"

Of all the skills we can teach a dog, my personal favorite is the "check in." This is when a dog—either on cue or on his own—stops what he is doing and voluntarily looks his human in the eyes for direction, feedback, or praise. The check in is a critical skill necessary to teaching many other skills, so it's one of the first skills I teach any dog, even young puppies. There are many ways to teach it—you can use the method below, but don't be afraid to get creative and use what works best for your dog.

I love this cue for so many reasons! It accomplishes an astonishing number of things:

♦ Interrupts undesired or potentially dangerous canine behavior
♦ Disrupts "stare down" situations with other dogs
♦ Teaches your dog that you are the path to what he wants
♦ Teaches your dog to look to you for guidance
♦ Gives your dog a calm response to use when exciting stimuli is present

♦ Puts the focus on the handler (the beginning of all obedience training)
♦ Empowers your dog know he can communicate what he wants and receive it (if it is safe for him to)
♦ Strengthens the human-canine bond and releases oxytocin (the "love hormone")

OVERVIEW

Teaching the Check In

- **Step One:** Reward and Reinforce Eye Contact

- **Step Two:** Have Short Practice Sessions Every Day

- **Step Three:** Add a Cue

- **Step Four:** Introduce Distractions

TEACHING THE CHECK IN

1 Place your treats and your clicker if you're using it on a tabletop and sit quietly in a chair. Every time your dog "checks in" with you, click or mark and give him a treat.

2 Once your dog understands that he will be highly rewarded for looking at your face, spend short, five-minute training bursts throughout the day working on getting a solid check in.

STEP ONE: Reward and Reinforce
Eye Contact
Begin teaching this skill when your dog is hungry (not on a full stomach). Place small, high-value treats out of the dog's sight—either high up on a table countertop or behind your back. Sit in a chair near the treats, ignoring (but watching) your dog. Every time she "checks in" (gives you direct eye contact), mark it with a "yes" or a click and toss a treat on the floor.

If your dog is very involved in "dog stuff" and doesn't seem interested, you can stand up, whistle, or clap a little to get her attention (don't repeat your dog's name over and over again). Watch for the dog's neck to turn as she focuses on you. Wait for her to look into your eyes, then immediately mark and reward the behavior.

STEP TWO: Have Short Practice Sessions
Every Day
Practice getting a check in without a cue in short five-minute sessions every day for three to five days. It is powerful for your dog to willingly offer you a desired behavior (without you having to demand it). If your dog checks in and you don't have treats handy, you can reinforce the behavior by giving praise and petting your dog.

Whenever you cue your dog for a check in (probably using their name), you want her to stop and turn all her attention to you.

Depending on what exciting thing your dog is watching out the window, it might be difficult to get their attention for a check in. If your cue isn't working with distractions, go back to practicing without distractions for a few days.

STEP THREE: Add a Cue

Once your dog offers you many check ins throughout the day, it's time to add a cue (I recommend using the dog's name). When you say your dog's name, you want her to stop what she is doing and check in. Your dog will be looking to you to find out what you need from her.

STEP FOUR: Introduce Distractions

While your dog is distracted, call his name and wait. If he is too involved with the distraction, try whistling, clapping, or even jumping to pull his attention away for the check in. The second the dog looks at you, mark and reward the behavior.

Begin trying to pull your dog's attention away from low-level distractions inside your home, first on leash, then off leash. Work toward pulling their attention from larger distractions like noise or activity outside the window. If you don't get a successful check in, go back to working without distractions to strengthen your dog's check-in behavior. Then try again.

Accidents happen and sometimes even the most cautious owner can lose a grip on their dog's leash but making sure you've taught your dog a reliable recall will help you interrupt your dog's natural drives, pull him back to you, and keep your best friend safe.

THE RELIABLE RECALL

A solid recall can be a matter of life and death. A dog following her brain's drive to chase other animals or stimuli can lead her into dangerous, harmful situations. Building a reliable recall gives you a chance to override this natural drive with training so you can quickly get your dog's attention and pull them back to you if they accidentally get loose or begin chasing something they shouldn't.

There is a lot involved in the process of a dog stopping its activity (no matter how interesting) and willingly returning to you, but it all begins with the check in—your dog hears your call and turns to look at you. Then it's all about making the act of coming back to you—even if delayed—a happy, exciting event for your dog. Even if you're frustrated, fake some joy. **Never punish a recall**—you want your dog to be enthusiastic about coming back to you, not afraid of punishment.

OVERVIEW

Teaching a Reliable Recall

- **Step One:** Enjoy Quality Time Together and Reinforce Your Dog's Check In Daily

- **Step Two:** Start Rewarding the Recall Sequence

- **Step Three:** Add Distractions, Perfect the Response, and Repeat Outside

- **Step Four:** Reinforce Your Dog's Skills with the "Come to Me" Game

- **Step Five:** Link Special Responses with High-Value Rewards

- **Step Six:** Practice Off-Leash Recalls and Be Cautious in Public Spaces

TEACHING A RELIABLE RECALL

1

First make sure your dog responds to his name with a solid check in every time—he should look directly at your face to await further instruction.

2

Start rewarding all natural recall behaviors—such as your dog excitedly coming to greet you when you return home.

STEP ONE: Enjoy Quality Time Together and Reinforce Your Dog's Check In

The most important part of a recall is your connection to your dog. The more time you spend with her enjoying the world and teaching her vital life skills, the better your dog's recall will be.

The most important skill to strengthen this bond is the check in, which should become a daily, routine occurrence. Once your dog offers a consistent check in, intermittently reinforce it with treats and always acknowledge the behavior with a happy and enthusiastic "yes."

STEP TWO: Start Rewarding the Recall Sequence

First reinforce a natural recall in which the dog comes to you on his own. For example, if you come home after being away and he is excited to see you again, use your recall word (I use "come") and then back up, clapping as he runs to you. Reinforce the behavior with food, play, or affection—whatever your dog loves the most. Repeat any time your dog heads toward you on his own.

3

Once your recall works well inside your house, try practicing in a fenced-in yard with low-level distractions.

STEP THREE: Add Distractions, Perfect the Response, and Repeat Outside

Once you know your dog understands that "come" means he should come to you, slowly increase the distractions in the area, for example, have another person stand in the room.

At first, this second person should be quiet and ignoring your dog. Get a lot of solid recalls away from the newcomer to you. Then ask the person to move and make sounds without looking at or engaging with your dog. Continue practicing recalls, raising the distraction level as your dog's recall improves.

Once you've perfected the behavior inside, practice outside in a secure, fenced-in yard. Repeat the process, slowly adding distractions.

■ TIP

If you don't have a second person to help with recall training, try using a stuffed toy or some other interesting new object. Cue her to come back to you from the item. After you get a successful recall, encourage her to go back and investigate the new object—you'll reinforce for her that if she does what you want first (the recall), she can do what she wants after (sniffing the new item).

Play the "come to me" game by first having a friend or family member gently restrain your dog as you walk or run away from him to build his excitement (left). Once you've cued your dog to "come," your partner-in-training will release him into the recall (right).

STEP FOUR: Reinforce Your Dog's Skills with the "Come to Me" Game

Use the "come to me" game to really ramp up your dog's excitement for recalls. Gather three to four people in your fenced-in yard and make sure your dog is off leash and hungry.

First, one person should engage your dog while the rest of the group ignores her. This person will then run away and use the cue word one time. When your dog comes to the first person, that person will reinforce the behavior with petting and treats.

Then, this first person will gently hold your dog's harness to build excitement while a second person runs away and cues the dog. As soon as the cue word is said, the person holding the harness will let go, your dog will run to the second person, and that person will give treats. Repeat several times and play the "come to me" game often to strengthen your dog's recall.

If only two people are available, skip right into the second part of the game (with the harness being gently held and building the dog's excitement to reach the human and the treats).

STEP FIVE: Link Special Responses with High-Value Rewards

Reinforce "special" responses—super-fast recalls or demanding recalls. Teach your dog that a super-fast recall earns the very best treats (such as their favorite meat or cheese) while slower responses might earn only a regular dry biscuit. If your very good boy is successfully recalled

5

Use your dog's favorite treats (like special jerky sticks or cheese cubes) to let them know that responding quickly gets them the best treats!

6

Leashes provide safety for everyone, including your dog.

from something super tantalizing to him (like a squirrel, for example), give him a "jackpot" reward of several high-value treats in a row and exuberantly praise him.

STEP SIX: Practice Off-Leash Recalls and Be Cautious in Public Spaces

A wise trainer once noted that off-leash dog control is the equivalent of a PhD education for your dog. Continually practice and reinforce off-leash recalls at home throughout your dog's life. Only when her recall is rock solid, and you can successfully recall her from every distraction should you take it on the road.

Always use a leash in public spaces until you know your dog is well-trained. As soon as you choose to unhook your dog's leash, you hold all the responsibility for anything that might happen.

If you want to hike with your dog off leash, use a variety of long lines in varying weights to practice recalls in public places where off-leash walking is allowed (certain parks, hiking trails, etc.). Some of these lines are as long as 30 feet (don't use long lines if other dogs are running loose as they can cause injuries). Work your way up to using a very light leash (so the dog feels almost off leash). If your dog "goes deaf" during this practice, give him a few seconds to "remember" to listen to you. If he doesn't come, turn in the opposite direction, and cheerily say "let's go!"

After you practice, practice, practice on leash, unhook your dog in a safe area and practice recalls as you walk with your dog. Give your dog valuable rewards every time he comes back to you on cue. If you unhook and your dog runs for the hills, you'll know you still have work to do on leash.

Recall Tips

- Wisely choose times to practice recalls with your dog that will set him up for success and reinforce the behavior you want.

- Perfect your dog's recall in a calm, controlled, indoor setting and slowly build up.

- Don't repeat the cue to come to you—only say it once. Instead clap, whistle, or jump to get their attention.

- Use your recall word for meals, treats, puzzles, walks, and anything else the dog will find rewarding.

- Don't use the recall for un-fun or possibly stressful activities like nail trims or baths.

- Don't put your dog into potentially dangerous situations—even the most highly trained dog can ignore a recall cue.

- If you think you have practiced a recall enough, practice 100 more times. You can never rehearse the recall skill enough.

- Never use force such as a shock collar in training of any kind.

Use your recall word for fun activities only—such as getting ready to go for a walk or playing a mind puzzle. Do not use your recall word for activities that may stress your dog, such as nail trims.

You cannot practice a recall too many times and rehearsing too few times can put your dog in danger. If you think you've practiced enough, practice 100 more times!

Create a secure home life that makes your dog feel safe—you'll set your dog up to be a resilient problem solver!

PROBLEM SOLVING AND RESILIENCE

I've never seen a dog training class centered on teaching problem solving and resilience for dogs—and that's a real shame. Resilience begins before the dog is even born. It starts with the parent and grandparent dogs and even further back. How safe and secure your dog's ancestors felt will affect your dog's genetic expression. We have little control over our dog's genetic makeup, but we do control their environment. It is crucial that we create a home life for our dog set up for maximum resilience and problem solving.

OVERVIEW

Creating a Resilient Dog with Problem-Solving Skills

- **Step One:** Create a Home Space That Provides a Sense of Safety and Security
- **Step Two:** Allow Your Dog to Make Choices Throughout the Day
- **Step Three:** Ensure That Your Dog Receives Quality Physical and Emotional Attention Every Day

CREATING A RESILIENT DOG WITH PROBLEM-SOLVING SKILLS

1

Make sure your dog has his own quiet space where he feels safe and secure.

STEP ONE: Create a Home Space That Provides a Sense of Safety and Security

Create a standard daily routine so your dog knows what to expect each day. Ensure that she has her own quiet space she can access whenever she chooses. Always supervise young children around pets and make sure everyone in the house respects his canine body language.

2

We've taken a lot of agency away from our captive dogs. Build resiliency by giving your puppy or dog the right to make choices throughout the day with your guidance.

3

Make sure your puppy or dog gets the mental, physical, and emotional enrichment she needs to become a confident member of your home.

STEP TWO: Allow Your Dog to Make Choices Throughout the Day

All animals seek control over their environment and when we remove all control, they often begin to show behavior problems. This doesn't mean you should allow your dog to destroy your home or garden. It means you should allow your dog to make safe choices, like staying outside if possible, napping uninterruptedly, walking away from a petting session, etc.

Never force your dog to do something it absolutely doesn't want to do. You can lure, praise, redirect, or try again another day—there are so many options that don't require force. Getting your dog's consent is important.

STEP THREE: Ensure That Your Dog Receives Quality Physical and Emotional Attention Every Day

Maybe the weather is terrible outside, but you can still engage the dog inside with mind puzzles, find-it games, tug, fun obedience work, or nose work. You don't have to spend hours and hours making sure your dog has daily enrichment, but smart owners will see to it that their dog's needs are met on a daily basis. You know your dog best and each dogs' needs are different. My two cattle collie mixes need a high level of engagement, physical activity, and quality napping time. If they don't get it, we can tell—they invent their own games, like bringing into the house and shredding every tree limb they can find in the yard. They also begin to wrestle too assertively with one another if they are not well exercised or if they don't get enough nap time in during the day. Smaller dogs also need adequate enrichment, but it may look different for a teacup Chihuahua than it does for my herding dogs.

There are many aspects that create a resilient dog and all need to be examined to add quality control when and where we can. Components of resiliency include environmental, genetic, developmental, and psychological factors. Social support from the human (and other family canines in the house) is as important to your dog as it is to us. Ensuring your dog is not experiencing chronic stress makes for a happier life for everyone in your home.

If properly reinforced in a safe, relaxing environment, dogs can develop useful skills for calming themselves.

THE ABILITY TO SELF-CALM

Studies have shown that dogs can experience hyperactivity, impulsivity, and inattention—the same symptoms of ADHD in humans.[1] These ADHD-like behaviors in dogs are often linked with obsessive-compulsive behavior, aggressiveness, and fearfulness. It's important to know the difference between normal and abnormal canine behavior in these cases and to teach your dog ways to self-calm. All dogs can benefit from learning calming behaviors (even if some need it more than others).

OVERVIEW

Teaching Your Dog to Self-Calm

- **Step One:** Reinforce the Natural Calm Behaviors You Want to See More Of
- **Step Two:** Teach "Go to Mat"
- **Step Three:** Teach "Take a Breath"

TEACHING YOUR DOG TO SELF-CALM

Reinforce the calm behaviors you want to see in your dog—if he's resting but awake, mark it and give him a treat.

STEP ONE: Reinforce the Natural Calm Behaviors You Want to See More Of

Once your new dog has settled comfortably into your home and lifestyle, begin reinforcing the calm behaviors that you like in your dog. When he is resting but awake in a natural down position or offers a sit, say "yes" or click and give him a treat.

Get creative and mark and treat the dog any time he is totally relaxed—I'll treat a dog if he's relaxed on his back with all four feet in the air or if he's calm and has all four paws on the ground. The behavior you reinforce will increase, so repeatedly and frequently reinforce calm behaviors while your dog is learning about their new way of life with you.

1   Alexandra Larkin, "Dogs Can Show Human-Like ADHD Behaviors, Study Finds," *CBS News*, October 16, 2021, https://www.cbsnews.com/news/dog-adhd-behavior-study/.

2

Teaching your dog to relax on a mat gives you a very useful tool. Once your dog associates his mat with relaxing, you can use this "trick" on the road so he can calmly accompany you to outdoor restaurants, friends' houses, and other social spots.

STEP TWO: Teach "Go to Mat"

Begin with a comfy bathmat or dog-sized mat and place it on the floor in an area where there are no other major distractions. Every time your dog looks at the mat, walks toward it, or puts a paw on it, say "yes" or click and give her a reward. Then change the criteria—first withholding the reward until all four of your dog's feet are on the mat, then withholding the treat until she lies down on the mat.

Toss a treat away from the mat to get her to step back off every time, then pick up the mat and set it back down on the floor. Wait for your dog to lie down on the mat, then mark it and reward her. You can also cue her to "down" if she knows that trick, but it's better if your dog offers the "down" on her own—she'll learn by figuring out the behavior you want.

Slowly start to build the skill—asking her to "stay" and "down" on the mat for longer and longer periods of time. Encourage her to stay on the mat by giving her an especially delicious chew toy that is only available on the mat. The goal here is for your dog to associate the mat with quiet, calm, relaxation, and great treats.

3

"Take a breath" might seem unusual at first, but it can make all the difference for your dog. When your dog's mouth is closed, her nostrils will flare when taking a breath—this is when you treat to reinforce deep breathing.

STEP THREE: Teach "Take a Breath"

Taking a series of deep breaths can calm dogs down as much as it can calm humans down. Deep breathing can change the physiology of the dog and help the dog feel calmer. A dog is fully capable of learning that taking a breath feels better for him than anxious barking or pacing. This technique also gives a dog some measure of control over how they feel when faced with a scary or stressful situation.

To teach this behavior, you'll first have to recognize when your dog is taking a breath. Dogs cannot pant and sniff at the same time, so look for a closed mouth. Like us, when dogs take a breath with their mouth closed, their nostrils flare. Look for this side flare when teaching this skill.

Start in a small room with few distractions and a hungry dog. Sit in a chair or stand in front of your dog and hold delicious treats in one of your hands. Let your dog sniff this closed hand—you'll notice he naturally closes his mouth as he sniffs. Mark this breath with a "yes" or click and feed him one treat. Back your hand out of the dog's reach and wait for his lower jaw to shut. Mark and treat whenever you see the telltale nostril flair. As your dog learns, add a cue to the behavior (I use "breathe").

A "Take a Breath" Case Study

I once worked with a large, rare-breed dog who had a human bite history (and I'll never forget it). This recently adopted dog was sent to me for evaluation (he had been thoroughly examined by a veterinarian already) to see if I could help him to calm down. He was anxious all the time and would erupt in sudden, unexpected bouts of aggression at anyone within reach—there was no obvious cause to his biting behavior.

This dog was so explosive in his responses—it was one of the very few times I didn't ask anyone else in my family to come near or assist me. I've never been bitten by a dog in my 20-year career, but I knew in an instant this was a dog who could very well bite me. I could not get close to him at first—he would lunge and growl at me (with clear menace). It was not a direct threat so much as it was telling me what he would do if I continued to approach him.

The thing that eventually allowed me to work with him was teaching him through his wire kennel to take a deep breath. It just clicked with him—he loved to breathe deeply and began offering breaths freely. You would see his entire body shift—he would become a soft, tail-wagging dog after every 10-minute session.

I do still believe this dog had a genetic cause or a chemical misfire in his brain and that he still posed a bite risk, but his adopters had no children and they decided to keep him and continue working with him. While I might not have made the same decision, it was a joy to see him learn to self-regulate and to love breathing deeply. It was the first step toward a new way of living for him.

The key to teaching a dog to "take a breath" is to watch for a closed mouth and observe the top and sides of the dog's nose flaring while the dog takes a deep breath in.

THE LOOK AT THAT (LAT) GAME

The "look at that" game is one of my personal favorites. It was created a few years ago by the brilliant trainer and author of *Control Unleashed*, Leslie McDevitt[1] as part of a much larger program she first developed for sports dogs. LAT teaches your dog to look at something in her environment quickly and then look back to you (alerting you to things in the environment). It's a wonderful tool for all dogs, but it's especially useful for reactive dogs. The dog learns that she can safely look at a potentially triggering object without having to interact with it and that she can look back to her handler for support.

Use LAT when you see something up ahead that might trigger your dog. It's a simple but brilliant form of communication between dogs and humans that also helps you learn your dog's threshold level with specific triggers. If your dog is unable to look at an object or can't refrain from staring at it to the point of refusing food, you'll know you need to create more distance between your dog and the trigger for her to feel comfortable.

Perhaps the best part of this skill is that it changes an environmental trigger into a cue. As your dog learns she is safe from the trigger, she'll begin to associate it with a quick and tasty treat from you. Some dogs learn this very quickly and eventually don't even bother to look at the trigger—they flick an ear or just barely move their eyes in its direction. McDevitt says this skill changes your dog from a reactor to a reporter—instead of reacting to the trigger, she instead calmly indicates it to you.

LAT also strengthens the bond between human and dog—the dog is saying she is willing to take her eyes off the trigger (a potential danger), turn away from it, and face her handler. It's a show of trust on her part.

The goal of the "look at that" game is to have your dog look at something in the distance—an oncoming leashed dog, for example—and then look away from that object and back to the handler.

OVERVIEW

Teaching Look at That (LAT)—Overview

- **Step One:** Start Off Leash in a Quiet Indoor Space with a Neutral Target
- **Step Two:** Add a Leash and Train in a Secure Outdoor Space
- **Step Three:** Make Sure Your Dog Feels Safe During LAT Practice

---

1 I personally first learned of LAT from trainer Leslie McDevitt. I have in recent years been made aware of other trainers in other parts of the world using something similar to LAT (but referred to with a different name) in their training protocol. They created their own versions independent of learning it directly from one source.

A "Look at That" Case Study

One of my favorite real-world stories about LAT happened to a client of mine in the mountains of Colorado. My client was an active mountain runner, and she adopted a puppy that looked much like a Black Lab to be her running partner. The puppy ended up weighing in at well over 100 pounds and looking more like a Great Dane. As he grew, he discovered he loved to chase wildlife—a dangerous game for dogs in Colorado. We taught him LAT so he would stop first to tell her when he saw or smelled wildlife on their mountain outings.

On one secluded run, her running buddy suddenly stopped in his tracks and the fur on his neck and back stood straight up. He refused to move forward and started playing LAT over and over again. He was looking at a grove of pine trees in the distance. Thankfully my client honored his communication and began to turn around and head down the mountain. Out of the corner of her eye she, too, saw the movement in those trees. It was a mama black bear and her two cubs—had her very good boy not known to use LAT as a way to communicate with her both my client and her dog could have been hurt or even killed that day.

TEACHING LOOK AT THAT (LAT)

Start training LAT with a neutral target, such as a can of beans. If the target is too high-value, your dog might get overly excited and won't be able to focus and learn.

■ LAT **TIPS**

- If the can or object you choose turns out to be exciting to the dog, let her sniff it before you begin teaching. If she jumps wildly to get closer to the can, choose something else.

- Be sure your timing is clear so your dog can figure out the behavior you're trying to reinforce. At first, mark and treat as soon as she looks at the can, then shift to only marking and treating once she looks back to you.

STEP ONE: Start Off Leash in a Quiet Indoor Space with a Neutral Target

Begin teaching in a quiet, controlled space like your bedroom or living room with your dog off leash. Use an uninteresting object (don't use a tennis ball with a ball-crazy dog, for example). I usually grab a can of tomatoes or beans from the kitchen. Get your dog's attention while holding the can behind your back. Move the can to your hand, then move your hand out to the side. This motion will cause your dog to look to where your hand moves to. Mark and treat when she looks at the can. Repeat several times a day for one to two days.

At first, your goal is for your dog to orient herself toward the can. Once she consistently offers this looking behavior, pause when she looks at the can instead of marking and treating. Wait for her to look back at you, then mark and treat to reinforce that eye contact. You may need to whistle or make noise at first to redirect your dog's gaze. Once your dog consistently looks at the can, then back to you, tie the behavior to a cue (generally I use "look at that").

2

You will need to train LAT more slowly when practicing outside because there are a lot of distractions for your dog—so many interesting sights, sounds, and smells to investigate!

3

Make sure your dog feels safe from her triggers before you try to practice LAT.

STEP TWO: Add a Leash and Train in a Secure Outdoor Space

Once your dog's LAT behavior is consistent and tied to a cue, add a leash to your indoor practice and begin working on leash in a secure outdoor space, as well. You'll want to practice in a place with some low-level activity (such as a yard where neighbors and other dogs occasionally walk past). Repeat the same training process used inside, but go much more slowly—there are a lot more interesting distractions for your dog outside than there are inside.

Some trainers begin cuing their dogs by asking "where is the dog?" or "where is the person?" Dogs can certainly learn these human names for things with enough repetition. I stick with "look at that" for anything moving within the dog's eyesight then I narrow it down to potential triggers, such as other leashed dogs or kids on skateboards.

STEP THREE: Make Sure Your Dog Feels Safe During LAT Practice

Set your dog up for success and try to not teach or practice LAT in situations in which a trigger can directly approach your leashed dog. I am always prepared to come in between my dog and any oncoming dogs, for example.

It is critical for your dog to understand that she is safe from the threat. You're trying to change her perspective, so you need her to feel that the trigger cannot invade her space. You are trying to convince her, in fact, that seeing the trigger equals a reward.

Teaching a chin rest is a wonderful way to give a dog the ability to consent to animal husbandry tasks like vet checks.

THE CHIN REST

A dog's consent is not something many dog owners consider but allowing the option to consent is probably the fastest and most comprehensive means to help your dog achieve resiliency. Dogs who know they retain control over their lives are better adjusted. Most people have been taught that dogs must do as we demand or else. Thankfully dog training continues to progress, and we've learned ways to work cooperatively with our dogs.

I love the abundance of consent games that have popped up over the past decade—one of my favorites is the "chin rest." In the chin rest, a dog learns to freely place his chin on your hand or a chair. While it is simple to teach for most dogs (it can take longer for a dog that is fearful toward humans), this beautiful skill does so much for the dog-human relationship. The chin rest demonstrates in black and white to your dog that he is free to remove his chin and walk away from a situation if he is uncomfortable, building a sense of trust. It helps calm anxious dogs by giving them a means to communicate their anxiety.

Think of all the times we tell our dogs what to do and invade their space. We put on collars, harnesses, and leashes, brush their teeth, trim their nails, take them to the vet and to the groomers, and even dress them up in costumes. We are up in their business all day every day—and your dog has no words to tell you if he needs you to stop. The chin rest gives the dog the ability to say "not now" or "no." It's genius!

■ ■ ■ ■ ■ ■ ■ ■ ■ ■ **OVERVIEW**

Teaching the Chin Rest

- **Step One:** Hold Treats in One Hand, Reward Movement Toward Your Empty Hand

- **Step Two:** Get a Full Chin Rest and Add a Cue

- **Step Three:** Show Your Dog How to Communicate with the Chin Rest

TEACHING THE CHIN REST

1

Use truly delectable treats to teach the chin rest—try chunks of cheese or meat rather than dry biscuits.

2

When your dog places his chin on your hand, mark or click and give him a treat. Slowly extend the time between when your dog first rests his chin on your hand and when you reward him.

STEP ONE: Hold Treats in One Hand, Reward Movement Toward Your Empty Hand

Begin in a quiet room with your dog off leash. Place your chosen training treats in a vest pocket or bait bag behind your back. Sit in a chair and wait for the dog to come to you, then put a few treats in one hand and put your other hand out flat toward the dog.

Mark or click and reward any movement toward your flat, open hand. Repeat until your dog "gets it"—she'll begin touching your hand with her nose.

STEP TWO: Get a Full Chin Rest and Add a Cue

After your dog starts consistently touching her nose to your flat hand, add a pause and wait to mark and treat until she puts her chin on your hand. You can use the treats in your other hand to lure her into the chin placement if needed. If you have a shy dog or one who might have experienced pain from a human hand in the past, ask the dog to put her chin on a chair seat instead of your hand.

Ask for a chin rest several times a day for 10–14 days. Continue to practice every week and add the cue word of your choice. Then build up the duration—have your dog keep her chin rested on your hand for longer periods of time before marking and rewarding.

3

Once your dog is able to rest his chin in your hand for a longer duration, start using grooming tools and "pretend" vet checks. If your dog removes his chin, stop what you are doing right away to show him that he controls these interactions.

Teaching your dog the "chin rest" strengthens your bond and gives him another tool he can use to communicate with you.

STEP THREE: Show Your Dog How to Communicate with the Chin Rest

Practice the chin rest with another person in the room. At first this person should ignore your dog. Ask your dog for a chin rest. When he has his chin rested on your hand or a chair, the other person should come up to your dog from the side and put a hand on his back. Continue to feed small treats and giving reinforcement the whole time the is still and in the chin rest. The person should pet the dog gently for a bit and then retreat.

Repeat the process a few times and gauge how your dog reacts to the petting. Have the person return and touch or pick up the dog's foot or touch their tail or ears. Continue to reinforce with small treats the whole time the person is touching your dog and stop as soon as the person leaves.

If at any time your dog walks away or stops eating the treats, have the person back up. If your dog removes his chin, take a break, or try again the next day. This is a great opportunity to watch closely for any signs of anxiety in your dog (like not eating, panting, wide eyes, yawning, etc.) and to honor these responses. The important piece of this puzzle is for the dog to be in control of his body and to know he can show you what he finds acceptable.

A Note on Luring and Chin Rests

Luring often gets a bad rap, but it can help communicate what you're asking your dog to do. If your dog is confident with putting her chin on your hand, you don't need to lure. If you do need to lure your dog at first, slowly phase it out as her confidence grows.

THE BUCKET GAME

Another fun method for allowing dogs to show consent is the "bucket game." It's a brilliant technique created by Chirag Patel, a skilled trainer who speaks at conferences worldwide and runs a training and behavior consultancy practice in London called Domesticated Manners (see Recommended Training Academies and Certifications in the United Kingdom/Ireland on page 234).

Like the chin rest, the bucket game gives dogs a way to tell us they need a break or that they want us to stop what we are doing. This is useful for husbandry-type handling like nail trims, giving ear drops or medicine, and veterinary work, but it is also helpful for behavior issues. The bucket game can be used, for example, to teach a shy or nervous dog to accept and even enjoy petting again. This game also teaches impulse control and concentration and helps to calm dogs.

OVERVIEW

Teaching the Bucket Game

- **Step One:** Introduce the Bucket at a Distance Using Low-Value Treats

- **Step Two:** Move the Bucket to the Floor

- **Step Three:** Slowly Build the Duration

- **Step Four:** Add Movement, Touch, Physical Examination, and Grooming

TEACHING THE BUCKET GAME

Introduce your dog to the "bucket" but don't feed him from it or let him put his nose into it. Start with it out of his reach and mark it or click and reward him for staring at it.

STEP ONE: Introduce the Bucket at a Distance Using Low-Value Treats

Have your dog off leash in a quiet environment. Start with treats that aren't terribly exciting to your dog (dry biscuits rather than their favorite meat or cheese, for example). Place them in a small bucket or container that is one solid, mostly opaque color—you don't want your dog to clearly see the treats inside.

First, teach your dog not to rush at the bucket. Start with the bucket set high on a counter or held in your hand at chest level. Mark or click and give your dog a treat every time he looks at the bucket. Place the treat directly in your dog's mouth, making sure to pull your treat-delivering hand away from the bucket after you deliver the treat.

Repeat several times with the bucket at this height, then move it to knee level or place it on a chair. You want your dog to be quiet and about 1–2 feet away from the bucket. It's also important for her to have "four on the floor"—she can sit, lie down, or stand, as long as all four of her paws are on the floor.

If your dog barks or jumps up toward the bucket, do not mark, click, or give a treat. Stay silent and either move the bucket farther away or place your hand over the top. Practice two to three times a day with the bucket at different heights and limit the sessions to about 3–5 minutes. Don't rush this process—you want your dog to understand that you want her to look at the bucket, not at you or anything else.

Some trainers have moved away from putting food in a single bucket and prefer to use multiple objects such as cones or items in different dog-visible colors (this alternative was first created by Canadian trainer Sue Alexander). They teach that one object means "go" (or continue) and the other object means "stop." The dog can look at or walk to the object that expresses what he is feeling in that moment.

2

Set the bucket on the floor a small distance away from your dog. If he stares at the bucket, mark it or click and give a treat. You can pick the bucket back up as you deliver the treat—each time you put it back down the dog will likely orientate toward it.

STEP TWO: Move the Bucket to the Floor

Once your dog can quietly look at the bucket at the lower level, move the bucket to the floor a few feet away from him. Your dog might naturally move forward (since putting the bucket on the floor might look like you are placing a meal down), so you need to quickly place the bucket on the ground and mark or click and reward as soon as he looks at the bucket. Quickly pick up the bucket as you deliver the treat.

Repeat this process several times until your dog understands that you want him to stay with four paws on the floor even when the bucket is on the ground. If your dog has trouble here, go back to the point at which he was doing well (the bucket being at knee height, for example) and train more there.

It's important to not give cues such as "down" or "stay." You want your dog to choose to give the behavior you are seeking rather than just responding to a command. Remember, it is a game of consent!

3

Slowly increase the duration by waiting for your dog to stare at the bucket for longer amounts of time before you mark or click and reward.

4

Once your dog can hold his gaze on the bucket for up to one minute, begin to introduce some care techniques, such as touching his ears or feet, while he continues to look at the bucket. If he gets up or stops looking at the bucket, it's a sign that he is too uncomfortable to proceed. Take a break or try again the next day.

STEP THREE: Slowly Build the Duration

Now start to lengthen the amount of time your dog must look at the bucket on the floor before you mark or click and give him a treat. Go slowly here! At first, silently count to around 3–4 seconds (1–2 seconds if your dog needs to start with a shorter duration), then mark or click and reinforce with a treat.

Your dog should start to look right back at the bucket after receiving his treat. This will show you that he is understanding the game. Try to randomize how long the durations last. If your dog gets antsy during longer intervals, go back to reinforcing the behavior after short intervals for a bit and work back up.

STEP FOUR: Add Movement, Touch, Physical Examination, and Grooming

Once your dog can look at the bucket on the floor and remain calm with all four paws on the ground for 10 seconds or more, begin adding husbandry and touch. Dogs can give subtle signs of discomfort at any stage of the bucket game but they're most likely to occur when you introduce touch.

■ TIP

Be sure to keep your hands still while you wait to reinforce and give the treat from the bucket.

Introducing Touch to a Nervous or Concerned Dog

If your dog is particularly observant or concerned about hand motion, begin moving your hand near her without touching her at first. You should also look at the bucket rather than making eye contact with her. You want your dog to become comfortable with this sort of movement around her body. She'll probably look at your hand movement at first but be patient—as soon as she looks back at the bucket, mark it or click and give her a treat.

Slowly begin to briefly touch her where she is most comfortable (often the back or chest). As you're touching her, wait for her to look back to the bucket, then mark or click and give her a treat.

If your dog cannot focus enough to look at the bucket, stop what you are doing. Your dog might even choose to walk away and that's ok. Give her a minute to come back and reengage, then start again, always allowing her the control to disengage and stop the game if she needs to. If you find a spot that makes your dog uncomfortable (often the ears), spend less time there, focusing instead on areas where she is comfortable. The goal is to be able to touch your dog for at least 10 seconds while she looks at the bucket.

Then move on to physical examinations and using grooming tools. Begin to slowly touch her ears, around her eyes, lift her tail, pick up each paw, etc. Pay attention to which areas are more sensitive and go more slowly with those. If your dog stops looking at the bucket, pulls her body part away from you, or gets up to leave, stop what you are doing. If she returns and reengages, continue. If she does not, stop for now and let her relax on her own. Start again the next day and focus on less sensitive areas

for a while before attempting a more sensitive examination again.

Go as slowly with this process as your dog needs. You can really ruin the trust you've built up by doing this too quickly. If she indicates a definite NO about you touching certain body parts or performing certain types of grooming, stop the game and call in a professional dog expert to help with this. You don't want to cause your dog anxiety while trying to build confidence and trust.

Ask an Expert

Trainer and Behavior Consultant Mikkel Becker on Why She Is Optimistic for the Dog-Care Industry

This interview has been edited for length. Please see https://foxchapelpets.com/positive-training-dogs/ to read the full interview.

Mikkel Becker's dog, Indiana Bones, demonstrates the calm results of modern canine care programs like Fear Free.

▶ **Are you optimistic or pessimistic about the way dogs are currently being handled by both trainers and veterinarians? Why?**

I'm extremely optimistic, because I believe the affection people have for their dogs resembles that which is felt for human children (dogs both intellectually and emotionally are indeed similar to human toddlers), and the growing science-based applications of behavior and behavior modification methods together with this affection are increasing the need and value of more humane, human-like treatment for pets.

Dog training and behavior concepts are no longer being based on a pseudoscience of myths and misconceptions that at one time justified using unnecessarily harsh and even abusive methods. Instead, such outdated and scientifically unsound methods are being steadily overtaken by approaches that understand the complex physical, mental, and emotional lives of pets and advocate for the enhanced well-being of the pet. Reward-based methods are imperative for helping the dog to not only act better on the outside, but to also feel better emotionally and be in a better headspace on the inside. In other words, humane, reward-based training methods provide a stronger foundation for dogs to begin with and offers a deeper healing and longer lasting resolution when issues already exist.

As such, dogs are getting higher quality care that addresses the root causes for their reactions, such as fear, anxiety, and stress or physical discomfort and pain. For training to be successful and safe, it's important for the underlying issues that might be causing the outward "bad behaviors" to be addressed, rather than merely masking the root issue and temporarily treating only outward symptoms.

Failure to meet the dog's real needs and inner motivation will result in frustration and likely failure at resolving the issue (at best), and far too often will result in a compromise of trust, a break in the human-animal bond, and an increased risk of the dog being surrendered or even euthanized. By

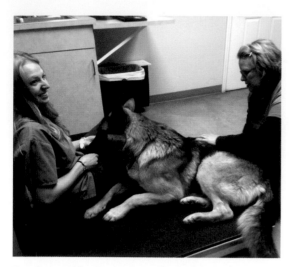

Fear Free certifications help create a network of professionals with known skill—veterinarians and trainers can feel confident about recommending one another.

treating the root cause, the Fear Free approach works with, rather than against, the dog. Punitive and intimidation-based methods almost treat dogs as adversaries who need to be controlled, rather than the deeply emotional and intelligent creatures they are.

Dogs, like children, need and deserve to be treated with ethical respect and a kind, scientifically sound approach. More and more pet owners are being educated by trainers, veterinary staff, and quality educational materials on how to better understand their dog's behavior, body language, and species-specific needs. As such, pet parents now have more information to back up why certain approaches to training and pet care "feel" wrong. They now have the evidence-based understanding to recognize signs of emotional distress in their pet's body language, and know the better training methods, like clicker training, that can teach their pet to behave without harmful physical force. Thankfully, there are now way more effective ways to train pets—training never has to hurt or be scary for the dog to learn.

As a trainer and as the daughter of a veterinarian, I've directly felt the strained relations in times past between veterinary professionals and training or behavior experts. However, with the emergence of Fear Free and other educational outreach programs that tie trainers and behavior consultants together with veterinary teams, I'm seeing a more partnered approach that works for the good of the pet. This teamwork-based, collaborative approach between trainers and behavior professionals and the pet's veterinary team is for the betterment of the pet, as they're able to receive more effective, well-rounded care that ensures good health from the inside out.

These efforts also increase the understanding of preventive methods as well, demonstrating that socialization efforts and early reward-based training guidance can help proactively guide the pet toward more desirable behavior from the very start. Yes, there are still veterinary professionals who use outdated methods and have a shallow understanding of behavior and training methods, but they are becoming fewer and far between as educational programs like Fear Free offer scientifically sound knowledge and practical guidance for how to treat the entire pet kindly and humanely, including physical health, but also emotional and behavioral health.

Education about animal learning and behavior is becoming a greater part of the standard curriculum for veterinary students. For instance, many veterinary colleges encourage, and some even require, Fear Free Certification for their veterinary students (Fear Free Certification is complimentary for all DVM students and veterinary nurse students). As such, veterinary professionals are now learning emotionally protective methods for handling, interacting with, and guiding animal behavior from the very start of their professional careers, where in decades past there may have been very little, if any, talk about emotional health and behavior.

Because Fear Free Certified Professionals are required to take ongoing Fear Free continuing education, it also means that those who earn Fear Free Certification are kept up to date on emotionally protective practices and other behaviorally friendly methods of providing quality care for pets. Such ongoing training includes educational materials for better partnering with training and behavior professionals, guiding pet parents toward using more effective preventive and management-based strategies, offering enrichment programs in-home and in-hospital to improve animal welfare, and advocating reward-based training.

On the opposite side of the spectrum, many veterinary professionals have had negative experiences with trainers and behavior professionals, as the industry in the past was like the wild west in terms of what the veterinarian could expect when referring out or working with such professionals. Working with unfit trainers or untrained "behavior experts" not only puts the veterinarian's credibility on the line, but also does a disservice to dogs, since certain training and behavior modification methods can be extremely detrimental and dangerous.

More and more pet owners are learning about their dogs' body language and how to approach and protect them if they're showing signs of distress.

Thankfully, this, too, is progressively changing as more and more training and animal behavior organizations are offering high-quality education that's rooted in humane, reward-based approaches. These organizations are creating higher standards of care and expanded knowledge and experience requirements for those calling themselves trainers or behavior consultants. Increased availability and advocacy for certifications, the establishment of higher-level animal training education programs (like the Karen Pryor Academy, The Academy for Dog Trainers, and the Victoria Stilwell Academy), and an increasing dedication to humane, reward-based methods and partnership with the pet's vet (such as the Fear Free Animal Trainer Certification) are increasing the veterinary professional's trust and close working relationship with training and behavior professionals.

In the past, it was much more difficult for veterinary professionals to know who they were referring clients to, but the industry has changed and there is now an increasing and ongoing commitment for professionals to maintain a baseline level of education and certification, to commit to ongoing education, and to seek certification through educational institutions that have more established standards for their members. As such, it's becoming more and more standard for veterinary providers to have a trusted referral base of trainers and behavior experts that clients can be directed toward. And, when issues exist, they are more often addressed and resolved in a partnered, collaborative, and cohesive way that is more protective of and effective for the pet.

What Not to Do in the Name of Training

It's unbelievable and heartbreaking to me how many people are willing to use force, pain, punishment, and fear to stop a dog's unwanted behavior. To help your dog in positive ways that improve his life rather than harm him, we need to take a long look at what can cause that harm and what harm looks like to a dog. In this chapter, we will take a closer look at exactly what not to do and why.

This chapter explains why the following things are harmful for your dog and counterproductive:

Veterinarians also take an ethical oath:

Being admitted to the profession of veterinary medicine, I solemnly swear to use my scientific knowledge and skills for the benefit of society through the protection of animal health and welfare, the prevention and relief of animal suffering, the conservation of animal resources, the promotion of public health, and the advancement of medical knowledge.

I will practice my profession conscientiously, with dignity, and in keeping with the principles of veterinary medical ethics. I accept as a lifelong obligation the continual improvement of my professional knowledge and competence.

Dogs are counting on us to treat them with kindness and avoid causing them harm. Veterinarians are held to a certain standard of care; it would help dogs immensely to also require a certain standard from trainers and owners.

Because there are no requirements for people to list themselves as dog trainers, you must do your research. Once you've chosen someone and training begins, pay attention to your dog's body language to make sure the training isn't causing any distress.

Just as medical doctors pledge to do no harm when they sign the Hippocratic Oath, veterinarians sign a similar ethical oath. Owners and trainers, however, are not currently required to pledge anything. There are no official standards of care, education, or certification for dog trainers in the United States. There are, of course, laws in place that apply to animal cruelty and inhumane practices, but they are often not adequately or consistently enforced.

The lack of standards for dog trainers and behavior consultants is appalling; it permits and even causes harm to dogs. Many owners are likely to just do an internet search and hire a trainer that is nearby or affordable without knowing if that trainer has any type of education or experience in training dogs or working with serious behavior concerns. In this chapter, we look at serious training "don'ts" so owners can more easily recognize improper training and how it can harm their dogs.

DON'T PUNISH THE DOG

In essence, punishment is a harsh way to tell your dog what not to do—punishment seeks to stop or interrupt a behavior. On an entirely different level, punishment stands every chance of damaging the human-canine bond. Why even have a dog if ruining the bond is your goal?

A review by Dr. Gal Ziv of The Zinman College of Physical Education and Sport Sciences, Wingate Institute, looked at scientific literature on dog training methods. His conclusion was that people should use reward-based methods to train their dogs:

> Despite the methodological concerns, it appears that aversive training methods have undesirable unintended outcomes and that using them puts dogs' welfare at risk. In addition, there is no evidence to suggest that aversive training methods are more effective than reward-based training methods. At least three studies in this review suggest that the opposite might be true in both pets and working dogs. Because this appears to be the case, it is recommended that the dog training community embrace reward-based training and avoid, as much as possible, training methods that include aversion.[1]

In addition to other studies that came to this same conclusion, major groups from the American Veterinary Society of Animal Behavior and the ASPCA to trade organizations such as the Pet Professional Guild have all written statements advocating for positive methods that do not use

---

1   Gal Ziv, "The Effects of Using Aversive Training Methods in Dogs—A Review." *Journal of Veterinary Behavior* 19 (May–June 2017): 50–60.

tools or methodologies that include pain, force, or fear.

Sadly, humans can get quite creative when it comes to thinking up ways to harm dogs and call it training. Here are a few tools and methods to avoid at all costs (note that these will probably be troubling to read about):

♦ Electric shock collars (which are illegal in many countries outside of the United States)—these go by many creative names like e-collar, e-touch, training collar, stimulation, stim, tap, and, most misleadingly, clicker collar
♦ Prong or pinch collars (even flat collars can cause throat damage if used harshly)
♦ Leash "pops" or corrections
♦ Hitting or kicking
♦ Kneeing or jabbing
♦ Hanging a dog by a leash
♦ Shaking a dog or employing the drastic so-called "alpha roll," in which someone violently throws a dog to the ground and rolls it to "prove who is boss"—this is outdated, ill-informed, and greatly damages the canine-human bond—it's horrific
♦ Shouting or screaming
♦ Spraying a dog with a spray bottle or water hose

Many professional organizations and trainers do not support the use of shock collars for any kind of dog training or behavior counseling.

♦ Throwing a chain or any object at a dog
♦ Using "dominance methods" based on the false idea that dogs are always striving to achieve leader status over humans
♦ Chaining a dog (now illegal in some states)
♦ Excessive isolation on chains—in backyards, basements, homes, kennels, or crates
♦ Flooding a dog—flooding attempts to reduce an animal's fear by "flooding" the animal with that which they fear, making the animal stay in proximity to their fear source for a period of time without the ability to escape. This might not cause physical damage, but it is a dramatically harmful exposure protocol that inflicts a great deal of stress and is not humane.

The pitfalls of using punishment in training dogs are numerous and can include:

♦ Harming or breaking the human-canine bond
♦ Stopping or decreasing an unwanted behavior only when the owner is present
♦ Causing the dog discomfort and increasing the dog's fear or anxiety
♦ Causing the dog to lose trust in you and potentially all humans

Horrific and pain-inducing collars like this are never necessary to train a dog or address behavior concerns.

- Causing fear of humans, especially a human hand as used in punishment
- Increasing defensive and aggressive canine behaviors
- Creating confusion and causing unusual behaviors such as spinning, tail chasing, chewing or licking themselves, or loss of urine control as a displacement behavior
- Causing behavior problems through the use of inappropriate or excessive punishment

Punishment does not diminish fear or anxiety, does not help the dog learn desired behaviors, and does not give the dog a feeling of safety or help to create a resilient dog. Veterinary behaviorist Dr. Karen Overall wrote in her book *Clinical Behavioral Medicine* that:

> The single most devastating advice ever given to people with dogs is that they should dominate their dogs and show the problem dogs "who is boss." Under this rubric, untold numbers of humans have been bitten by dogs they have betrayed, terrified, and given no choice. And for dogs that have an anxiety disorder that involves information processing and accurate risk assessment, the behaviors used to dominate a dog (e.g., hitting, hanging, subjecting the dog to dominance downs, alpha rolls, and other punitive, coercive techniques) convince that troubled, needy, pathological dog that the human is indeed a threat, resulting in the dog's condition worsening.

DON'T HAVE UNREALISTIC EXPECTATIONS

When I interviewed dog trainers as I was writing this book, I asked many of them what they want the most from owners and time and time again they said owners need to have realistic expectations for their dog. This goes paw in paw with understanding the genetic influences of your dog's breed—a Doberman is not a Schnauzer, a Schnauzer is not a Pug, and a Pug is not a Springer Spaniel. We've bred dogs to do certain tasks and that affects their genetic coding even if they don't actually do those tasks anymore.

Sometimes an owner obtains a new puppy with big dreams of winning agility titles together. Many owners imagine a perfectly happy Golden Retriever who will calmly allow the grandkids to climb all over them. A different dog owner wants a tireless dog to go with them on long daily runs. And other owners want low energy snuggle bugs. We get dogs for a reason, and we need to consider how well those reasons fit the needs and desires of the dog well before that cute puppy enters our home.

There is nothing wrong with wanting a sport dog or a house companion. Where we quickly run into conflict is when the dog has other internal desires or health or behavioral problems that put the kibosh on all your plans. You can research the perfect breed and find the perfect breeder who does everything right for the mother dog and the newborn puppies and there still might be a valid reason why that particular puppy is unable to fit your ideal.

Sometimes reactivity to other dogs shows up as the dog matures, even if there wasn't a single incident that helped to create it. It could be that once the dog reaches social and sexual maturity, the reactivity develops along with it. Or it could be an underlying health issue that hasn't been diagnosed yet, such as hip pain or a neurological concern. Perhaps your dog has zero interest in your hobby and participating in it causes a lot of stress for the animal. When these things happen, it is often disappointing for the human involved.

So, what are we to do? When you bring a dog into your home—a 10- to 20-year commitment—understand the potential downsides and risks. Be mentally and emotionally prepared for the possibility that your big dreams may not work out with this particular dog and have a plan in case that happens. This plan can and should include working with your veterinarian to rule out medical causes and bringing in a well-trained, force-free

It's crucial to have realistic expectations about behavior and personality when you bring a new puppy into your home.

professional dog trainer or behavior counselor. Give the dog in front of you every chance to see if there is a solution.

Once you determine your plans won't work with this dog, you have an important decision to make—and it is critically important to the dog. You have options:

- Let go of your original ideas and accept him for the dog he is.
- Keep working with professionals who can help you find a win-win solution for you and the dog.
- Rehome the dog into a more appropriate home (I applaud this difficult choice if you can truly find a great home that works for both the new dog owner and your dog, though it will still cause some stress for the dog).
- Take the dog to a shelter or rescue (which is a far better choice than dumping a dog on a city street or in the country, but definitely not a great option).

Taking your dog to a shelter or rescue is the option that will cause the most stress for your dog—the one you chose to bring into your home and your life and loved, or at least wanted to love. Working in shelters or rescues can be a heartbreaking job—shelters are a stressful place for many dogs no matter how kind the workers, and these animal lovers see heartlessness and a lack of commitment from owners every day (not to mention those sad cases where loving owners with health or financial concerns have no alternative).

I am glad shelters and rescues exist, but they are not there to serve as dumping grounds for owners unwilling to make a serious effort. Dogs become attached to us. Bringing home a dog is an enormous responsibility, so it's on us to use all our resources to do what's best for our dog.

An "Adjusting Your Expectations" Case Study

When my husband and I rescued and took in two cattle collie siblings who had been removed too early from their mother (at five weeks) and kept alone in a backyard (where they acquired worms and fleas and began learning to fight over resources), I knew very well that they might become unhappy with living together as they matured.

They lacked desperately needed guidance time with their mother and were left to their own devices as tiny, vulnerable puppies. Their early life was a first-class prescription for troubled behavior later in life. I was aware of the possibilities. I decided before I even brought them home that, should they start to fight or harm one another and if I was unable to stop it, I would find a more suitable home for one of the dogs and provide him with a lifetime of counseling and training. It would have hurt like hell to have to choose which dog to rehome since I loved them both—but I would have done it for their sake.

Thankfully, I didn't have to. My husband and I took the situation seriously from day one. The brothers were already roughhousing extensively with one another and were growling and showing frustration within days of coming home. We developed an all-consuming plan to separate them often. We put them in separate crates for naps and overnight. We separated them when they had toys, food, and even sticks they brought in from the yard.

We also put them together a lot and let them play, stopping them if they began to tip into fighting behavior. We interrupted them what felt like 1,000

Separate, safe, comfortable crates are indispensable if you're trying to teach troubled dogs or puppies how to happily coexist.

times a day at first. We redirected. We ensured they had plenty of downtime, naps, and play dates with safe puppies and adult dogs to help teach them things only another safe dog could teach them. If you could talk to any of our neighbors from that time, they would confirm that my husband and I looked like new parents of human twins—because we were exhausted!

All our work and intervention paid off. They are happy, well-adjusted brothers who now sleep next to one another and rarely need to be separated. They can play with toys, eat meals, and enjoy treats right next to one another. It was a ton of work, but we owed it to them. Can you imagine if a busy household with young children had adopted these puppies? There would never have been enough time to give them the help and guidance they desperately needed.

DON'T MISUNDERSTAND CANINE COMMUNICATION

Do you know when your dog is happy by looking at his body language? Most of us can recognize the big, sweeping tail movements and wiggly butt of a happy dog, but what does your dog's mouth do when he is happy? His ears? His eyes? Likewise, most of us recognize that when a dog's tail is tucked tightly under his body, he is probably scared. But what does his mouth do when he is scared? His ears? His eyes?

What happens just before a dog bites? In most cases, dogs give ample warning that they are stressed, humans just don't interpret their language very well. Generally, when a stressed dog bites, it is not to do harm for no reason (the exceptions being dogs with medical issues or—very rarely—truly aggressive dogs). The dog usually first attempts to get away from the situation. If that fails, they might start blinking more, scratching themselves, or suddenly become overly interested in smelling the ground. She might lick her nose or tuck her tail. Her eyes may grow very wide and, if we are paying attention, we'd see the whites of her eyes clearly. She might clamp her mouth shut hard and put her ears back.

A dog communicates through its body movements. My dog, Finn, is showing happiness and delight through his relaxed, open mouth, forward-facing ears, soft eyes, and big doggie smile.

This dog's body language is telegraphing that he is happy to see his owner.

This dog's body language is saying he is uncomfortable, nervous, and scared to see his owner.

All of these are canine behaviors indicate frustration, stress, anxiety, or fear. If these signs are ignored, what choice does a dog have? Some shut down and get very still, trying to make themselves as small as possible. Others desperately increase the "volume" of their communication—becoming stiff and possibly growling and air snapping. If we don't acknowledge their language, they feel they must bite to relieve their stress and to force the cause of the stress to back off. The world would make a lot more sense to our dogs if we were all better educated on canine body language.

Thankfully, there are countless free resources on the internet that can quickly get you up to speed on canine body language. You can visit YouTube and search for "canine body language" to find hundreds of free tutorials.[1] You can visit websites for organizations like the American Veterinary Society of Animal Behavior (AVSAB) for free information as well. Many of the force-free dog training groups and academies listed in the Resources for Owners section beginning on page 233 provide a vast number of free resources and paid webinars on their websites.[2]

Please keep in mind that context is everything. For example, a dog might do a "shake off" to remove excess water from its coat after swimming, but a dry dog performing a "shake off" might well be "shaking off" something that is of concern to him—it could be an early warning signal that you need to remove the dog from the situation.

A fearful dog can show subtle or not-so-subtle signs of fear. It's important for dog owners to recognize and help a dog who is showing fear. Signs can include pulled-back ears, a stiff body, whites showing around the eyes, and a closed, hard mouth. Fear without relief can lead to a trigger-stacking incident in which his environment pushes the dog over threshold.

DON'T DELIVER CONFUSED TRAINING

Trainers often see confused and frustrated dogs. Sometimes it happens when there are two dog owners and one dog parent indulges an undesirable behavior, like barking, because it looks cute. Or maybe Dad doesn't permit the dog on the couch, but Mom loves to have the dog nap with her on the couch on Sundays. How is the dog supposed to

---

1   The Fear Free Happy Homes channel's *Dog Body Language 101* video is one good example. See www.youtube.com/watch?v=siy0eog48ys. Fear Free also provides free downloads that are very helpful in teaching about canine body language. See www.fearfreepets.com/toolbox/body_language_and_signs_of_fas_in_dogs_and_cats

2   The International School for Canine Psychology and Behaviour is just one example. See https://www.theiscp.com/resources-webinars.

You might not allow your dog on the couch, but if your partner thinks it's cute and allows it when you're not at home, your dog will end up confused and unable to understand and learn the rules.

Always praise and treat a recall, no matter what. The skill is that important. Also don't use recalls to lure your dog into situations the dog might hate, like baths or nail trims. It's far fairer to the dog to work on making these activities less traumatizing in the first place—it's less stressful to use cooperative care for necessary grooming sessions.

Dogs also often receive confused training when it comes to jumping up to greet humans. Dogs want to sniff your face to say hello and to get to know you if you are new to them—it's often how they greet their dog comrades. The problem is, of course, that we are much taller than they are. I am often called to owners' homes because of jumping problems and the first thing I observe is usually the owner either talking enthusiastically to the dog in greeting (inadvertently encouraging their excited dog to jump up to say hello). Avoid talking to your dog in an excited voice when entering the house.

Many owners use the old human stand-by—pushing their knee into the dog's chest. For many dogs, that knee equals attention, so they back up and come running at you again for more of this "attention." Owners often send mixed messages to their dog—come say hello as I greet you excitedly, but also, I am mad and will yell at you and push you away when you do so. Dogs observe us constantly and they repeat the behavior that works for them—an observant dog might learn to see a lifting knee as a cue to jump.

Lifting your knee into them and pushing them away isn't kind, it doesn't foster security for the dog, and it works against you. Instead, train a reliable sit since sitting is an incompatible behavior—the dog cannot both sit and jump at the same time. Also be prepared and have tasty treats ready. Toss them on

understand that the couch is open on weekends but not on weekdays? One human can easily undo the training and expectations set by the other human in the home without even being aware of it. It's best to have an agreed-upon training plan and settled house rules well before your dog comes into your home.

Another place where confused training is common is in teaching the recall. As discussed in chapter 7, a solid recall can make the difference in life-or-death moments. A confused recall often results from situations that may seem benign to us but not to our dog. The worst is when an owner calls and calls for his dog, then, when the dog finally hears the request and returns, the owner punishes the dog. The owner views this as a punishment for running away and not listening, but the dog most likely views it as a punishment for returning. If you punish the dog for doing what you asked—even if it is performed on the dog's schedule and not your own—what have you taught your dog? Most likely that you are crazy or unreliable.

A reliable recall is a must-have skill for every dog. We encourage owners to always reinforce a dog for coming to you with treats, praise, or toys.

Behaviorist Dale McLelland allows her rescue dog Pezz some time and space to decompress. Getting adequate rest and sleep is as important to our dogs as it is to us.

the floor when you come in from a long day at work or have guests over and ask your dog to "find it!" The dog will begin to associate a person coming into your home with a fun game of "find it" instead of the fun game of "jump up and say hi."

Owners often give confused training when on walks with their leashed dogs. For most dogs, a leash indicates a fun walk through the interesting sights and smells of the world outside, but if their owner constantly yanks on the leash, it can also represent pain and conflict. The solution is to use clear leash communication and never use the leash to punish.

Dogs love to sniff and sniff and sniff some more on walks. Please stop yanking dogs by the leash when they stop to sniff. Work out a win-win situation for your dog that allows time for sniffing without letting your dog pull your arm out of the socket. It is unfair to a dog to not permit sniffing time on a walk—that is where they get the most amount of pleasure and it is their walk, not just ours alone.

Dogs are also often confused by the human response to reactivity on walks. If your dog, for example, lunges and barks at a passing dog and you yank hard on his leash and exasperatedly yell "NO," what have you taught him? You have succeeded only in increasing your dog's anxiety and apprehension at seeing other dogs—seeing a scary, strange dog now includes punishment from a scary, angry owner. It's double the trouble for your dog. Punishing your dog's reactivity does not help and damages his sense of safety and trust. Chapter 4 provides a few modern techniques you can use that will actually help lessen your dog's anxiety upon seeing his triggers.

DON'T TERRORIZE SMALL DOGS

One type of video I see far too often online involves terrified small dogs being recorded as they

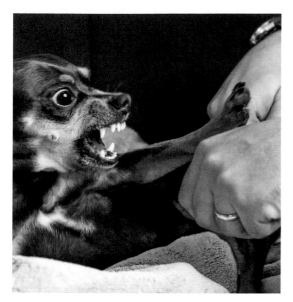

Small dogs deserve to have their body language respected—if they clearly indicate they are uncomfortable with a situation, back off and help them regain their sense of security.

essentially scream in dog language for others to back off—barking, snarling, and trying to escape. Why some people find this to be amusing I will never understand. It is not funny—it is cruel. Stop doing this. If you wouldn't laugh at a Rottweiler doing the same thing, then you know it isn't funny to do to a small dog either.

Small dogs deserve agency over their bodies just as much as large dogs do. When we pick them up, hug them, or put them up to our faces, it actually terrifies many little dogs. If they are not comfortable with it, they have few options.

Small dogs need extra protection because they are so vulnerable, but you need to plan ways to protect your little friend that won't make him even more afraid. Acclimate your dog to small spaces like carriers or strollers before placing him in there. Listen to his body language and behavior. If he indicates that he isn't comfortable in certain spaces and situations, do counterconditioning or desensitization work or get professional assistance to help them become comfortable. If you're not willing to do this, stop putting them into the stressful situations. Also, just because your dog might be small and airplanes will allow him onboard, seriously evaluate whether he can emotionally handle being on a loud plane for hours.

DON'T ELIMINATE YOUR DOG'S AGENCY

Many of us tend to over-command our dogs throughout the day—don't do this and don't do that—all while expecting them to be perfect, quiet angels that love all other dogs and humans. Micromanaging their every move leads to growing frustration and dogs begin seeking their own methods of relief. They also do not learn to solve problems on their own. They look to us or wait to be told what to do—many might call this a highly trained dog, but is it a happy dog? I'd call it a neurotic or anxious one that is shut down—a shut-down dog may look obedient, but it has little to no day-to-day pleasure in life.

All animals seek control over their lives and their environments. The more often we guide a dog to the best choice for us and for them and the more we allow them to make daily choices, the happier and less prone to behavior issues the dog becomes. We can stop many behavior problems from ever occurring by being guides for our dogs rather than dictators and encouraging them to think their way out of low-stress situations (finding hidden toys, having freedom to explore a fenced-in yard, etc.). When dogs become daily problem solvers, they gain confidence and resiliency that will serve them (and their owners) well when they need to quickly make decisions in high-stress situations.

Ask an Expert

Trainer and Behavior Consultant Andrew Hale Discusses Trauma in Dogs, Communicating and Connecting with Troubled Dogs, and Helping Stressed Dogs

This interview has been edited for length. Please see https://foxchapelpets.com/positive-training-dogs/ to read the full interview.

Trainer and behavior consultant Andrew Hale with his soul dog, Milo. Hale rescued Milo but says that Milo really saved him!

▶ **You said something once in one of our conversations that intrigued me: "I assume dogs (and people) that I meet have trauma." Could you expand on that and explain what you mean?**

Yes, I make that assumption with many of the dogs I have met. Sometimes that trauma can be obvious and caused by known events in the dog's history. Most caregivers (owners) can recognize the probability of trauma developing from the certain events, like deliberate cruelty or being attacked by another dog. However, trauma can be triggered by events that are unknown and often unseen by the caregiver. Given that trauma, to whatever extent, is often a contributor to many behavior challenges, it cannot hurt to presume that it is a factor. Following a trauma-informed process will not do any harm, and indeed underpins a dog-centered approach anyway since this approach seeks to learn more of the dog's emotional truth. Not starting with this assumption, however, risks missing something very fundamental to that animal's emotional experience.

▶ **You have a background in human psychology. How do you use that knowledge to help owners communicate or feel a connection with their dog, especially a troubled dog?**

Understanding the psychology of judgment and expectations

is so important when trying to help a caregiver explore the support and care needs of their dog. *Perception is everything.* What the caregiver thinks is the issue will very much dictate their perspective. That perception can sometimes be 180 degrees away from the actual challenges faced by the dog. For example, many caregivers will view the behavior of the dog on the usual "good to bad" continuum, which supports the notion of reward and punishment. This, in turn, can promote a more "task-orientated" approach to these challenges. For example: "My dog's barking is bad (the judgment). I must stop my dog's barking (the task)." A task-oriented approach might be to punish the barking or reward the dog when it's not barking. But what about the dog? What triggered the barking in the first place? What relief might that dog be seeking?

Understanding that the caregiver will likely be making these quick judgments based on their view of how a dog *should* behave is crucial. We need to find a way to connect through emotional experience, so they can relate to their dog's care and support needs. This shifts the focus away from a task-orientated approach to a care-orientated one.

The key here is to understand the abstract nature of the emotional experience and use that as the main point of reference. To do this I invite the caregiver to share their thoughts and feelings first, before even meeting the dog. This way I get an insight into their world view and belief system and get to hear their emotional truth. They will often share feelings of anger, embarrassment, frustration, guilt, etc.

The next step is to talk about the emotional experience in a neutral way, discussing the importance of cognitive processing and the role of the nervous system. I use analogies for all these—such as the "bucket analogy" for stress (an empty bucket represents the nervous system and the water in it represents the amount of stress a person or animal is carrying). I can then go back and discuss their emotional experience again with them, referencing these principles and analogies (for example, "your bucket must

have been filling quickly in that situation"). Now we have a vocabulary and perspective we can apply to the dog when I meet him or her for observation. I can use the same language, analogies, and references, which helps the caregiver connect their emotional experience with that of their dog. This encourages more empathy and supports the care-orientated approach. Once the caregiver's perception changes, so does their ability to offer the care and support the dog really needs.

▶ **What are three important ways owners can help a dog find relief from their stressors (in general terms, since every stressor and every dog is unique)?**

First, we need solid observations. We need to be aware of our own judgments and biases and allow the dog the time and space they need to give us the information we need to support them.

Second, we need to look for general ways to offer relief that might not be directly associated with the central challenges. For example, making sure the dog has a good diet, is getting enough rest, etc. I ask all my clients to look at their dog over a seven-day cycle, not just one day—thinking about the activities and everyday stressors that come up during that week. We should always look to remove as many of the avoidable triggers as possible, or to compensate for them by allowing adequate decompression time after exposure. Sometimes that is not measured in hours, but rather days and weeks!

Finally, once the core triggers have been identified, including physiological or cognitive aspects, as many methods as possible to provide relief need to be found. That might mean removing exposure to a trigger for a period of time or offering the dog more time and space to process the trigger (giving them more of a chance to come up with a self-regulated response).

The biggest takeaways here are to slow things down, learn from the dog, and allow a structured process for piecing the puzzle together.

Day-to-Day Living with a Troubled Dog

Dogs have a serious problem—at the end of the day, if they are not able to mesh and flourish within our human lifestyles, the outcome can be devastating for them. Shelters and rescues have great difficulty keeping up with the rising number of dog intakes. The human-canine bond is not thriving in many homes—it is barely surviving. We have choices to make on an individual level and on a societal level. This chapter starts with an in-depth look at what it can be like living with a troubled dog and then discusses the following lifestyle and environmental issues we can control to help our dogs.

CHOICES: DOG DAY #1 VERSUS DOG DAY #2

Imagine you are a dog. You are quite good-natured, and you tell all your dog friends that you do, indeed, have the softest, shiniest coat of all the dogs in the neighborhood. You aim to please and you are an agreeable sort of canine. Which of the following dog days would you prefer?

Think about an ideal day for a dog—it's more than likely this perfect day includes spending a lot of quality time with their human family.

We should strive to make every day an enriched day and not just another, boring sad day for our dogs.

Sample Dog Day #1—A Bad Day

You need to do your "business," but the humans are still snoring. You know from experience that barking makes the humans behave strangely, so you wait as long as you can. Finally, nature calls and you pee on the back of the dining room chair, the one closest to the back door.

Dad human finally gets up, stumbles to the kitchen, and yells, "MAX! What did you do?" He grabs you by the collar, throws open the back door, and shoves you outside, all the while muttering mean-sounding human words. It's cold outside, but you quietly lay down on the cement stoop by the door. He lets you back in after a while.

The humans frantically get their day going while you try to stay out of the way. You give them pleading soft doggie eyes as they eat breakfast. The little human pets you on the head and kisses you goodbye as she carries her yummy-smelling lunch out the door with her. Everyone leaves at once. They forgot to feed you breakfast again.

You look out the window and bark at anything that moves for a few hours until you get bored. The trash truck arrives. It hurts your ears and is scary, so you run to the adult humans' bedroom and try to hide under the pillows, knocking a few onto the floor. In a few hours your stomach is growling. You shred the pillows to try to calm your stomach and cure your loneliness.

Then you remember the kitchen trash can. You know for some reason that messing up the kitchen trash can make the humans cranky, so you eat the bathroom garbage instead (thinking you have made a wise choice and no one will be mad at you). You need to pee, but you can't get outside, so you hold it, again.

Hours and hours later the humans return. You are SO HAPPY to see them again! HELLO! HELLO! But they knee you, yell at you, and stomp away from you.

Someone finally lets you out in the backyard and dad human puts down a bowl of the same kibble you've been eating every day for the past five years. After the human activity dies down and the people are in their bedrooms, you go check on them to see if they will pet you.

When you walk into the adult humans' room, mother human is holding up one of the pillows and yelling at you, "MAX! What did you do?" You don't know why she is yelling but you turn tail and go visit the nice little human. She is nearly asleep, but you softly put your head on her bed. She pets your ears and says, "I love you, Maxie. Sorry we didn't get to walk today. We will walk this weekend, I promise." She rolls over to go to sleep. You turn a few circles and go to sleep by her bed since there is nothing else to do.

Sample Dog Day #2—A Good Day

You wake up in bed next to your human dad and softly nudge him with your nose at precisely 5:45 a.m. He wakes up and says, "Is it time to go outside already, Max?" He opens the doggie door to the backyard, and you run out, do your business, and then chase the birds.

You come running back in the doggie door and observe that dad is making you a yummy breakfast of meat, veggies, fruit, and kibble. You are so excited that you get all wiggly, and dad laughs as he pets you and tells you what a good boy you are. You devour your delicious breakfast.

You like to take a little nap after eating, so you head to your favorite plush blanket on the couch. When you wake up, human mom and dad notice

Happy dogs make for the best companions! The author's dog named Monster happily waits to go on his daily "Sniffari" (sniffing safari) walk with her.

and say, "Want to go on your morning walk, Maxie?" First, they put in you in the car with them so you can all drop off little human at her school. She gives you a big hug and tells you she can't wait to play together when she gets home from school. Then they drive you to a new area you haven't been before; they enjoy the morning sounds, and you enjoy the morning smells.

You go home, and the humans leave you a frozen toy packed with cream cheese and sardines when they go to work. You are happy and tired, and you don't even notice the trash trucks. Mom checks on you when she comes home for lunch, but you are napping away.

When you wake up, mom is gone but you spy the tasty toy. You take it to your favorite safe place—your crate! It's full of comfy pillows that you don't need to destroy because you have a delicious treat to chew on.

You know your humans will be home soon because they stick to their routine. When they do get home there is a joyous reunion—it's one of your favorite times of the day.

Then, even better, you and little human spend time outside in the backyard together. Sometimes she throws the ball for you, hides treats for you to find, or sits in the grass, petting you and telling you all about her day. Dinner time comes around, with more tasty food, and then you spend more time outside before you're tired and ready to go to bed. You can't wait for tomorrow!

Fact 1: Neither dog has any choice about the home they live in.

Fact 2: Day #1 is closer to how many dogs are currently living than Day #2, and millions of dogs also receive punishment on top of these stressful and boring days—exacerbating behavior problems.

It's crucial that we provide for all of our dogs' needs.

Fact 3: Day #1 sets the dog up for failure as he does his doggie best to relieve his stress and boredom. Day #2 gives the dog a routine he can trust and provides human connection, exercise, and enrichment.

Fact 4: Either of these two dog days could put stress on an already stressed or anxious dog, but Day #2 gives the troubled dog the chance for normalcy and relief.

Fact 5: If Day #1 sounds like a good dog day to you and Day #2 sounds like too much work, you are, in fact, not ready to share your life with a dog. The humans in Day #2 still lived their lives BUT they made sure their dog's needs were met as well.

We are responsible for ensuring the happiness of our dogs.

"Umwelt" and The Importance of the Dog's Perspective

I share this blog post from British Behaviorist Lisa Hird (with permission) on the concept of **"umwelt"** in dogs in response to concerns I've heard about "anthropomorphizing" a day in a dog's life (as I did above):

As a companion to humans, the domestic dog is naturally interpreted from a human-centered perspective. When we anthropomorphize, we attribute human thoughts, intentions, and personalities to nonhumans, most frequently, to our dogs. We do this in an effort to understand our dogs, but anthropomorphism falls short. An animal's sensory world is different from ours.[1]

To understand what is going on with our dogs, we need to understand the concept of **"umwelt."** Umwelt is the part of the world that an organism can detect—how the world appears via their unique systems. Humans view the world through human perspectives. A bee views the world through an ultraviolet lens. Dogs can hear high-pitched sounds that we cannot. Birds can see ultraviolet.

For dogs, the world is made up of numerous smells, and a dog's umwelt is determined by what he can perceive, by his history/experiences and by what matters in the world to him. Canines have a three-dimensional sense of smell—they can discern so much from scent that they gain an olfactory worldview. *Exploring and understanding our dog's umwelt or inner world means taking our dog's perspective. We can then ask ourselves what might be causing my dog to do a certain behavior? What is my dog experiencing from this event? What could my dog be seeing, smelling, and feeling at this moment?*

According to American author and scientist Temple Grandin, when a dog sniffs a tree, he is receiving a wealth of important information. If we can begin to understand what dogs think about, what they can see and smell and experience, we will have a better understanding of what it is like to be a dog and be able to empathize with them and advocate for them.[2]

---

1   Temple Grandin, *Thinking in Pictures* (New York: Vintage Books 1995, 2006). Google Scholar.

2   Additional references for this blog post include the articles by Temple Grandin: "My Mind Is a Web Browser: How People with Autism Think," *Cerebrum* 2, no. 1 (Winter 2000): 14–22 and "Do Animals and People with Autism Have True Consciousness?" *Evolution and Cognition* 8 (2002): 241–248; and the book Animals in Translation (New York: Scribner 2005), written by Temple Grandin and Catherine Johnson, all accessed via Google Scholar.

Make Your Dog's Day Perfect

So how can you create a win-win day for your troubled dog? This isn't an ideal answer, but it is a common one in dog training: it depends. It depends on your dog's triggers and the severity of her behavior, your dog's medical health and age, her genes, if you live in a loud city apartment or in the country, your level of patience, your budget, etc. It all depends! Dogs are individuals, of course, but hearing "it depends" isn't always helpful. Use the general steps below as a starting point to build a better day for your troubled dog, and adjust them as needed.

BUILDING A BETTER DOG DAY

Dogs new to your home need time and space to settle in—after all, everything is new to them!

STEP 1: Make Sure Your Dog Feels Safe

Don't give a new rescue free range of the house until he's had time to settle in. That doesn't mean he's locked in a crate for hours. Maybe he stays near you in your home office with lots of interesting things to sniff and chew on. Maybe he stays in a laundry room

.... OVERVIEW

Building a Better Dog Day

- **Step One:** Make Sure Your Dog Feels Safe

- **Step Two:** Seek Professional Help as Soon as Possible

- **Step Three:** Avoid or Slowly Introduce Outdoor Time and Focus on Enrichment Alternatives

- **Step Four:** Observe Your Dog and Plan for His Triggers

- **Step Five:** Always Comfort and Never Punish Your Anxious Dog

or in a large X pen when you need to leave the house (again, with toys and treats to occupy him).

A dog who is new to your home will do best on a routine. Please allow him the time he needs to settle in—it'll be different for every dog. Also protect your new dog from well-meaning humans—not every dog wants to be touched by strangers. *Always* supervise dogs and children when they are together.

STEP 2: Seek Professional Help as Soon as Possible

The earlier you call in qualified, professional help, the better the outcome for your dog. Rule out contributing medical problems with a veterinary exam. If there is a behavioral issue, call in a truly qualified, force-free trainer now (see chapter 10 for a discussion of whom you can trust and what to look for). It's a lot more complicated and potentially deadly for the dog if you wait to call us in after a bite has occurred.

3

Take outdoor adventures slowly with your new dog. Give them time to acclimate. Here I am enjoying some outdoor time with a lovely Borzoi who came to me for recall training.

5

Always comfort your dog if he is experiencing distress— you want to reinforce for him that he is safe with you.

STEP 3: Avoid or Slowly Introduce Outdoor Time and Focus on Enrichment Alternatives

Consider not walking your new or newly troubled dog. There are so many safe and calm things we can do to keep a dog's mind and body busy and content in the safety of our homes, such as nose work, "find-it" games, snuffle mats, treat-filled toys, mind games, and more. A public walk is not a positive thing for a reactive dog who is hypervigilant and sees a threat around every corner.

Conversely, if your new housemate seems to be adjusting just fine, begin to take him out on short, safe walks and observe his body language and reactions. If he handles the experience well, congratulations! Be sure to enjoy many more walks together all the while remembering it is your responsibility to show your new friend that he is safe in your presence and out in the world.

STEP 4: Observe Your Dog and Plan for Her Triggers

Carefully plan for what to do if you come across something that startles your dog or if she overreacts to something (such as a broom, a loud noise, or guests in the home). Set your best friend up for success by anticipating these things and being ready to address them in real time.

For example, if the vacuum cleaner scares your dog, separate her from the vacuuming at first by putting her in the car, garage, or a separate room, or having another person take them for a walk when you are vacuuming. Gradually let her get acclimated to the loud noise. If you see you are getting nowhere, call in a professional right away to save yourself and the dog a lot of stress and heartache.

STEP 5: Always Comfort and Never Punish Your Anxious Dog

It's always okay to comfort your dog—please do! Despite widely held misconceptions, it will not reinforce your dog's anxiety.

It is not okay to punish your dog—please don't! See chapter 8, What Not to Do in the Name of Training starting on page 170.

Ask an Expert

Behaviorist Lisa Hird Shares How She Helped a Troubled Puppy Mature into a Happy Family Member

This interview has been edited for length. Please see https://foxchapelpets.com/positive-training-dogs/ to read the full interview.

Jack's behavior concerns showed up early in his puppydom, but he is now a happy, well-adjusted family member.

▶ **What behavioral issues worried you the most in terms of being able to help Jack?**

Probably his lack of confidence, his unpredictability toward unknown dogs, and the beginnings of noise phobia. Jack could easily become aroused and display over-the-top behaviors or suddenly be fearful of noises. He had started to air snap at other dogs if they got too close to him when out for walks.

To really compound matters, we had said goodbye to our older male dog who was diagnosed with cancer and a month later we moved from rural Scotland back to urban England. Suddenly there were lots of dogs and people around, fence-running dogs barking on either side of us, and a whole lot more noise. To make matters worse, Jack was attacked while on leash by a dog and then a cat. A week later, he ended

up with emergency surgery for a blocked stomach! During his recovery at the veterinarian, they had building work and construction going on, which compounded his noise phobia. In short, he became a very fearful boy.

▶ **What do you feel out of your vast repertoire of canine behavior knowledge helped him the most?**

I talk about the Five Cs with my clients, and they worked for Jack!

Calm: lots of calming activities such as scent work and avoiding highly arousing games. Being over-stimulated does not feel good. If a dog is not calm, he cannot learn.

Connection: we worked a lot on connection. We looked at connection rather than control, dropping all the cues that are often used to "manage" behavior. This is fundamental to changing behaviors and to allowing dogs to be dogs.

Choices: providing dogs with choice in their lives is essential. The choice to interact, the choice to observe something, the choice to move away. If we try to force a dog to do something we can actually increase their fear and anxiety. Choice helps build resilience and self-confidence and as we humans control all the resources, we can easily provide choices. Dogs that are anxious about nail trimming, veterinary treatment, etc., can be empowered by using techniques such as Chirag Patel's Bucket Game or Chin Targeting, although we must ensure we are not using coercion.

Consistency: consistency is essential and something we humans need to learn!

Confidence: all the above can lead to confidence and a more positive outlook!

In terms of reactivity and fearfulness around other dogs, BAT training was phenomenal (Behavior Adjustment Training is a confidence-building program created by American trainer Grisha Stewart[1]). Prior to using BAT, Jack would see another dog at a distance and freeze, tail tucked under, body tense, and changing his breathing. Dogs need to be able to process the information around them. We used distance and lots of opportunities to observe other dogs at a safe distance.

▶ Can you share with us a sample "day in the life" of Jack as you were helping him heal?

First, Jack had a thorough veterinary exam to ensure there were no pain issues underlying his behavior issues. I also stopped using cues! I had trained Jack using clicker training as a pup and he had a vast repertoire of cues for various behaviors and performed them all perfectly. Did it make him better behaved? Absolutely not—so we ditched them a long time ago!

After breakfast and a rest, Jack would have a session in our large garden. This might be ACE free work [discussed on page 69 in chapter 4], Sprinkles, treat searches, scent work, or similar activities. Lots of calm sniffing activities. We used a white noise machine to mask some of the external noises to avoid triggering his noise sensitivity.

Twice a week we would practice some connection skills on and off leash in the garden or games like Scottish Trainer Chirag Patel's counting game[2] or American Trainer Suzanne Clothier's breadcrumbs game.[3] These are both great management games if another dog comes out of nowhere or comes too close, too fast.

Jack would then sleep until lunchtime. His walk in the afternoon would be somewhere quiet, with plenty of space. Some days we would just sit at a bench to watch the world go by, other days we would just observe at the edge of a park.

Jack developed interest in a neighbor's male Akita, pausing as we walked past to observe him at the window.

We did a number of parallel walks with him, and this really bolstered Jack's confidence. Any time we saw dogs on a walk, we would do an impromptu BAT session, gaining sufficient distance for him. After his dinner, he would have some form of enrichment.

Twice a week we worked on chin targeting [discussed in chapter 7] and handling skills as he had developed a fear of anything veterinary-related following his emergency operation. We did happy visits to the vet's office, starting in the car park without going in, building up to seeing his vet, then introducing handling with her.

▶ Can you share his current day in the life?

After breakfast and a rest, Jack still has a session in our large garden. This might be ACE free work, Sprinkles, treat searches, scent work, or similar. Lots of calm sniffing activities. Jack still sleeps until lunchtime, but we no longer need the white noise machine. He has a calm sniffy walk in the afternoon. We now hope to meet other dogs rather than trying to avoid them.

We sadly said goodbye to our senior female Staffordshire terrier. Jack became very depressed and lethargic when we lost her. We have since adopted and integrated a young, troubled female Staffie and they adore each other. Jack is now back to his happy, confident self again.

Whenever we see dogs now, his body language is much more confident, and he has play bowed at a number of different dogs when we meet them. If a dog reacts toward him, he just observes them and then walks by. We do still parallel walk with the neighbor's dog when we meet them and have lots of off-leash sessions at the local park. After his dinner, he still has some form of enrichment.

Jack recently had a suspected mast cell tumor removed at the vet. Thankfully it was benign. The veterinary staff were amazed at how happy and confident he was. Jack is a much more confident and relaxed boy at the age of 10.

---

1   See https://grishastewart.com/training/.

2   See www.youtube.com/watch?v=Ra8TKCwTDbk.

3   See www.suzanneclothier.com.

When your troubled dog is able to take a break and play, you'll know you're making progress

FOCUS ON PLAY TO REDUCE FEAR

Play and fear are incompatible. Using play is a powerful tool for working with troubled dogs because play has a positive effect on emotions. Fearful or anxious dogs can respond to play even better than food. Since dogs can't tell me about their physical and emotional state, I like to use play as a way to get important feedback from them.

Some dogs (such as puppy mill dogs) have suffered so much trauma that they are unable to play—they are too hypervigilant or shut down from fear. Other dogs might be in too much physical pain to want to play, such as in cases of severe arthritis or hip dysplasia. (As with all training, please make your first stop the veterinarian's office to rule out a physical condition that might impair your dog's ability to play.)

Think about coming close to something that terrifies you—say sharks in the ocean or rattlesnakes on land—can you imagine yourself feeling carefree

and wanting to be playful? It would not be possible. It is the same for dogs. When we reduce a dog's stressors and give them a sense of security, we often see play coming back into their lives—it's a joy to behold. When a formerly shut down reactive or aggressive dog does display play behavior, I breathe a sigh of relief as this tells me we are making progress.

I've used play with my cattle collie dog siblings who love to bark and chase delivery trucks (from their side of the fence). They love playing fetch and tug, so when I know the delivery truck is on the way, we go outside and play. Both of those games are higher priorities for them than the "bark and chase" game. You can use fun trick training and positive reinforcement obedience training in the same way if your dog is in a calm headspace, but for my two, playing tug and fetch ranks much higher than obedience work. For them, playing works better to draw their attention from the delivery trucks.

There is another "condition" not related to pain or trauma that can inhibit play, which I call the "super

A Play Case Study

I used play to help a very serious working dog, a Blue Heeler named Pete. He was adopted as an adult dog from a rescue by a single, middle-aged woman who lived alone and revolved her life around him. They were a match made in heaven, or at least they were until her new boyfriend moved in. He loved Pete, too, but that love was not reciprocated. Pete did not approve of this new addition to his already perfect lifestyle. He was very stiff around the boyfriend and circled the couple whenever they hugged or were affectionate. They called me when Pete escalated to growling.

Was Pete practicing resource guarding toward the owner? Perhaps. Did he not like the boyfriend or was he afraid of men because of something that happened in his past? I don't know. What I did learn was this: Pete was a V-E-R-Y serious dog. He took his role as protector and "look out" for his owner seriously. I could get him to sit and do small tasks with good food reinforcers, but his

body remained stiff, and he always kept his eyes toward his owners. He was having zero fun, and neither were we, frankly.

I asked his owner if she ever observed him being playful. Her face lit up and she said that he loved fetching a tennis ball. I stood up, put my bait bag on the table, and dug out some tennis balls. Pete instantly transformed into a new dog. I tossed the ball for him several times and he'd fetch it and run it back to me, happily doing a massive, whole-body happy shake. His mouth, ears, and eyes were relaxed and joyful. He even let me pet him for the first time and seemed to like the petting as long as he had the ball in his mouth.

We came up with a new plan. I had the owner turn over all fetch games to her boyfriend (at least for a little while). Whenever her boyfriend came in from work, he'd hold a tennis ball in his hand, and he'd go straight to the backyard for a game of fetch with Pete. He'd do the same thing when he came out for a cup of coffee in the morning and when they went on walks.

The boyfriend became linked in Pete's mind to a fun game of fetch and after a few weeks this positive feeling remained even when the boyfriend wasn't playing fetch with him. When Pete—that hard-working boy—let the boyfriend into his doggie circle of trust but continued exhibiting the "protection" behaviors (protecting them as a couple from all newcomers, even on walks), they simply had people entering his space hold tennis balls. The problem was solved.

My Border Collies Echo (on the left) and Radar (on the right) loved to play, but only after a swim in the pond. Each dog decides what they find rewarding or aversive—not us.

serious working dog" condition. My two sibling Border Collies, Echo and Radar, had it. They were very serious working-breed dogs who had no interest in play. Throw a ball and they would look at you with confusion and disdain. Later in life they would chew on quality bully sticks, but that's not exactly playing. I was so desperate to get them to play as puppies that I tied fleece from our sheep to toys hoping to inspire them (to no avail).

Both dogs were excellent herders, loved to be petted, and followed me everywhere, but playing was not in their wheelhouse for many years. A lot of this involved breeding—their genes wanted them to herd sheep all day and that was one of their main joys in life. Some of this probably stemmed from their first eight weeks of life—they were kept in a dark horse trailer with their mom and had no human connection or socialization.

They did finally learn to play at six years old after we moved to a property that had a pond. They loved to swim in the pond, shake off, and then playfully chase one another before quickly getting back to work. Their lack of joy in playing, however, wasn't because of fear or from being shut down—it's just who they were.

AVOID FOOD-RELATED CONFLICT

We positive trainers are always encouraging owners to train their dogs with highly reinforcing food motivators. In training for obedience, I suggest using both food and toy/play reinforcement. There are countless blog posts about if, when, and how to remove food when training obedience skills. In general, it is good advice to reinforce new skills a lot in the beginning and then, as your dog is able to do these skills in different locations with a lot of stimuli in the environment, switch to giving treats intermittently.

None of that really applies when working with behavior cases, however. Often a terrified or anxious dog is so upset by her environment (or her genetic coding or pain issues) that the last thing she wants to do is eat anything. Her body is on high alert and food isn't helpful. Training goes out the window when a dog is overloaded. It's better to remove your dog from the situation, allow him time to recover, and try again somewhere that feels safer for him. Dogs with severe separation anxiety will often not want or be able to eat anything when their owner is away without behavioral help.

Food can also become a source of conflict for a nervous dog. Let's say your dog is fearful of men. You don't know the dog's history, you just know what you observe—when he sees a man, his hackles go up, he tries to back away, and, if cornered, he will growl and show his teeth. If a man tries to hand your dog a delicious piece of steak, there can be an internal

Go slowly when introducing your dog to new people. If you find that treats cause over-arousal or conflict for the dog, trying switching to toys for reinforcement. Behaviorist Mark Bridger-Pescott works first and foremost to establish a bond and trust with every new client.

I became very interested in canine nutrition after losing far too many dogs to pancreas or liver problems. When I had my own health crisis in 2005, I clawed my way back to good health through years of work and a lot of trial and error. What I learned about my body and my personal health needs was that I thrive on a low-carbohydrate, high-fat diet with quality protein: the ketogenic way of eating. I reversed my prediabetic diagnosis and resumed a normal, highly active lifestyle. The food I was eating fueled my good health and reversed decades of poor health.

Seeing the significant way diet changed my health, coupled with my background as a journalist, led me to question the multibillion-dollar-a-year pet food industry. Any time big business can make our lives easier and more convenient, the products in question can quickly become "must-haves." It is faster and easier to open a bag of highly processed kibble and put it in a bowl twice a day. Done and done! More time for us to watch our favorite shows, go to the gym, etc.

conflict—he smells and sees the steak and it looks so good, but the scary man is holding it. Even if the man tosses the food to the floor, your dog may still be conflicted. Teaching your dog to be less fearful of men might need to involve toys instead of high-value food, at least at first.

PROVIDE GOOD NUTRITION

What we feed our dogs is also a controversial topic. Some owners swear by raw feeding. Others say feeding a dog the same kibble throughout his life works fine. High-quality food can be pricey but feeding your dog cheaper food can also become pricey if the food plays a part in your dog becoming ill. At the end of the day, each owner must decide what is best based on their knowledge and experience of their dog. I am not a canine nutritionist, but I want to share my personal journey exploring nutrition as a dog owner. See Nutrition Resources on page 235 if you'd like to dive deeper into the subject.

Choosing the best food for your dog can feel overwhelming—high-quality food can be pricey, but you also want to make sure your furry friend is getting the best nutrition for him.

Nutrition is as critical for our dogs as it is for us—how your dog's food makes his body feel (sluggish and tired or energized and healthy) affects his behavior.

That convenience comes at a steep price—the potential health of our dogs. I will always be the dog owner who prefers fresh food to kibble for my dogs just as I prefer fresh food for my own diet. While dogs have some similar dietary needs to humans, they are their own species and have their own needs. Making food for them at home requires an investment of time and education. One popular argument for the packaged-kibble diet is that it at least ensures that a dog's vitamin needs will be met. Unfortunately, dog food companies are not required to list certain nutritional information, like sodium content or carbohydrate levels, on their packaging. Unless I fully know what the ingredients are, what the nutritional content is, and the macronutrient breakdown, I don't want to feed it to my dogs.

Animal health workers are seeing a concerning rise in animal diabetes cases:

"It's estimated that **1 in every 300 dogs and 1 in 230 cats** will develop diabetes during their lifetime—and those statistics keep rising. The 2016 State of Pet Health Report shows an upward trend in the prevalence of the disease, rising nearly 80% in dogs and 18% in cats over a 10-year period."[1]

An 80% increase in diabetes in dogs is unacceptable. The question, though, is why is it happening? There is enormous debate on this complex issue, so it's best to investigate the reliable resources listed below for yourself and look deeply at what you are feeding your dog.

If a person feels sluggish and tired and experiences dramatic blood sugar changes throughout the day, their behavior will be affected, and dogs are the

---

1   "Pet Diabetes Facts," *VetSource*, October 31, 2018, https://vetsource.com/news/pet-diabetes-facts/.

same. That is why nutrition is critical: how a dog feels affects how they behave. As the quote often attributed to Hippocrates says, "let food be thy medicine and medicine be thy food."

RESEARCH VACCINATIONS

Which vaccines to give when and how often to give them is yet another hot topic in the dog community. Many of us who work with behavior issues are concerned about the effects of vaccines—some scientific evidence indicates that we have been greatly over-vaccinating our dogs and that some vaccines influence behavior.[2] And anecdotally, many of our clients have told us that they believe their dogs have had extreme reactions after some vaccines.

Dog vaccines are put into two categories: core and non-core. Core vaccines (including those for parvovirus, distemper, canine hepatitis, and rabies) are recommended for all dogs, while non-core vaccines (like Bordetella and Leptospira) are more often recommended based on the dog's lifestyle, health, and environment. You must make the decision about which vaccines your dog needs. Begin by asking your veterinarian a lot of questions:

♦ Do they administer multiple vaccines in one visit? *I prefer to spread vaccines across multiple visits for my dogs.*
♦ Do they accept titer testing? *Before I decide whether to vaccinate my dogs against a specific disease, I have the level of antibodies against the disease in their blood measured with a titer test.*
♦ What effects will the shots have on your dog if she is older, very small, or is facing some other health challenge?

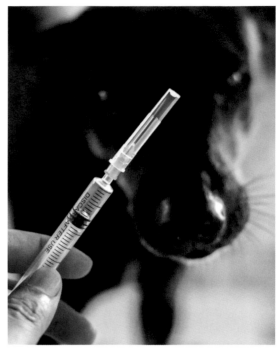

It's important to ask your vet many questions about the vaccinations they recommend and how often they should be administered. Also make sure to ask about any common side effects and concerns specific to your pet (age, size, etc.).

♦ Do they administer the same dose to dogs of every size? *Small dogs can have adverse reactions if given doses meant for large dogs.*
♦ How often do they recommend administering the core vaccines?

If at any time you feel you are not being taken seriously, find a new veterinarian willing to answer your questions. I highly recommend vets who are Fear Free Certified.

2 "Are You Over-Vaccinating Your Dog or Cat?," *The Pet Health & Nutrition Center*®, https://www.pethealthandnutritioncenter.com/blogs/natural-pet-health-education/are-you-over-vaccinating-your-dog-or-cat.

Ask an Expert

Behaviorist Dale McLelland Shares How She Helped a Once-Troubled Dog Learn to Trust People Again

This interview has been edited for length. Please see https://foxchapelpets.com/positive-training-dogs/ to read the full interview.

Scottish Behaviorist and Canine Expert Dale McLelland taking an afternoon break with her beloved Old English Sheepdogs. We encourage letting dogs be dogs, and that includes getting in plenty of downtime throughout the day.

▶ **Introduce us to Mr. McBitey, aka Pezz. I have thoughts on his name, but how did he get it?**

Pezz is a 6-year-old male Bedlington Terrier, but we fondly refer to him as Mr. McBitey! It is a nickname given with affection, though. A family illness forced his owners to rehome him, and I have no doubt he was struggling to cope with this emotional turmoil.

▶ **What behavior concerns brought Mr. McBitey's owners to see you?**

The reported behaviors were "unpredictable biting or charging" mostly at his guardians and seemingly without warning or for any real reason (as far as they could tell). This "unpredictability" made living with him quite difficult, and they felt that they were treading on eggshells around him. He also had significant skin issues and what appeared to be an unusual gait. While this had been investigated, the causes were never fully identified.

▶ **What were the first steps you implemented for him?**

We can never underestimate the time it takes for dogs to adjust from a major change in their lives. Predictable routines were important as was the establishment of a safe and secure base. I endeavored to give him as much freedom to choose when to go outside and where to sleep and I absolutely established a hands-off approach.

Most importantly, I didn't use any form of bribery, such as food, to get him to engage with me. I wanted to be sure that it was his choice entirely. Trust is not transferable; we have to earn this with every dog that we work with while using close observation skills to understand the range of his responses and meet his needs. There were some obvious flash points, such as reaching toward him while he was resting. Others seemed less obvious but understanding the early signs of his worry or discomfort meant that these could be noted and avoided.

▶ What does a typical day under your care look like for Mr. McBitey?

We live in the countryside, so things are quiet here. He has his own space to retreat to and he generally isn't a "morning person," so I have to give him time to wake up gradually. He likes his breakfast before venturing out, which he is always reluctant to do if it's raining! We go for wanders in my paddock, where he can sniff and explore and will often meet a variety of dogs who come here for boarding and daycare. He engages with them all and will have short periods of play if he feels like it!

We avoid any kind of training activities that involve food rewards as he becomes fixated; this food fixation stops him from being able to make those choices to disengage when he isn't comfortable. He enjoys his free work sessions and walks across the fields with my dogs. It's a pretty good life for him, I believe.

He also has to have regular baths and treatments for his skin condition, which he doesn't love, but he is much more comfortable with handling and touch now, so I get the impression that he accepts it, content in the knowledge that he can choose to walk away if he needs to.

▶ How is Mr. McBitey doing today? What are his biggest improvements and accomplishments?

He is doing really well! I should say that his pet name of McBitey, isn't actually justified anymore—he is a clear communicator and while he does start to worry at times,

Mr. McBitey—also known as Pezz—has become a lovely housemate after receiving professional care from Behaviorist Dale McLelland

he now has the skills and experience to remove himself from the situation rather than freezing and snapping (his prior responses). The biggest achievements are too many to list; it's his ability to make choices that never ceases to amaze. In the early days, he growled when his collar was put on—he had to be distracted by food, he stiffened and braced himself when he was touched, his posture was tight and hunched, but now he can meet new people without too much tension and knows that he can disengage at any time.

Many of the more obscure "triggers" simply disappeared once he relaxed and learned a new approach. Life is so much easier now that I can show him his collar and he trots right over to have it put on—no need for bribing, no tension, just a positive association for something that once worried him greatly.

For him, I would say that his biggest achievement is being able to exercise choice. He feels safe, I am sure of that, and his life has opened up vastly; new experiences are no longer worrying, and I hope that he sees me as his secure base throughout.

UNDERSTAND THE IMPORTANCE OF THE HUMAN-CANINE BOND

We don't need science to tell us that the bond between humans and dogs exists. This bond is a mutually beneficial and rewarding gift. Do we treat our dogs as treasured gifts? If we think we do, would the dogs agree?

As far as dogs loving us goes and the benefits this provides, that has been studied extensively. A 2019 survey of recent studies[1] made note of the many health-related benefits dogs can provide humans:

♦ Pet owners report higher levels of physical activity, better adherence to a heart-healthy diet, and lower levels of blood glucose and diabetes.

♦ Dog ownership correlates with significantly higher overall cardiovascular health scores compared ownership of non-canine pets or no pets at all.

♦ Dogs boost their owners' physical activity and mental health.

♦ Bringing a dog into the home can improve adherence to an exercise regimen, enhance fitness, and reduce visceral adiposity (dangerous fat that surrounds your abdominal organs).

♦ The strong emotional bond between a human and a dog has powerful therapeutic effects on both mental health and heart health.

♦ Higher levels of physical activity, exercise, and fitness not only improve cardiovascular disease outcomes but also curb anxiety, hostility, depression, and emotional distress.

♦ In single-person households, dog ownership has been associated with significantly lower risks of both all causes of death (33% lower) and cardiovascular disease deaths (36% lower).

The powerful bond between humans and dogs is well documented and we know how dogs show us love.

♦ Over the past 40,000 years, humans and dogs have become evolutionarily adapted to fill a niche in each other's environments—a relationship that has translated into contemporary health benefits.

♦ We know from other studies that oxytocin—the bonding or love hormone—increases in both dogs and humans when they interact in a way similar to that of a mother and infant staring into each other's eyes.

In other words, dogs are excellent for your heart, your overall health, and your happiness. If you want to improve your life, get a dog (even a troubled dog provides benefits and their own unique contributions). Look at all your other relationships (with your partner, your children, your parents, your siblings, your boss, etc.)—do these relationships inherently make your heart happy? They might, of course, but dogs can often understand and

---

1   James H. O'Keefe, MD, et al., "The Human-Canine Bond: A Heart's Best Friend," *Mayo Clinic Proceedings: Innovations, Quality & Outcomes* 3, no. 3 (September 2019): 249–250, www.ncbi.nlm.nih.gov/pmc/articles/PMC6713833.

The human-canine bond keeps us healthier and happier both physically and mentally. It's important to give dogs access to the activities they love, and many dogs, including my dogs Echo (left) and Monster (right), love to swim.

(See chapter 1 for an in-depth look at why modern dogs are so stressed).

Author and former professor emeritus of animal behavior, cognitive ethology, and behavioral ecology at the University of Colorado, Boulder, Marc Bekoff, PhD, said this about dogs and love: "If you define love as a long-term commitment—meaning they seek one another out when they're apart, they're happy when they're reunited, they protect one another, they feed one another, they raise their children together—then, of course, non-human animals love each other."[3]

Those of us who have experienced tight bonds with dogs already know that dogs are capable of love, both toward one another and toward us. Science has proven it and canine body language clearly shows it: an exuberant, tail-waving dog with a relaxed face and wiggly-all-over body is clearly expressing a positive emotion toward her human. Call it joy, love, happiness, attention-seeking—call it whatever you like, there is no denying there is a strong bond between humans and dogs.

Lately, however, that bond has become more tenuous, at least from the dog's perspective. A human can spend a lot of money purchasing a dog, installing a fence, buying expensive dog food and toys, and visiting the vet, only to keep the dog alone and bored in his crate for 10 hours a day. This owner considers this to be "love." I call it abuse and neglect: the opposite of loving care.

What does a caring owner need to provide to actually convey love to her dog (beyond the all-important sense of safety)? We know from the brilliant work of neuroscientist Jaak Panksepp that mammals have seven primary emotional

bond with us better than anyone else, including other humans.

What does love (or happiness, or joy, etc.) look like from your dog's perspective? There is an immediate and unbalanced power relationship between humans and dogs. We have most, if not all, of the power. Ethicists have even argued that the human-dog relationship wavers between the extremes of "pampered" and "enslaved."[2] Dogs have evolved to—mostly—cooperate with humans. But many human lifestyles no longer work for our dogs and the result is skyrocketing behavior problems.

2   Judith Benz-Schwarzburg, et al., "How Dogs Perceive Humans and How Humans Should Treat Their Pet Dogs: Linking Cognition with Ethics." *Front. Psychol.* 11:584037 (December 16, 2020). https://www.frontiersin.org/articles/10.3389/fpsyg.2020.584037/full.

3   Erin Meisenzahl-Peace, "Dogs Can Feel Rejected and Fall in Love Like Humans," *Vice*, February 16, 2017, https://www.vice.com/en/article/j5emeg/dogs-can-feel-rejected-and-fall-in-love-like-humans.

For the relationship to be healthy for both species, we must consider what makes a dog's life a good one—from the dog's perspective. My dog Echo loved hiking off leash in the mountains near Durango, Colorado. I taught Echo an excellent recall so this fun activity could also be a safe one.

systems: seeking, care, play, lust, fear, sadness, and anger. Owners should strive to provide a home environment that puts a high importance on the first three emotions: seeking, care, and play.

The primal urge to mate (lust) is a biological need that we take away from most dogs. Controlling their mating partners creates problems. There's no concrete solution to this real problem, but breeders must put just as much importance on temperament and health as they do looks. Puppy mills and large breeding kennels that cannot properly socialize puppies need to be shut down—they are cruel and creating deeply troubled dogs. I am hopeful that the ethical breeders working to breed resilient dogs will become the most popular option for dog owners (other than shelters and rescues). We as customers need to support quality breeders—if we continue as we are now, our dogs will remain troubled.

Just as human parents (no matter how hard they try) cannot keep their children from experiencing

the negative emotions—fear, sadness, and anger—even the best owners can't keep their dogs from experiencing these emotions. Life is not a continual party for any of us and these emotions exist for good reason. If a housemate passes away, a bonded dog will feel sadness. We can't change the existence of death or loss, but we can work throughout the dog's life to build resiliency and we can be there to give support and comfort.

So how can we improve our dogs' well-being? We can start by acknowledging that they have emotions, needs, and desires all their own and that, like us, they have a right to these things. We can work to reduce their daily frustrations. We can prepare a plan ahead of time for guiding our dog through difficult times in life, like moving or losing a friend. We can even take precautions, including them in our wills to make sure they will still have what they need even after we are gone.

We need to support and promote the positive breeders working to create happy, resilient puppies that can grow into healthy, confident dogs—it's time for us to shut down unethical breeders and puppy mills for good.

Ask an Expert

Applied Ethologist and Family Dog Mediator Kim Brophey Discusses How to Strengthen the Human-Canine Bond and Why It Is Crucial

This interview has been included in its entirety.

Kim Brophey with her happy and well-adjusted family dogs in Asheville, North Carolina.

▶ **What contributed to creating the human-canine bond? Why do you feel it is so strong and unlike any other relationship we have with an animal (cats and horses are similar, but horses don't sleep in our beds and cats, well, they run their own lives it seems)?**

I think it's the unique evolutionary history between humans and dogs. I think we became inextricably connected in a way that probably was a bit similar for horses as they were similarly valuable to human existence and success. But then after a while with the advent of other modes of transportation, it just didn't continue in the same way. And it didn't have as many complicated layers to it, I think, as ultimately the relationship with dogs did.

It would be really different if the horse lived in the house and if you were in the same social group all day, every day. I wonder what it would be like if I moved into the barn with the horse. How would our relationship be different?

Part of it is the fact that we became interdependent for access to resources 10,000–40,000 years ago and that changed how we survived. We needed each other in a way that was really unique evolutionarily, particularly for humans, as dogs opened up so many new possibilities for us in terms of things like hunting strategies, alarm systems, and resource protection. And then that diversified to so many other areas over the years, giving way to livestock management, pest control, and more. I think that fact that we brought them into our social group and even integrated them into our culture in a way was different from any other animal. We developed them genetically and behaviorally in a way that constantly increased the load of that demand and therefore the potential for effective communication, understanding, and complex relationships. And I just think that it's been a very interesting and unique evolutionary story.

▶ **What are three ways humans can increase the bond with our dogs?**

Accept them and meet them where they are, with the L.E.G.S. model [discussed in more depth on page 73] being elemental to helping people do that. When we change our expectations, it then changes our experience in relationship with our dogs. I think that is the most critical moment. Of course, you're going to be frustrated if you're expecting things go a certain way that might not be realistic or possible. So, we have to back up, get humble, and find out where the dogs actually are and why they are there before we can move forward. And it's a game-changing piece.

The next one is to challenge yourself to abandon the cultural concepts of obedience and training and to explore the concept of "relationship." Relationships include mediation and conflict resolution—finding ways to dialogue and have more effective communication, then finding agreements as a necessary parent or guide for your dog in the modern world. The point being that you shouldn't just swallow the concept that dogs need to obey and must be trained exclusively to do so. Remember, for 99% of our 10,000- to 40,000-year history with dogs, there were no dog trainers. We were totally successful in our relationships between the two species without dog trainers. So, think about emphasizing relationship communication, dialogue, and agreements over obedience, conditioning, and training.

All our relationships have terms and many times there are unspoken terms. I trust that my husband's not going to go out and start romantic relationships with 50 other people, but those things need to be established and understood. Sometimes we have conflict only because we have different expectations and haven't created any clear agreement yet.

The last one is to talk to your dog as if you were raising a child. It changes so much about your dynamic, your behavior, your dog's experience with and trust in you, your facial expressions, body language, and gestures, etc. I think because we have this cultural idea that because dogs don't understand what we're saying, we don't talk to them. If you didn't talk to a baby just because they didn't understand what you were saying, it would create learning dysfunctions and a lack of bonding. You've got to remember that dogs are a social species (like humans), and they need that sense of social referencing, dialogue, conversation, etc. Beyond that, they are also capable of learning to understand many words and phrases, not just the basic obedience commands. The more information we give them, the better off they're going to be. It increases their ability to predict and anticipate what's going to happen next because we're keeping them informed—and that really can lower anxiety and help with a lot of behavior problems.

▶ **What advice can you share for those dog owners and trainers who now fully understand the harm caused to dogs through a lack of knowledge and from blind adherence to only working with observable behaviors? How can we live with the guilt of our actions or inactions when it's affected dogs for generations?**

It's the same thing I tell my clients about behavioral euthanasia should it become necessary—you didn't ask to be in the situation any more than your dog did. We are dealing with the repercussions of choices that were made by our ancestors. We have a cultural structure and framework around dogs at this point that is not likely to change, so now we must work with what we have. And the most important thing is compassion for your dog and yourself in that process. Your ancestors may have hyper-manipulated and controlled animals but that wasn't your choice. Move on and do the best you can with what you have. Do as much damage control and as much compromising and mediation as you can to ensure that all parties' needs are met.

▶ **What are three gifts we can use our human intelligence for to give to our dogs to improve their lives?**

I think creativity is number one. That's the biggest thing that jumps out for me—be creative. Think outside the box. And that dovetails with using your critical thinking and not buying into any set ideology. That requires a willingness to challenge your belief systems. I think we should strive to use our human brain power for open-mindedness, creative problem solving, and critical thinking, which are kind of the enemies of ideology.

Canine Enrichment

Canine enrichment is the practice of satisfying your dog's needs and natural instincts in ways that are safe, fun, and appropriate for him. It puts an emphasis on a dog's physical and mental well-being. I would dearly love to see puppy classes teach owners all about creative and inexpensive ways to provide enrichment throughout their dog's lifetime. Enrichment, for me, is a higher priority than obedience training (although I don't advocate throwing behavior training out the door).

One of my all-time favorite books on canine enrichment is *Canine Enrichment: The Book Your Dog Needs You to Read*, a small but mighty book by British behaviour counselor and trainer Shay Kelly. Kelly also began one of the most positive and largest canine groups on Facebook with over 450,000 owners and trainers happily sharing enrichment ideas.[1] Kelly describes enrichment as "giving dogs something interesting to do. It's lighting a spark. It's giving them an engaging and fulfilling life." And I would add that it's way more than just a daily walk.

Kelly divides the elements of canine enrichment into five categories:

Safe Environment: A scared or reactive dog facing or recovering from a trigger is not a dog who can enjoy enrichment in that moment. It's the same for a noise phobic dog when fireworks are booming outside. If a dog is fearful, it will not be an enriching session for the dog.

Natural Behavior: Dogs love to sniff, so we can use that to our advantage when envisioning enrichment ideas. Kelly notes that it's our role to guide them to investigate safe environments with their powerful noses. We can play all sorts of indoor and outdoor sniffing games to light up their need to seek. Other natural behaviors we can work with include digging, chewing, retrieving, and the need for socialization.

Companionship and Bonding: Dogs are social animals, just like us. Solitary confinement is one of the worst punishments for humans and it's true for dogs as well. Dogs crave our attention, and engaging with them and making it clear that we are their family strengthens the bond.

Non-food Enrichment: Sometimes bringing in food can create an undesired conflict for the dog. Luckily there are countless ways to use enrichment without needing food. Toys are just one example: tugs, chew toys, rubber rings, squeaky toys, balls, knotted ropes, soft toys, and fetching items.

Food Enrichment: Kelly writes that food enrichment is an exceptional tool that offers endless opportunities. Food is a primal need, after all. One of Kelly's favorite ways to feed his dog is to separate his dog's meal between 10 inexpensive bowls and then hide the bowls throughout the house. The "find-it" game is one of my favorite food-based activities. As long as you are providing healthy, species-appropriate food and using safe containers or toys, there's no limit to the fun food games you can play.

---

1   See the Canine Enrichment Facebook group at www.facebook.com/groups/137561280156280.

Ask an Expert

British Behaviorist and Author Shay Kelly Shares His Favorite Enrichment Activities and Explains Why Enrichment Is a Top Priority for Dogs

This interview has been edited for length. Please see https://foxchapelpets.com/positive-training-dogs/ to read the full interview.

UK Behaviorist Shay Kelly is the author of two books and is considered around the world to be the "Canine Enrichment Guru." He runs a very popular canine enrichment group on Facebook.

▶ **You write in your book that from a dog's perspective, not everything done to help a dog is actually enriching for the dog, such as nail trims or stressful groomer or vet visits (even though these things do improve the quality of their lives). How do you describe things that are truly enriching for a dog?**

What is truly enriching for a dog are those activities that increase their positive affective state and emotional well-being. It's not just giving dogs something to do, and it's not only about providing something "extra." *Fundamentally, enrichment is about providing for a dog's behavioral needs.* When we start to think about what these behavioral needs are we see that an enriched life is about much more than a particular activity. For example, dogs need to be able to have some choices.

At first this can sound strange; why do dogs need choices? Humans tend control everything—what time to go for a walk, where to walk, who they meet, the training class, enrichment activities, what they eat, when they eat, and almost everything else in the dog's life. There are good reasons why we are the ones making many of the choices, but no animal on earth evolved to have all their decisions made by another species. Choice can be provided for in simple ways, for example, allowing the dog to stop and sniff as much as they want to on walks, or providing additional sleeping places around the home so the dog can choose which room they want to sleep in.

▶ **Why do dogs need enrichment? Can they provide their own enrichment or is it up to the owner to do that for the dog?**

Dogs make fantastic companions, and we don't usually think of them as being captive animals; however, the fact remains that their freedoms are fairly limited when compared with how they might behave if they had the freedom to do as they pleased. I realize that people are increasingly opposed to keeping animals in zoos; however, it is expected that animals that are kept in zoos be provided with suitable enrichment. If zoos neglected to do so, it would be unlikely for the zoo to retain their license to operate. Why should we expect less for companion animals?

Dogs have a fantastic brain that is capable of so many amazing tasks. We just need to look at the number of roles that dogs have been employed for by humans over the years to see just how smart that brain is. However, in many homes, the dog's brain is left unemployed. Enrichment fulfills it. Enrichment gives the dog's life meaning, without which depression can easily become the norm (although often going unrecognized in dogs). Essentially enrichment may be the difference between poor mental well-being and good mental well-being, and who doesn't deserve the latter? I don't believe that dogs can provide their own enrichment. The very reason enrichment is needed is because they live with us. Wild animals spend a great deal of their time acquiring food and surviving; this need has been removed for dogs by us humans, so it is our responsibility to fill the behavioral void with enrichment.

▶ What are some of your personal favorite enrichment activities using food? And what are some of your favorites that don't involve food?

I weigh their food out each day and keep it in a container so I know exactly how much they are eating. With some of it, I will make a scavenger hunt by hiding it around the house and sending the dog to find it. I also hide items with particular scents on them (I like to use catnip for this) to find and for doing so they receive a handful of their food. For me, there is nothing in the dog world so awesome as watching a dog homing in on a scent. Apart from this, I like items I can stuff with wet food, such as the Toppl or K9 Connectable. These allow the dog some independence as they work to get the food out.

Enrichment can be as simple as throwing a handful of food or a few treats on the floor to create a quick mini treasure hunt!

For non-food enrichment, I like to just stand and watch the dogs sniff when out on a walk. I also like to find things that suit the particular breed. For my Labrador (Mr. B) this might be splashing about in a shallow stream. On the other hand, my West Highland Terrier (Daisy) loves a sandy area where she can dig. I love to use food for enrichment, but it is important to remember that it shouldn't always be about food—just sitting on the floor giving the dogs a belly rub can be a great bonding experience.

▶ Can you please share some free or inexpensive ways to provide enrichment for dogs?

Probably the greatest difference we can make is simply allowing dogs the time to stop and sniff when out walking, and of course giving them a safe environment and making them part of the family. Dogs don't need a lot of expensive enrichment equipment; what they need is their human to treat them respectfully and take responsibility for meeting their needs. You can literally throw a handful of food across the floor and create a great experience for the dog, searching around for every last piece. Another favorite is to place a handful of food in old cereal boxes and let the dog rip them open, before recycling them. Some caution is needed here however as we must ensure the dog will not consume the cardboard and that it is free of toxins.

RESPECT OUR COVENANT WITH DOGS

Find out how your dog loves to play. Is it a game of chase with you? Is it jumping into a pond? Is it digging? Maybe it's all three. If the thing that floats your human boat is a dog sport, just make sure your dog also enjoys it. It is unjust to drag a dog through any activities that terrify or frustrate him—no matter how deeply you wanted to win blue ribbons. Don't let your ego turn dog sporting activities into something that is only about you and your needs. Find a dog who loves the same things you love, and both of your lives will be enhanced.

> Find a dog who loves the same things you love, and both of your lives will be enhanced.

Dogs want a sense of control, so how do we provide it? One way is to be predictable. Don't giggle at the dog, sound happy, and pat him on the head one time when he jumps up on you, then get mad when he does it again the next day. Show them and reinforce what *to* do instead of what *not* to do. Have a solid routine in place so your dog knows what to expect. Dogs make predictions about their worlds so help them anticipate having a safe, fun, and rewarding home.

One of the best things you can do for your dog is to transform the leash from a scary, painful restraint into a symbol of freedom, play, exploration, and togetherness.

We need to allow dogs to make choices. Positive reinforcement training is *not* permissive, but what works best for both species is for the owner to coach their four-legged housemates on how to follow the house rules. There is a world of difference between taking on the role of a friendly guide and furiously punishing any missteps because of the mistaken idea that dogs act out to "dominate you." This incorrect concept (known as "pack theory" or "dominance theory") has been completely and thoroughly debunked by scientific research, but it continues to harm dogs.[1]

One major thing we can do for our dogs is to change the leash from a possibly painful restraint into a dog's best friend. The leash provides safety for your dog and for any other dogs and people you might meet in public places. A leash can be a trap that causes tension and stress for your dog, or it can be a liberating tool that allows you to take your dog with you. Change what the leash means to your dog. Put the leash on in the house and play with your dog. When you go outside with the leash on him, use truly motivating reinforcers anytime the dog "checks in" and looks back to you. Make the leash a symbol for your dog representing the freedom to play, seek, and explore together.

Veterinary behaviorist Dr. Karen Overall hit the nail on the head when she said what we need to strive for with troubled dogs is a negotiated settlement. I would take it even further—we make negotiated settlements with everyone, every day. To be able to start any negotiation, you must have the ability to imagine the situation from the other

We owe it to our dogs to honor the "covenant" (the primal, unspoken cooperation and love) between humans and dogs. Expert puppy trainer Christine Young and her dog, Pekoe, enjoy a happy, positive life together in California.

person's perspective. How many of us ever bother to look through our dog's eyes? Dogs have crossed a significant evolutionary threshold to be by our side, something that no other animal ever has. We owe them our gratitude, our love, and our patience. We need to remember to be teachers and guides for our dogs.

---

1   Victoria Stillwell, "Pack Theory Debunked," *Positively*®, 2014, https://positively.com/dog-training/myths-truths/pack-theory-debunked/.

Ask an Expert

British Behaviorist Mark Bridger-Pescott Explains Why Labeling Dogs' Behavior as Troubled Creates Problems for Owners

This interview has been included in its entirety.

Trainer and Behaviorist Mark Bridger-Pescott ensures his rescue dogs Ava and Bear receive daily walks and enrichment. This walk is at local spot, Climping Beach in West Sussex.

▶ **What first drew you toward working with troubled dogs?**

I've always had a dog around me for my whole life; my first dog was a mixed breed, when I was around 8 years of age, and he was my very best friend. I started to help a German Shepherd rescue in my teens by doing home-checks, walking, collecting, etc., so I saw first-hand what rescue dogs were going through. That experience broke my heart, and I knew I wanted to try and help as many dogs stay with good families as possible. This experience started my journey toward dog training and behavior. I currently help several rescues by offering discounts, webinars (to help raise funds), and giving more up-to-date advice, based on the latest scientific findings, on how to deal with dogs.

I don't see a "troubled dog," I see a "dog"—an entity, a personality, a living being with emotions. When I am called to go and help a person with their dog, I'm looking to see how I can help repair their relationship while helping the dog overcome whatever it is that is making both the dog and guardian unhappy. In a lot of cases, once you repair the relationship, the behaviors improve too.

▶ **What are the most common troubling canine behaviors you are seeing in these modern times?**

I don't see "troubling canine behaviors," I see troubling responses to those behaviors. Dogs only do "dog things," and the main issue with that is that humans don't like some dog things (behaviors). I see that as a human issue and not a dog issue. If we can understand what the dog needs, then we can help them to behave in ways we do like. We tend to think the dog is being "naughty" or doing things on purpose, so we tend to respond in a negative way to what we (as guardians) perceive as being a negative behavior. This usually only serves to make the behavior worse and damage the relationship further.

The most disturbing issue for me is when people tell the dog off for growling—they take it personally. I explain that a growl is a wonderful noise, as it is an extremely clear indication that the dog is not happy and that we need to back away. If we do back away, we can teach the dog that we are able to listen to them and act accordingly, which in turn will build trust. (We obviously need to work on why the dog has growled, so we can avoid this situation in the first place, though.)

▶ What do you wish owners knew about working with a troubled dog that they might not know?

Most people will not actively choose to take on a dog that has behavioral issues, but they may take on a dog that develops issues at some point. These can arise for several reasons, including past experiences, genetics, or even just the fact that their entire world has just changed. This could be a puppy, a rescue dog, or a dog that someone can no longer look after who needs to be rehomed.

The first thing I urge people to do is to research the particular breed of dog they are getting—is that breed the right fit for them? And, equally importantly, are they the right fit for the dog? If they are the sort of people who like to relax in the evenings and weekends watching films, then don't get a Collie or Springer Spaniel, for example.

The second thing I ask people to do is to learn about the basic body language of their dog—learn to understand what they are trying to tell you and how to respond in the right way. It's important to understand the dog's basic needs first, and then build on that so they can help the dog become a well-rounded member of the family.

▶ What are the top three things troubled dogs need from their owners to begin to unravel their stressed or anxiety-ridden behaviors?

First, employing the services of a qualified, modern, science-based behaviorist is a must. Get the right treatment plan for your individual dog and follow that advice. Providing the following three pieces to the dog will be necessary no matter what.

Understanding—for anyone, being understood and listened to is extremely important, as it helps us to feel as though we can effectively communicate how we feel. When we know we're understood, we no longer feel the need to escalate our behavior. Imagine trying to explain to an animal that you are not well, or that you're in pain. How frustrated would you become if you couldn't explain how you felt to another species because they didn't understand you? And then how would you feel if that animal thought your actions were negative and reacted to you negatively in response? You would either just have to be quiet, shut down, and put up with it, or increase your behaviors to try and explain harder—neither are good outcomes!

Compassion—if we have compassion for our dogs and understand that they may be having a hard time (and aren't intentionally giving us a hard time), then it becomes easier for us to help them. They will be behaving due to a perceived problem in their world, so we need to understand that to help them overcome it.

Time—any issue, especially anxiety or stress-related issues, will take time to overcome, just as with humans. We have to work on the emotions behind the behavior first so that the dog is better equipped to cope in the first place, then they can improve.

▶ Are you optimistic or pessimistic for the future happiness of pet dogs?

I have to be optimistic, we all do, as it helps to drive us forward to spread the new modern ways of dealing with dogs that don't involve pain, force, or fear.

Slowly, the outdated ways will fade and there are so many new, young behaviorists coming through that have learned and continue to learn the right way of doing things. There are, of course, still organizations promoting the outdated ways and I fear they will always be around, but they are rapidly becoming the minority.

It's looking good for dogs as people are starting to see the benefits of treating dogs with kindness and respect; they are starting to ask questions regarding trainers and behaviorists and their methods and not just accepting that "this is how things are done." In some cases, this leads to the behaviorist looking into alternative methods, too. Furthermore, owners are also looking more into the food they feed their dogs, rather than just accepting that dog food is dog food. They are seeing the benefits of good quality food on the dog's behavior and health and seeing the link between nutrition and the "internal and external condition."

All in all, things are looking up for dog welfare in general as far as I'm concerned.

How to Find Help for Your Dog

As we've discussed, trainers and behaviorists in the United States and elsewhere are mostly unregulated, so there is a very real threat that an untrained or poorly trained dog trainer or behavior consultant could harm your dog and call it "training." (Also see chapter 8, What Not to Do in the Name of Training, on page 170.) I side with the countless professional academies, organizations, and industry professionals who understand the importance of training dogs without the use of fear, pain, or force.

Often, we are brought in after other trainers have used harsh treatments and escalated the dog's behavior concerns and anxiety levels.

If your trainer is using fear, force, or pain, interrupt them and stop it from happening. We know that dogs need to feel safe, and we know that harming them does the exact opposite: it destroys the human-canine bond. It is abusive—never tolerate anyone hurting your beloved pet for any reason.

There is so much incorrect and harmful information in the world. I've heard "trainers" say the most absurd things: "your

Our relationship with our dogs must be built on trust, and it is our responsibility to meet a dog's emotional and physical needs. A healthy relationship does not involve the concept of "dominance."

I wrote in my first book (*The Midnight Dog Walkers*) that I am happy (at no charge) to help you research and find a truly force-free, qualified trainer to help you. It's still true—I am *always* willing to do so, and my email address is *Annie@Phenixdogs.com*. There is a shortage of qualified force-free trainers, but they are out there, and going to the right trainer the first time can save you a lot of heartbreak.

You are your dog's best advocate, so ask many questions of anyone handling your best mate.

dog is trying to dominate you," "your dog just needs to learn who is boss," "your dog is lazy, stupid, or willfully disobeying you," and the list goes on. Your dog is simply doing his best to survive using his natural dog skills.

The American Veterinary Society of Animal Behavior has a free downloadable position statement called *How to Choose a Trainer* that I highly recommend using as a starting point in your search.[1] The organization recommends observing the trainer first, if possible, and asking yourself the following questions:

- Does the behaviorist or trainer offer rewards-based training?
- Are they a good teacher?
- Are they respectful?
- Do you feel comfortable with the behaviorist or trainer?
- What is their stance on vaccinations?
- How does the behaviorist or trainer address problem behaviors?

THE QUESTIONS TO ASK AND THE ANSWERS TO LOOK FOR

I have a background in marketing and public relations, but also as a journalist. Both have trained me to look past the marketing and ask the right—sometimes difficult—questions. You must do the same with behaviorists and trainers (or anyone handling your dog)—you are the expert on your dog and your dog's protector. Any professional of any kind who objects to your honest questions likely has an ego problem, or, more likely, a lack of quality training. Ask many questions, including:

---

1 See https://avsab.org/wp-content/uploads/2018/03/How_to_Choose_a_Trainer_AVSAB.pdf.

- **What are your qualifications as a professional trainer or behavior consultant? I'd like to know about any titles, certifications, and hands-on training experience that you have.**
Some recommended training schools are listed starting on page 233. Investigate their responses and ensure that they have the certifications they claim to have.

- **Do you have experience with reactivity, fear, anxiety, etc., in dogs? If yes, what is the first thing you do to help such a dog?**
You want to hear that they work to create a feeling of safety for the dog and try to find out what the dog's stressors are and how they can reduce them.

- **What professional memberships do you hold?**
Some recommended organizations are listed starting on page 233. Take a deep dive online and learn if the organization permits members to use fear, pain, or force, or supports the concept known as LIMA, which stands for "least intrusive, minimally aversive." I don't want any aversive used on my dogs, even minimally—it should not be part of the conversation, period.

- **Do you use shock collars, prong collars, chains, leash pops, spray bottles, alpha rolls, or any pain- or fear-inducing tools?**
If yes, RUN.

- **What will you do if my dog gets it wrong?**
You want to hear that they will communicate better with the dog or change the positive reinforcers and will not choose punishment.

- **What will you do if my dog gets it right?**
If they say they will punish the dog, RUN. You want to hear that they will reinforce the right canine choices with food, affection, toys, or play.

Think of finding a behaviorist or training professional like conducting a job interview—you need to find the best candidate to help create a better life for you and your dog.

- **Do you offer a guarantee?**
If yes, RUN! Dogs are not machines, they are individuals. This sets you up for disappointment and gives you false expectations. Look instead for something like dog trainer Mallory Robinson's lifetime guarantee of owner support as long as harmful tools are not used on the dog.

- **What kind of behavioral issues or classes do you refer out to other behaviorists or trainers?**
If they say "none," RUN! No one person is an expert in every area of dog training. For example, I do not teach for dog sports as I am not an expert in that field.

Do you feel that dogs are trying to dominate us?
If the answer is yes, RUN. This is a fallacy, and it is not based in fact or reality.

Do you work with teaching dogs how to play?
You want this to be a YES.

Do you use food in training?
Yes, but they should also use toys and other reinforcers. The trainer should know that food can sometimes set up a conflict for the dog.

Are you a "balanced" trainer?"
If the answer is yes, RUN. This word is often used to mean the person uses both punishment (aversives) and positive reinforcement—setting your dog up to be confused and potentially riddled with anxiety.

Have you ever had a dog injured or pass away under your care?
If yes, ask for more details. Older dogs or those with unknown health concerns can become sick or pass away and rarely a trainer might encounter an accident, but these should be exceptions, not common occurrences. I've never had a single dog get lost or die under my care in the 20-plus years I have been working with dogs.

Have you been bitten by a dog you were working with?
If they say, "all the time," RUN. A quality trainer might get a bite or two over a long career, but it should be a rare occurrence. Trainers who have bite scars often push dogs too hard, too fast and are missing all the body language cues and canine behaviors that occur before a dog bites.

You have every right to ask questions to protect your dog. Your new, vulnerable best friend is counting on you to protect him. My sibling dogs learned to trust me after being harshly taken away from their mother at too young of an age.

You are paying good money and placing your trust in this person, so you have every right to learn about their philosophy and the tools they use. Go forth and question everything. Your dog will thank you.

Ask an Expert

British Canine Behaviorist and Training Expert Lisa Hird Explains What to Look for and What to Avoid When Hiring a Trainer

This interview has been included in its entirety.

UK Behaviorist Lisa Hird's lovely dog Jack began life as a troubled pup. With her compassionate guidance he is enjoying his senior years as a peaceful family member.

▶ **It can be so confusing for dog owners seeking qualified, professional help for their troubled dog. Beyond looking at credentials, what traits do you advise dogs owners to look for in a trainer?**

Be wary of statements such as the number of years' experience working with dogs. This does not necessarily mean the person has up-to-date knowledge, or indeed any knowledge at all. Statements that someone studied with an organization is not the same as completing and passing a course. Do check out what courses the professional has completed and how recent their learning record is. Most professionals will belong to a membership organization and their membership will be monitored to ensure they keep up to date with their knowledge and carry out a specified number of hours of professional development.

The training plan should be tailored to you and your dog. If you are not comfortable with any of the suggestions within the behavior or training plan, ask questions. Ask yourself whether you feel comfortable and happy with what the trainer is suggesting for or doing with your dog. Have a search for videos on any of their pages and websites. Watch how they interact with your dog.

▶ **What professional or volunteer experiences do you feel create an excellent trainer?**

This is always a difficult question. Many trainers gain their practical experience helping at rescues. I would be looking

Look for trainers who don't use aversive tools like shock collars—they don't work and usually just cause even more trauma to already troubled dogs.

to see if they help with any rescue centers or charities, but not everyone has the time to do volunteer work. Also look or ask for evidence of CPD (Continued Professional Development) training and certification.

▶ What marketing terms do you look for when searching for a truly positive trainer?

Some of the words I look for are fear-free, non-coercive, reward-based, and relationship-centered training.

▶ What marketing terms do you seek to avoid when searching for a truly positive trainer?

There are a few words that are red flags to me, including balanced, reward-based balanced trainer, "dogs will learn that their choices and behaviors can result in either pleasant or unpleasant results," pack leader, dog listener, alpha trainer, and LIMA. LIMA is an acronym for the phrase "least intrusive, minimally aversive." LIMA describes a trainer or behaviorist who uses the least intrusive, minimally aversive strategy out of a set of tactics likely to succeed in achieving a training or behavior change objective. This means that punishment and negative reinforcement can still be used.

▶ What are the most important questions to ask of any professional who will be handling your dog?

When considering enlisting a professional to work with you and your dog, ask them what happens if the dog gets the request correct, and what happens to the dog if they get the request incorrect. The answers you get will help you determine whether they use fear-free, reward-based, relationship-centered training, or whether they use aversive methods or coercion.

Aversive tools, coercion, and punishment are not necessary and have no place in dog training. If the person you are going to employ mentions shock collars, citronella or water sprays, Halti® headcollars, etc., please look for someone else who does not use force or coercion.

The Most Difficult Decision—Behavioral Euthanasia

If you are the kind of person who loves dogs and shares your life with many dogs, chances are getting higher all the time that one of those dogs may very well be an "unfixable" and, in fact, dangerous dog. Trainers and behavior consultants all over the world are talking about the huge increase in cases of troubled dogs. Some of them feel forced to forego teaching much-needed manners and puppy classes—their case load has become so overwhelming and filled with highly reactive and aggressive dogs.

Why is this happening? You've read all the reasons before: poor breeding practices, a lack of safe and secure breeding programs for mother dogs and young puppies, breeding for show rather than health and temperament, puppy mills, a lack of early socialization, dogs bred for illegal fighting schemes, etc. One large part of the equation is well-meaning rescues and individuals believing we can "save them all" and the dramatic increase in "street dogs" with no socialization or experience being brought into busy homes with brand-new stimuli (sometimes including children).

The end of life for our dogs is traumatic for those of us who love them so deeply. Even when your dog has naturally aged and you've helped them weather their health concerns, it still breaks your heart to lose

your constant companion. Making that decision for a physically healthy dog is unbearable. If you have shared your life for any amount of time with a severely troubled dog who is hurting themselves, other dogs, or humans, you know of the deep pain in even considering ending such a dog's life and I am so very sorry if you, too, are in this club.

The cruel criticism online and elsewhere when we eventually make this impossible, very personal decision increases the heartache. If you love dogs, want the best for them, and end up encountering a deeply disturbed dog for whom nothing works, you may come to see behavioral euthanasia (BE) as a gift—releasing the dog from a life of misery, pain, confusion, and harm.

I am not talking about dogs with obedience problems we can fix, a dog who has become inconvenient, or a dog who growls once to warn nearby children that he is stressed by their behavior. I am talking about dogs with health or genetic issues so severe that lives have been put into danger. It

Reactive and aggressive dogs deserve our time, hard work, and patience, but sometimes those things aren't enough—the aggression might come from an unfixable physical cause, for example. Behavioral euthanasia might be the best choice for a truly troubled dog living a life filled with pain, fear, and confusion.

could be the lives of other animals or humans, or the dog could be so troubled that he drastically and repeatedly self-harms and none of the many techniques available, including medication, have been able to stop the behavior.

When a caring owner reaches this devastating decision, they have already thought about it deeply and many have consulted with countless professionals in the animal industry. This is *never* a decision that is taken lightly, I can assure you.

ZEMI'S STORY

The troubled dog I shared my life with for two years taught me my own limitations as a professional dog trainer and proved to me that we cannot save or help every dog, no matter how much we want to. My experience with Zemi broke my heart and gave me enormous empathy for all owners of reactive and aggressive dogs.

Warning Signs

Even though I advise my clients to meet and spend time with the parent dogs, when possible, I made a fateful decision to accept a "free" purebred German Shepherd puppy without personally meeting the parents. I did so based on my trust of a friend who knew the breeder. I had also shared my life with many German Shepherds, both my own and foster dogs. It is still my favorite dog breed.

I remember a small, wise voice in my head telling me to pass on the opportunity because of my own time constraints and because the breeder lived in another state, but then the breeder started sending me videos of the adorably plush puppies. The breeder told me the puppies' parents had "exceptional" temperaments, and the sire was of West German descent and loved people and other dogs. She sent me photos and videos of him, and he did look regal and relaxed. They had good structure, and the breeder was working on getting titles for them. The puppies obtained good scores on the many health tests available. I moved closer to a "yes."

I learned the hardest lessons from this beautiful girl, Zemi. Even at this young age you can see some fear in her eyes even though she had a wonderful puppyhood with me.

A few weeks later, the breeder confessed that this was—in her words—an "oops" litter. I hated hearing that, anyone breeding dogs knows how puppies are made (and how to avoid mistakes). I asked how it happened and what she considered the "oops" to be. She told me that the dam was "too young" at only 16 months to have been bred. She had no titles, nor an x-ray on her hips as she wasn't finished growing yet. Otherwise, I was assured, she was a terrific dog from top, working German Shepherd lines direct from Germany. Red flags waved before my eyes, but

Is It Hyperactivity or "Drive"?

Trainer Leslie McDevitt, MLA, CDBC, CPDT, gives the best explanation of the difference between arousal and drive: "'Drive' is not an official or technical term. It is a description that dog people have of a dog who wants to work and who enjoys his work. People see intent behaviors that are arousal behaviors that are hyperactive behaviors and say, 'that dog must be high-drive.' They are mistaking the intensity of those behaviors for 'drive.' Arousal behavior is a physiological response to excitement. The dog might be running in circles, jumping, or barking and that has nothing to do with drive."[11]

---

1   Annie Phenix, CPDT-KA, "We Chat with Dog Trainer Leslie McDevitt, Author of Groundbreaking
    'Control Unleashed,'" *Dogster*, August 18, 2015, https://www.dogster.com/lifestyle/
    we-chat-with-dog-trainer-leslie-mcdevitt-author-of-the-groundbreaking-control-unleashed.

the videos and what I knew of this breeder's other quality dogs (not German Shepherds) kept pulling me in.

I kept my eye on one male puppy who was the only puppy to notice the people filming. He often came over wagging his tail to say hello to the humans behind the camera. He showed a calm, curious temperament. I asked if I could purchase that puppy and the answer for a while was "yes"—until it became a "no." The breeder decided to keep him, and she offered me the runt of the litter for free.

I have nothing against runts—they can be adorably cute (Zemi was indeed cute with her short legs—like a miniature German Shepherd). Runts, however, are the result of getting less nutrition in the womb. Struggling for sustenance even before birth has a chance of wreaking havoc on internal systems. Being the biggest or the smallest in a litter influences personality. In Zemi's case, the main concern was resiliency. Zemi would prove to have none.

I had recently begun working with a local search and rescue team's dog that had become reactive to other dogs after being attacked twice off leash during an official search. I became very interested in the team, and the fact that Zemi's dam came from Schutzhund lines appealed to me. But I also learned that Zemi's mother had been born on a plane from Germany. This is an awful thing to do to both the mother dog and the new puppies—imagine the stress of giving birth in a loud transport plane! That's a terrific way to guarantee a lack of resiliency in all the puppies (and subsequent litters).

After I mentioned that I was looking for a working dog prospect, the breeder took to saying that if she were younger, she'd sure love to keep the runt as it was "driven" and "feisty" and would "surely make a good working dog." This is a huge, waving red flag to me, but I overlooked it. Even if the breeder was mistaking hyperactivity for a good working drive (as so many breeders, owners, and even some trainers do), I knew I had the tools to work with that less-than-desirable trait.

The breeder wanted to fly Zemi to me, but flying young, vulnerable, and impressionable puppies on airplanes is a terrible idea and potentially very traumatizing. Instead, I drove 1600 miles over two days to pick her up. I brought my Border Collie along and also a crate so I could keep them separated but close enough to get to know one another. Once we got home, my other dog, Echo, wanted nothing to do with her from the moment they met, unusual behavior on her part. Echo had helped me socialize puppies for years—she was a master at it and seemed to truly enjoy it. Echo not wanting to interact with Zemi was just one more major red flag.

I immediately enrolled Zemi in several puppy and socialization classes so she could be around many new, safe dogs and their humans. I made good headway on the 88-item checklist created by the Pet Professional Guild to help owners positively introduce puppies to the world, including visual and auditory elements, people of all ages, human sounds, different physical surfaces, physical handling of the puppy, meeting other animals, and more.

Zemi's initial reaction to life was wide-eyed and she attempted to back away from anything new. I assumed she was a little shy or in one of the fear periods normal to most puppies. It is not normal, however, for a puppy to remain fearful of everything new if they are properly introduced over time—unless there is a genetic or physical reason for this fear.

I worked diligently to positively build her confidence levels, and, on some days, she did seem slightly more confident. I began to try to get her interested in toys, hoping to use the desire for toys to train her as a prospective search and rescue (SAR) dog, but she never displayed play behavior. In the puppy classes, everything overwhelmed her. I took many breaks to allow her a moment to calm down. I could feel her rapidly beating heart as I held her in my lap. She refused all food when training anywhere but at home. Her eyes remained dilated through every class. I soon stopped taking her to classes as it was overwhelming and not productive to her learning about the world.

I continued her socialization at a much slower pace. Her behavior was screaming that she was terrified of life itself. I felt as though I was trying to do the impossible—create neuroplasticity and resiliency in a dog born with none. It was the beginning of my heartbreak for her.

Troubling Behavior

One pleasant summer day, I brought Zemi down to the barn to keep me company while I worked outside. We lived on a 40-acre, semi-secluded farm where she could safely run and explore. Play she did, at least that's how I interpreted it at the time. She wasn't doing anything of the sort, however. It was only that evening talking over the day with my husband that I realized that Zemi never stopped moving for the entire four hours. She spent the whole time chasing real and imaginary butterflies and flying insects.

This had been summertime and there were bugs in the air, but her hunting went on season after season, even in winter. That day at the barn was her first display of OCD behavior. We were never able to stop this behavior, even with medications. If Zemi was outside, she'd begin her immediate and unstoppable hunt for imaginary bugs. It was not only painful to observe, her risky and repetitive behavior also caused three severe insect bites to her mouth. I was getting to know the ER veterinarians quite well.

The next behavior she offered caused me to immediately contact the breeder. At 15 weeks old, Zemi tried to attack my feeble senior Sheltie mix, Lacy. I let Zemi out in the fenced backyard in the middle of the night so she could go to the bathroom. I didn't realize that my husband had let Lacy out before he came to bed (she often preferred to sleep outside on nice nights). Both dogs came to me as I put my hand on the backdoor to allow Lacy to go into the main part of the house. As Lacy slowly walked through the open door on her creaky, arthritic legs, Zemi attempted to attack her. All my years of shelter work and dog training gave me quick responses. Without wasting a second, I grabbed Zemi by her collar and held her in mid-air (she was still a small puppy). She continued to snarl, growl, and air snap. She tried to redirect on me, and it was the first time it occurred to me that my own dog may just be the very first dog to bite me.

It was only then that I pulled out Zemi's American Kennel Club papers and began deeply researching her lineage. What I found crushed me. Her mother actually came from what appeared to be a German Shepherd puppy mill. I found many negative reviews online from anguished dog owners referencing aggression and health problems. Her father's lineage didn't tell me much except that he came from show lines.

The breeder surmised in an email that perhaps my puppy "didn't get enough of her father's genes" and was acting more like her mother—a very expensive dog she later gave away for free (only to have her shortly returned as being "unmanageable"). A year later, this supposedly "calm" perfect father attacked his own son (the dog I originally wanted) in the breeder's home while she was at work. The poor young dog needed surgery to repair serious damage caused by his father. Zemi's genes on both sides were stacked against her.

Seeking Solutions

After finally processing all the red flags, I asked the breeder to take Zemi back. To her credit, she said she would, and she wanted the dog flown back to her. Then I remembered that Zemi's mother (who had attacked another female dog in the past) was still in the home, and that the breeder used shock collars on her dogs. Because of all of my hands-on experience and research into current scientific studies, I knew that using a shock collar would push Zemi's unstable, fearful mental state even more off-kilter.

I sought solutions I might have overlooked from other trusted trainers around the country, enrolled her in my reactive dog class (which she bombed), spent 2–3 hours every day exercising her mind (walks were a no-go because of her reactionary OCD behaviors), took her to three veterinarians and a veterinary behavior expert, tried a wide variety of anti-anxiety medications, ruled out any other known medical issues (such as hypothyroidism), and spent months working on counterconditioning and desensitizing.

I finally decided to teach her nose work as a way to perhaps give her a job she could handle and some much-needed focus. She proved to be an incredible nose work dog. She even managed to pass an Odor

Genetics and Fearfulness

More than one study has demonstrated the importance of genes as they relate to fearfulness in dogs. The research shows that if even one parent shows a predilection for fearful behavior, the puppy will receive "fearful" genes. The puppies in one study remained fearful even if the other parent presented as a "normal" dog, and even if the fearful puppies were fostered and raised by a stable mother dog. Neither medication nor training resolved the fear in these puppies.[1]

1   University of Helsinki, "Fearful Great Danes Provide New Insights to Genetic Causes of Fear," *ScienceDaily*, May 29, 2020, https://www.sciencedaily.com/releases/2020/05/200529150627.htm.

Recognition Test (even though she did growl and lunge at the judge's table). I foolishly allowed myself to have some small hope for her.

I had her tested by three local SAR teams as a candidate because she was so gifted at finding odors and hidden people, but she failed to make the team each time. She always found what I asked her to find (despite the real or imaginary bugs beckoning to her) but an SAR dog who tries to bite the person she successfully finds just won't work. She was not a police dog candidate since she had no impulse control and violently lunged and snarled when meeting anyone new. She was too unpredictable and unstable to be a working dog of any kind. All the stimuli of life overwhelmed her.

Zemi's options for what Dr. Karen Overall termed a "negotiated settlement" were quickly narrowing. Even though I thought it would be impossible to rehome such an aggressive and troubled animal, I tried anyway, hoping I might find that needle-in-a-haystack home for her (and would offer ongoing, free training for life). I found a hardworking, single, 50-year-old man who wanted a companion dog to come home to after his long days at work. He had good dog experience. He wasn't interested in taking her to public places, he had no other dogs and he rarely had visitors.

We began a three-month trial period after Zemi accepted him at his first visit (she was still quite young and somewhat receptive to new people). He would take Zemi for weekend visits and, like my husband and me, he grew attached to our troubled girl. I shared with him Zemi's long list of issues and he still wanted to try. He took her on walks before 5 a.m. so she would not run into another person or dog. He loved her.

He did call to share his concern that she would not come in from the backyard, ignoring him to chase—for hours—imaginary bugs. Then he introduced Zemi (with my guidance) to his 80-year-old, dog-loving mother (who did want to visit her son now and again at his home). Zemi went into assault mode, circling her as she sat passively on the couch. It was the end to any negotiated settlement in that home.

I let my imagination drift to far-away corners in my desire to be able to keep Zemi alive and safe. I briefly considered moving to a mountaintop away from civilization where she and I would live together alone for the next decade. That was a poor settlement all the way through—I would miss my husband and the stable of dogs who worked alongside me every day helping other reactive dogs. I would miss my clients.

I also knew that nothing had been able to stop Zemi's OCD behaviors and it occurred to me that giving up my life, my loves, and my income to move to a mountaintop to live with a dog I could never stop from being frantic and unsettled was veering hard in the direction of crazy human behavior. I recognized that I had entered the bargaining stage of grief. The frank words of a veterinary behavior specialist I knew began to truly sink in and make sense: **"You might get to the point of understanding that this is not a failure of training; it is an acceptance of reality."**

I took her to another local veterinarian in my hometown, hoping she might have some answer I had overlooked. She was the only local veterinarian who had studied behavior after graduating from veterinary school. She read the lengthy report from the veterinary behavior specialist, as well as my novel of an email outlining everything I had tried to help Zemi. She wanted to try one more thing, putting Zemi on probiotics to see if any digestive issues contributed to her OCD behavior. Zemi did have on-again, off-again stomach issues, so I agreed to bring her in for the preliminary exam.

I muzzled Zemi for everyone's safety. I asked the vet to please never turn her body directly toward Zemi and to not look her in the eye. The vet did as I asked, but it didn't matter. I held onto the leash and collar while the doctor tried to examine Zemi's stomach with her hands. Zemi stiffened, leaned her head straight up and back into the vet, letting out a low, long, warning growl that left the hair on my neck standing on end. I saw the "death threat" stare in Zemi's eyes that I never want to see from any dog. She then attempted to bite my vet on the face through the muzzle. I pulled her away and took her across the room. Zemi laid down with her back to the vet.

This behavior was the last straw, even considering all the other countless last straws. The veterinarian agreed that Zemi was a dangerous dog and that I had tried everything possible to help her. She also said she never used euthanasia for behavior concerns—Zemi would be her first. We did still try the probiotics to see if it made any difference, but it didn't.

Saying Goodbye

My husband was out of town and asked to be present for the final appointment, so we scheduled it for two weeks later. I knew the last day of her life—it was marked on a calendar. It meant two weeks of sitting with her, weeping endless tears, and watching her run around in frantic circles trying to catch bugs that never existed. I would catch her, put her leash on her, and try to sit with her in the backyard. I begged her for a connection. I wanted her to be able to stop the noise inside of her muddled mind and be able to be present with me.

It was impossible for her. She'd whimper and pace at the end of the leash. I think so much was happening inside her brain that she needed the bug chasing behavior to shut out all the other stimuli, like some children will block stimuli by rocking back and forth. I took her inside and she'd collapse in a heap, as though just going outside in her own backyard was too much for her (even while taking high doses of anti-anxiety medication).

Neuroscientist Jaak Panksepp has noted seven emotional systems that all mammals have inside their brains: seeking, fear, rage, lust, care, panic and grief, and play. Observing Zemi's bizarre behavior, it felt on many days as though her brain was stuck on seeking (unstoppable, invisible bug chasing), fear (dilated pupils, rapid heartbeat, fur raised), panic (when she was a puppy she bolted from new stimuli, sometimes stimuli I couldn't detect in the environment), and rage (aggressive barking, growling, and lunging at other dogs and people). Those emotions seemed to take up so much brain space that she didn't have any room left to enjoy normal play or care.

Zemi was never a dog who liked to play. When I'd encourage her to run and play with my other dogs, she would become stiff, give the other dogs hard stares, and chase them down one by one. Eventually she would begin to drool and shake. I stopped taking her on our group runs—they clearly overwhelmed her, just like everything else in life seemed to. There is productive exercise and there is unproductive exercise—based on her reactions, life itself was an unproductive exercise and a trial for her.

I hugged my other dogs and cried with them, too, as their lives had been upended for nearly two years in my quest to heal an unhealable dog. I nearly backed out. I nearly packed for that imaginary cabin on the top of a mountain. I wrote to the veterinary behavior expert just to ask for the hundredth time if there was anything else we could try to help her. There wasn't. It was time. There would be no win-win negotiated settlement for Zemi.

We gave Zemi a very strong tranquilizer on the day of the appointment. We waited for the vet to come out to the car behind her office—it would be less stressful for Zemi than going inside and facing strangers. I was inconsolable. I lived my life to save dogs and I owed them so very much, and here I was, making the choice to end her life. The vet came out to give her another sedative shot since the first strong tranquilizer had had no effect on her. Zemi tried to attack the vet. My husband and I had to struggle to muzzle her. Even so, I was still telling myself I could call off what felt like an execution. As I was in my final pleading deliberations with myself, a stranger walked by and asked if I was okay—I was hysterical in my grief. Zemi roused herself and tried to attack him. Luckily her muzzle was still on.

I asked my husband to go get the vet. I had to end this dog's anguish and suffering.

And that's what we did.

My veterinarian showed great emotional fortitude that day as she had to step past my weeping to inject a dog who was trying to attack her through most of the process. She hugged me hard afterward. It was the hug of compassion and understanding. It was an embrace from someone else who had dedicated her life to saving animals. She sat in witness to my misery. She didn't have any tissues on hand, but that didn't matter—there would not have been enough tissues in the world.

I've never completely gotten over it. I have not had a German Shepherd since her death. I spend my days with my three remaining dogs. The dogs, my husband, and I slowly learned to relax again. I carry on with a hole in my heart and furiously work to help other dogs and their owners avoid this misery.

I started a German Shepherd puppy class that fall in Zemi's honor, in the hopes of reaching puppies at risk before behavior problems show up. I am more fully present for the few clients who face this agonizing decision for their beloved but deeply troubled dogs. I hold their hands and I cry with them, providing the empathy, compassion, and understanding I know they so desperately need.

I wrote this chapter with tears streaming down my face as an appeal to anyone who breeds dogs—I beg you to always breed for good health and solid temperament first and good looks second. Bad breeding destroys lives, both human and canine. Genes matter. What happens to puppies in utero matters. The treatment, well-being, and health of the mother dog matters. The temperament, treatment, and health of the father dog matters. How and where the puppy is socialized before it reaches 12 weeks of age matters.

And sometimes an owner can do everything right by their puppy and still end up with a distressed and dangerous dog.

I know I did.

Help for Owners

For far too long, both trainers and owners have felt alone in reaching the conclusion that their loved dog is dangerous to others or to itself. Thankfully many in the dog training community are now speaking up and sharing their own stories and (with permission) those of their clients. Books and podcasts are also available that address this tough issue. Know that you don't have to face this difficult discussion alone—see page 236 for a list of behavioral euthanasia and grief resources.

Ask an Expert

Trainer and Behavior Consultant Lee Desmarais Shares Her Personal Experience with a Dog We Couldn't Help

This interview has been included in its entirety.

Trainer and Behavior Expert Lee Desmarais shown in a calm moment with a troubled young dog she adopted from a client. This dog was beyond anyone's help as she had a brain tumor that severely affected her behavior. Neither trainers nor veterinarians can "fix" a dog that is dangerous to live with because of a massive health problem.

▶ **You have years of experience working with all kinds of behavior issues in all breeds of dogs. And in that work, you have had to counsel clients through the heart-wrenching decision of behavioral euthanasia. And then it happened to one of your own dogs. Tell us how you met this dog as a puppy and the behavior you observed in the young dog.**

I was originally hired by Winnie's guardians for puppy training when she was four months old. She was an eager little learner and a joy to work with, but from the very first session her owners spoke about her "puppy biting." I never saw it personally during our 10 training sessions, but I did see, as I often do, the evidence of it—bloody scratches on her owner's forearms. We covered all the common responses to that behavior: make sure she is getting enough sleep, make sure she has enough oral stimulation and intellectual opportunity, keep her arousal levels down, no over-stimulating play or touching, keep exercise reasonable to prevent any physical discomfort. You name it—we covered it.

For a while the interventions in place seemed to reduce the biting to some extent. We taught her to go to "place," building distance and duration. We taught her a solid "leave it" to distract her from the biting. Both skills were helpful to redirect her (sometimes) but by the time that Winnie was six months old her owners were still at a loss, and, to complicate matters, she had developed separation anxiety. They were not only unable to crate her, but they also couldn't leave her alone at all. Someone always needed to be home with her. (Sadly, this is a common theme with many COVID puppies whose owners were once home all the time.)

Winnie's owners felt that they had followed all the recommendations and strategies and had done their homework consistently day in and day out (and they did, they were very committed students), but that she just wasn't a good fit for their home. I offered to adopt her if they ever wanted to give her up. One Sunday afternoon, I got a frantic text message from Winnie's owner that she had attacked his wife. Winnie had been laying quietly on the couch beside her and suddenly jumped up and started biting her forearm. They were unable to redirect her verbally; they had hit a wall. The very next day, I picked Winnie up and brought her home.

▶ **Sometimes owners tell trainers that their dog "bit them out of the blue." That is what happened with this young dog. There were no warning signs or stressors. Can you describe the first few times she bit you?**

First, I would like to say that in all the years I have been working with behavior cases, I have never been bitten by a dog, much less one of my own. I clearly recall the first time I experienced Winnie's behavior—my partner and I were sitting on the couch one evening watching TV and Winnie was laying between us chewing on a chew toy. She suddenly leapt up and came toward me air snapping. I jumped up to put distance between us and she continued to come at me, and then just as suddenly as it started, it stopped. It lasted about 30 seconds. Over the next several weeks I slept on the couch with her at night because she couldn't be alone. Each day I worked with her on her separation anxiety and spent a great deal of time observing everything Winnie did, collecting data. Her eruptions continued to increase and were happening randomly throughout the day. I had never seen this behavior before. She would go offline; she was just simply not reachable during these episodes. Even though she was looking right at me, she wasn't seeing me at all.

▶ **Can you briefly share with us some of the many things you did to help Winnie, including working with a veterinarian?**

I have a very large, enclosed playground for my dogs. It has a natural landscape with a sensory garden, physical structures, a pool, and lots of things to explore and engage with. We spent hours every day just being together in that space the first couple of weeks, but I quickly saw that it was too over-stimulating for her to be in that space and the attacks were starting to happen there, too. We took daily decompression walks on a long line: Winnie led, and I followed. She was curious, fearless, and up for anything. But unless she was sleeping for the night, she had a very difficult time settling and she would quite easily become over-aroused, so I spent a lot of time using Dr. Karen Overall's Relaxation Protocol and doing scent work. But it didn't help.

I was completely beside myself. The attacks from her were increasing, becoming more and more violent, and lasting for longer periods of time. My vet considered that it might be an absence seizure disorder given the nature of onset and cessation, so, taking the most conservative approach, Winnie was put on a seizure medication. It made no difference, so it was discontinued after a few days. I started doing some research on rage syndrome. I had read about it briefly years before. I had never seen it personally, and knew it was rare, usually caused by a brain disorder such as a tumor. I convinced myself that was probably not what I was seeing; but nevertheless, I wound up going down a rabbit hole. Over a period of days, the more I read, the more I was convinced that was indeed what Winnie's issue was. I then reached out to a highly qualified veterinary behaviorist; she concurred that it indeed sounded like rage syndrome and said that only an MRI could tell us what was going on in Winnie's head.

▶ **Please explain the depth of injury this dog was capable of.**

All in all, Winnie made contact with my body approximately 18 times, breaking skin with puncture wounds and scratches, not including countless attempts and lots of air snapping. As fast as I could block her, she came at my face, abdomen, and extremities. Often leaving the room and closing the gate was the only option to remain unharmed. These episodes not only grew more frequent, but became longer in duration, and being alone with her had become a safety issue. The last time she went into a rage, we were alone, and she had me pinned in my dogs' playground against the chain-link fence. I had nowhere to go, and the only protection was a plastic lawn chair, which I used to stave her off, but even then, she was able to bite my ankles and ripped the chair right out of my hands. So, what was she capable of? I shudder to think.

▶ **The final, most difficult decision you made for her was behavioral euthanasia. It did turn out that she suffered from a debilitating medical condition that was the root cause of her aggressive behavior. What was that condition and how was it discovered?**

An MRI revealed a tumor in her brain stem and a lesion in her limbic system.

▶ **This case illustrates that even the most proficient behavior expert cannot fix a brain issue. Perhaps her story can help heal the pain of this choice for some dog owners, as it is clear we could not use behavior modification or medicine to stop Winnie's aggression. What words of encouragement can you share with anyone considering the painful choice of behavioral euthanasia?**

People struggle with euthanasia in general, even when there are clear-cut reasons for the decision. But it is much more difficult when it's behavioral because behavior isn't as concrete and doesn't seem to be a "real" enough reason. People feel like "oh, there must be something else I can try that just hasn't been tried yet." But sometimes there isn't. Sometimes it's bad genetics. Sometimes it's too many bad experiences. Sometimes it's a loose wire that is never going to connect. Sometimes it's a brain tumor. And

Winnie had a good puppy life, but a brain tumor changed her behavior. She began to exhibit aggression, including biting people. Sometimes there are such severe physical, emotional, or genetic issues that the kindest thing we can do as owners is the hardest—to gently let them go.

sometimes it is the kindest most humane gift we can give that animal—freedom from being a prisoner in their own head. Whatever the case is, no matter what the reason, it is always a heavy decision.

I often tell clients who struggle with this decision the words from an excellent book called *Facing Farewell* by Julie Reck, DVM: "All creatures have a day of birth and a day of death. Humans, in contrast to animals, know they will die someday. Humans uniquely perceive a straight timeline between birth and death and strive for the timeline to be as long as possible. Like us, animals are given a day of birth and a day of death, but unlike us their lifespan is not linear, but circular. Initially they are young, then they mature, and with time they age. Pets do not fear any stages of life and receive the onset of a gray muzzle and stiff joints with grace."

A Manifesto for New Words

I share the following manifesto (with permission) from trainer and behavior expert Dr. Laura Donaldson (whose program Slow Thinking is Lifesaving for Dogs is discussed in detail in chapter 4 starting on page 59):

There are paradigm shifts at work in the field of dog training these days—and one way to hasten this transformation is by changing the words humans use to describe their relationship with dogs and the training process more generally. I wanted to identify some key verbal shifts reflecting this new understanding. Changed words signify a reality that more closely emulates the partnership that I envision for the dog-human bond. So here are my new resolutions for dog training:

INSTEAD OF "attention-seeking" (as in attention-seeking behaviors), there is "connection-seeking."

INSTEAD OF "nuisance" behaviors (as in counter surfing, destroying the flower beds, or eviscerating couch pillows), there are innate canine behaviors used to seek relief, such as chewing, scavenging, and digging.

INSTEAD OF "just a dog," there is "what a dog," recognizing that dogs are sentient beings with a rich emotional life and cognitive abilities on a par with humans.

INSTEAD OF "my dog needs to do what I say because I say it," we substitute "my dog should have a say in what is happening to them." This is otherwise known as agency.

The language we use to describe canine behavior is important. Is your dog "lazy" or is it more that you are not communicating effectively with your dog?

INSTEAD OF micromanaging a dog's every move as the remedy for "reactive" behavior, we give dogs the time and space to process environmental information safely and in their own way.

INSTEAD OF dog behavior training being defined as "stopping unwanted behaviors" (a quote from a dog training business's website), dog training becomes an exercise in mutual learning and INTERSPECIES COOPERATION.

Resources for Owners

Navigating and evaluating the many resources available for dog owners is overwhelming at the best of times, but when you're trying to make life better for a troubled dog, it can be downright nerve-wracking. The following sections provide concrete starting points you can use to help make your life easier. First, you'll find a listing of quality training academies and certification programs that do not use force, harm, or fear. Then, I've listed a few resources you can use to make informed, educated decisions about your dog's nutrition. Finally, I've provided a listing of resources to help with the difficult discussion of behavioral euthanasia. Many of these resources are also applicable to grief in general. I hope the following sections make life better for you and your beloved furry friend.

TRAINING ACADEMY AND CERTIFICATION GUIDE

I have compiled a list of organizations and individuals who—to the best of my knowledge—do not promote or use force, fear, or harm in their courses. These are organizations and individuals with years of experience at all levels of working with dogs in need of help. This list is not exhaustive, but it is a great starting point. Always be careful about who you hire and continue to ask good questions of anyone who might be handling your dog (see The Questions to Ask and the Answers to Look For on page 215).

Recommended Training Academies and Certifications in the United States

The Academy for Dog Trainers: *www.academyfordogtrainers.com*

The American Veterinary Society of Animal Behavior: *www.avsab.org*

Animal Behavior Society: *www.animalbehaviorsociety.org/web/index.php*

BAT Certified Trainers: *www.grishastewart.com*

Catch Canine Trainer's Academy: *www.catchdogtrainers.com*

Companion Animal Sciences Institute: *www.casinstitute.com*

Control Unleashed Instructors: *www.controlunleashed.net*

Cooperative Paws Service Dog Education: *www.cooperativepaws.com*

Dr. Laura Donaldson's Slow Thinking is Lifesaving for Dogs course: https://www.cleanrun.com/product/slow_thinking_is_lifesaving_for_dogs_why_it_s_important_how_to_teach_it_on_demand_webinar/index.cfm?ParentCat=1300

Fear Free®: *www.fearfreepets.com*

INTODogs Pet Bereavement Support Facebook page: *https://www.facebook.com/INTODogs-Pet-Bereavement-Support-265974498591630*

Karen Pryor Academy for Animal Training & Behavior: *www.karenpryoracademy.com*

Peaceable Paws™ Dog and Puppy Training: *www.peaceablepaws.com*

The Pet Professional Guild: *www.petprofessionalguild.com*

Malena DeMartini School for Separation Anxiety: *www.malenademartini.com*

Northwest School for Canine Studies: *www.northwestschoolofcaninestudies.com*

Pet Industry Advocacy International: *www.petadvocacy.info*

Separation Anxiety Dog: *www.separationanxietydog.com/dog-pros*

Smart Dog University: www.smartdoguniversity.com

Suzanne Clothier Relationship Centered Training: www.suzanneclothier.com

Low Stress Handling® University: https://university.lowstresshandling.com/#/public-dashboard

Victoria Stillwell Academy for Dog Training & Behavior: www.vsdogtrainingacademy.com

Kim Brophey's L.E.G.S.® Applied Ethology Family Dog Mediation® Professional Course: https://kimbropheylegscourses.thinkific.com/courses/legs-applied-ethology-family-dog-mediation-professional-course

Recommended Training Academies and Certifications in Canada

Alberta Force Free Alliance: www.albertaforcefreealliance.com

BC SPCA (British Columbia Society for the Prevention of Cruelty to Animals) Speaking for Animals: www.spca.bc.ca

Cochrane & Area Humane Society: www.cochranehumane.com

Bravo Dog Training & Behavior: www.bravodog.ca

Recommended Training Academies and Certifications in the United Kingdom/Ireland

ACE (Animal Centred Education): www.tilleyfarm.org.uk

Association of Pet Dog Trainers (APDT) UK: https://apdt.co.uk

The Association of INTODogs: www.intodogs.net

CAPBT (COAPE Association of Applied Pet Behaviourists & Trainers): www.capbt.org

Domesticated Manners: www.domesticatedmanners.com/about

IMDT (Institute of Modern Dog Trainers) UK: www.imdt.uk.com

International Canine Behaviourists: https://icbglobal.net/

The Pet Professional Guild British Isles: www.ppgbi.com

Living with Bereavement: www.livingwithpetbereavement.com

UK Dog Behaviour & Training Charter: www.dogcharter.uk

The UK College of Scent Dogs: www.ukcsd.com

Victoria Stilwell Academy for Dog Training & Behavior: www.vsdogtrainingacademy.com

Without Worry Canine Education: www.withoutworrycanineeducation.co.uk

The Association of Pet Behaviour Counsellors: https://www.apbc.org.uk/?fbclid=IwAR2Iwqylmij7AlSLJ4McDKC42d6c3hpy3VDXJG4ybhxsQtr2oMwzBhi4NDQ

Recommended Training Academies and Online Certifications in Other Countries

IMDT (Institute of Modern Dog Trainers) Australia: www.imdt.com.au

NUTRITION RESOURCES

The following sections include a few useful resources you can use to begin your own research into nutrition options for your dog. When researching this topic, it is important to ask a few vital questions, including:

♦ Who is paying for the nutrition research and studies cited?

♦ Are the studies peer reviewed?

♦ Who has something to gain from the information being shared?

♦ What do "health nutritionist" certifications actually require of certificate holders?

♦ What are the requirements to be a "canine health" or "nutrition" coach?

♦ What "natural claims" are backed by quality science?

Nutritionists, Veterinarians, and Veterinary Schools

American College of Veterinary Experts: *https://acvn.org/*

Clovis and Company: *https://www.clovisandcompany.com/professionals*

Cornell University College of Veterinary Medicine: *www.vet.cornell.edu/hospitals/services/nutrition*

Cummings School of Veterinary Medicine at Tufts University: *https://vetnutrition.tufts.edu/*

Darwin's Natural Pet Products: *www.darwinspet.com*

Dogs First: *https://dogsfirst.ie/*

Dog Food Advisor®: *www.dogfoodadvisor.com*

Dr Judy Morgan: *www.drjudymorgan.com/*

Monica Segal: *www.monicasegal.com*

NC State Veterinary Hospital: *www.cvm.ncsu.edu/nc-state-vet-hospital/small-animal/nutrition*

North American Veterinary Community (NAVC Pet Nutrition Coach Certification): *https://navc.com/Certifications/*

Susan Thixton's Truth about Pet Food: *www.truthaboutpetfood.com*

The Canine Nutritionist: *www.caninenutritionist.co.uk*

Veterinary Medical Center of Central New York: *www.vmccny.com/clinical-nutrition*

Veterinary Nutritional Consultations, Inc.: *www.vetnutrition.com*

WellHaven® Pet Health: *www.wellhavenpethealthmk.com/nutritional-counseling*

Books and Magazines

Linda P. Case, *Feeding Smart with the Science Dog* (Independently published 2022)

Linda P. Case, *Dog Food Logic: Making Smart Decisions for Your Dog in an Age of Too Many Choices* (Dogwise Publishing 2014)

The Woof Brothers, *Dog Nutrition & Cookbook: The Simple Guide to Keeping Your Dog Happy and Healthy* (Admore Publishing 2019)

Scott Shanahan, *Easy Dog Food Recipes: 60 Healthy Dishes to Feed Your Pet Safely* (Rockridge Press 2020)

Dr. Connor Brady, *Feeding Dogs: The Science Behind the Dry Versus Raw Debate* (Farrow Road Publishing 2022)

Lew Olson, *Raw and Natural Nutrition for Dogs, Revised Edition: The Definitive Guide to Homemade Meals* (North Atlantic Books 2015)

Rodney Habib and Karen Shaw Becker, *The Forever Dog: Surprising New Science to Help Your Canine Companion Live Younger, Healthier, and Longer* (Harper Wave 2021)

Amy Marshall, *Why You NEED to Feed Your Dog a Raw Food Diet: A Complete Introduction for Beginners* (CreateSpace Independent Publishing Platform 2018)

Judy Morgan DVM and Hue Grant, *Yin and Yang Nutrition for Dogs: Maximizing Health with Whole Foods, Not Drugs* (Thirty Six Paws Press 2017)

Animal Wellness magazine: *https://animalwellnessmagazine.com/category/dogs/dog-nutrition*

Dogs Naturally magazine: *www.dogsnaturallymagazine.com*

Whole Dog Journal: *www.whole-dog-journal.com*

BEHAVIORAL EUTHANASIA AND GRIEF RESOURCES

No matter the cause for your grief, know that you are not alone. I hope you will reach out and use some of these incredible resources if you are grieving a loss or are facing behavioral euthanasia. If you do reach out to an industry professional and they begin by shaming you, move on, and find someone with more real-world experience. Do not allow anyone to shame you during this very difficult time.

Support Groups and Counseling Resources

INTODogs Pet Bereavement Support Facebook group: *https://www.facebook.com/INTODogs-Pet-Bereavement-Support-265974498591630*

Living with Pet Bereavement website: *https://livingwithpetbereavement.com/*

The Ohio State University Veterinary Medical Center Behavioral Euthanasia fact sheet: *https://vet.osu.edu/vmc/sites/default/files/import/files/documents/pdf/vmc/Behavioral%20Euthanasia%20fact%20sheet.pdf*

The University of Tennessee Knoxville Veterinary Social Work program offers services from veterinary social workers who can help you process your grief: *https://vetsocialwork.utk.edu/*

Colorado State University Support and Pet Loss Resources: *www.vetmedbiosci.colostate.edu/argus/pet-loss-support/*

LSU School of Veterinary Medicine Best Friend Gone Project: *www.lsu.edu/vetmed/veterinary_hospital/services/counseling_services.php*

VetVine® Virtual Pet Loss Support Services offers a safe online space to talk about pet loss in sessions led by compassionate facilitators: *www.vetvine.com/article/657/vetvine-virtual-pet-loss-support-services*

Losing Lulu Facebook group offers a well-moderated space and first-class support for owners who have made the decision to euthanize a pet for behavioral reasons. If you've ever felt alone in this painful decision, this compassionate group will prove to you that you are not alone: *www.facebook.com/groups/losinglulu*

Association for Pet Loss Bereavement: *www.aplb.org*

Podcasts and Webinars

An in-depth and personal discussion between me and podcaster Kajsa Van Overbeek on her Ruff Around the Edges podcast talking about my experiences with Zemi and all we did to try to help her: *https://kajsavanoverbeek.com/ 014-ruff-around-the-edges-with-annie-phenix/ ?fbclid=IwAR12Rrn68TvLtpwfTVL5ZDekp3xm ZSI4KJkPTn6Bc2xY0qH1kFmvgrGEWhw*

Drinking from the Toilet podcast's *#125: Behavioral Euthanasia with Dr. Chris Pachel* episode features a discussion of behavioral euthanasia between trainer Hannah Branigan and veterinary behaviorist Dr. Chris Pachel: *https://hannahbranigan.dog/podcast/125/*

Veterinary behaviorist Dr. Chris Pachel offers a webinar, *Navigating Difficult Conversations: When Euthanasia for Behavior Is a Consideration* for $29.95: *https://aggressivedog.thinkific.com/ courses/navigatingdifficultconversations?fbclid= IwAR1TOldWjsTTGL3f5nAfYau7DZL5 zwYptD1BeiSbyUAl6aome_4RxyqyUwQ*

Books on Grieving the Loss of Pets

Julie Reck, DVM, *Facing Farewell: Making the Decision to Euthanize Your Pet* (Dogwise Publishing, 2012)

Patricia McConnell, *The Education of Will: Healing a Dog, Facing My Fears, Reclaiming My Life* (Atria Books 2018)

Jeannie Wycherley, *Losing My Best Friend: Thoughtful Support for Those Affected by Dog Bereavement or Pet Loss* (Bark at the Moon Books, 2018)

Ken Dolan-Del Vecchio and Nancy Saxton-Lopez, *The Pet Loss Companion* (CreateSpace Independent Publishing Platform 2013)

Gary Kowalski, *Goodbye, Friend: Healing Wisdom for Anyone Who Has Ever Lost a Pet* (New World Library 2012)

Lucy Hone, *Resilient Grieving: Finding Strength and Embracing Life After a Loss that Changes Everything* (The Experiment 2017)

Jenny Smedley, *Dogs and Cats Have Souls Too: Incredible True Stories of Pets Who Heal, Protect and Communicate* (Hay House UK 2018)

Jon Katz, *Going Home: Finding Peace When Pets Die* (Random House Publishing Group 2012)

Garth Stein, *The Art of Racing in the Rain: A Novel* (Harper Collins 2008)

Adrian Raeside, *The Rainbow Bridge: A Visit to Pet Paradise* (Harbour Publishing 2020)—for children

Cynthia Ryland, *Dog Heaven* (Blue Sky Press 1995)—for children

Index

N

nails, 70

negative punishment, 101

negative reinforcement, 101

negotiated settlement, 109, 211, 226

neuroimaging of dog brains, 60, 65–66, 66n3, 67–68

noise phobia, 93, 110, 115–17

nose work and sniffing, 25, 95, 106, 180

nutrition, 197–99, 235–36

O

obesity, 24–25

obsessive compulsive disorder (OCD), 24–25, 86–88, 96, 224, 226

off-leash recalls, 99, 145–50, 179

O'Heare, James, 40

O'Moore, Denise, 136–37, 251

Overall, Karen, 109, 115, 174, 211, 226, 230

owners, as part of care team, 42–45

P

pack theory, 211

Panksepp, Jaak, 203–4, 227

Patel, Chirag, 163

paw pads, 70

Pete (dog), 195

Pezz "Mr. McBitey" (dog), 71, 200–201

pica, 82, 86

Pike, Amy, 26–27, 246

pinch and prong collars, 17, 173

play for fear reduction, 194–96, 224, 227

play pens. See crates and crate training

positive punishment, 101

positive reinforcement, 101, 211

predatory aggression, 38–39

predictor (communication) cues, 54

Premack Principle, 107–9

professional trainers. See trainers and training

prong and pinch collars, 17, 173

PTSD, 68, 79, 133–34

pulling on leash, 105–9

puppy mills, 13, 14, 204, 225

puppy raising, 118–37

    about, 118

    adolescence, 130–33, 136–37

    maternal aggression and, 38

    prenatal and neonatal care, 12–14, 118–24, 204, 222–23

    rescue puppies, 133–35

    socialization and training early, 16–17, 124, 125–29, 223–24

R

Radar (dog), 196

raising puppies. See puppy raising

reactivity. See also fear behavior

    aggression vs., 21, 40–41, 67

    methods for reducing, 56–58 (See also Animal Centered Education; Dog L.E.G.S.; management)

    sight or sound reactivity, 83

    trends, 21

recall training, 99, 145–50, 179

Reck, Julie, 231

relaxation and calming behaviors, 63–64, 153–55, 192

rescue puppies and dogs. See also day-to-day living with dogs

    expectations and, 175, 176

    taking it slow with, 133–35

resiliency

    autonomy, 129, 152, 192

    bonding and, 204

Photo Credits

Unless otherwise noted, all photography by Annie Phenix.

Shawna Henrie/Bleudog Fotography: back cover, 99, 100, 102, 112, 115, 120 right, 122, 134, 135 left, 141, 143, 147, 148, 150, 152, 156, 161, 162 left, 163, 165

Tica Clarke Photography: 8 top left, 34

Sarah Fisher: 69 left, 72 left

The following photography was provided by the Experts: 20, 126 right, 246: Helen St. Pierre; 24, 108, 136, 177 right, 251: Denise O'Moore/Might Dog Graphics; 26, 246: Dr. Amy Pike; 32, 180 right, 200, 201, 250: Dale McLelland; 47, 48, 249: Dr. Marty Becker; 50, 52, 55, 167, 168, 249: Mikkel Becker; 60 top, 65, 68, 247: Dr. Laura Donaldson; 77, 205, 247: Kim Brophey; 94 right, 140 bottom, 149 right, 192, 218, 252: Lisa Hird; 113, 248: Malena DeMartini-Price; 123, 251: Jane Ardern; 128, 211, 248: Christine Young; 182, 252: Andrew Hale; 197 top, 212, 253: Naomi Bridger-Pescott (Mark Bridger-Pescott); 208, 253: Shay Kelly; 229, 231, 250: Lee Desmarais

The following photography is from Shutterstock.com: 1: Grisha Bruev; 5: Erik Lam; 7: Roman Chazov; 8, 110, 117 right: smrm1977; 9: Annabell Gsoedl; 11: Patrick H; 12: Avphoto.av; 13, 33: Ezzolo; 14: Anna Hoychuk; 15, 202: Ksenia Raykova; 16: MDV Edwards; 17: Canon Boy; 18: Lisa Eastman; 19: Pixel-Shot; 21: Anake Seenadee; 22: Bachkova Natalia; 23: Aleksey Boyko; 25 top, 125 top, 237: Jaromir Chalabala; 25 bottom, 81 top, 121 right: Jus_Ol; 27: Tetiana Yablokova; 29: Sue McDonald; 31: Bonsales; 35 top: Olimpik; 35 bottom, 57: Ryan Brix; 36: Susanna Photo; 38: olgagorovenko; 39: Fercast; 40: Semiglass; 41 top: Scott E Read; 43: Bianca Grueneberg; 44 top: Chester-Alive; 45: Pressmaster; 49: SeventyFour; 51: ImYanis; 53: Iris_forest; 54: Konstantin Zaykov; 58 top: phonecat; 58 bottom, 204 bottom: Rita_Kochmarjova; 59: Yuri Kravchenko; 60 bottom: BublikHaus; 61 Agnes Kantaruk; 62: Cindy Hughes; 63 left, 87 right, 145, 188 top: alexei_tm; 63 right: Africa Studio; 64 left: silverkblackstock; 66: Bogdan Sonjachnyj; 69 right: wernimages; 70: showcake; 71: candy candy; 72 right: Donna Heatfield; 75: Paapaya; 76: dien; 78: Erickson Stock; 79: marcinm111; 81 bottom: Daniel Besic; 82: Annabelle I; 83: NeonSparrow; 85: katamount; 87 left: Hryhchyshen Serhii; 88 right: Ilona.shorokhova; 89, 209: sanjagrujic; 90 left: 4 PM production; 90 right: Reshetnikov_art; 91 right: Art_man; 92: Andrzej Mielcarek; 93 top: Valeriya_Chistyakova; 93 bottom: GoodFocused; 96: Candy299; 97 left: Konstantin Tronin; 97 right: The Vine Studios; 98: Ryan Jello; 105: encierro; 106 right: Christine Bird; 107: Vlad Linev; 108 bottom: VI Studio; 109: Lorenzooooo; 111 left, 112 left: Andrey_Popov; 111 right: Blaj Gabriel; 116: Scorpp; 117 left: George Fairbairn; 119: otsphoto; 120 left: Duet PandG; 121 left: Jan Dix; 124: Dora Zett; 126 left: elebeZoom; 127 top: Christian Mueller; 130: Paul's Lady; 131 right: Melounix; 133: Anna Hoychuk; 135 right: Mary Swift; 137: Ryan Brix; 139: Soloviova Liudmyla; 140 top: Tara Lynn and Co; 142: Branislav Nenin; 144 left: elbud; 144 right: CL Shebley; 146 right: LNbjors; 149 left: Cheryl Ann Studio; 151 top: New Africa; 151 bottom: Przemek Iciak; 153 left: etonastenka; 154 right: ViChizh; 155: Cristina Conti; 157: The Bohemian Lens; 159 left: Oksana Kuzmina; 159 right: FellowNeko; 162 right: My July; 166: Eric Isselee; 169: Mary Swift; 171: SakSa; 172: pavel zubenko; 173 top: Vera Aksionava; 176: Sari ONeal; 179: elina.nova; 181: Piotr Wawrzyniuk; 185: Volodymyr TVERDOKHLIB; 191 right: Albina Gavrilovic; 194: Maila Facchini; 195: Zenotri; 197 bottom: Irina Senkova; 198: Switlana Sonyashna; 199: Numstocker; 210: SeaRick1; 216: Evgenii Panov; 219: Hector Roqueta; 221: The Len

About the Experts

I wish to thank the contributors and include the states or countries in which they work so that dog owners near them who are looking for quality help can reach out. Contributors are listed in order of appearance in the book. If there is a particular expert in this book whose interview resonated with you, please contact them even if they are in another country. So many of us now provide remote, online support for you and your dog.

A special and humbled thank you to these amazing professionals: it was you who returned to me my love of working with dogs—I have been given new hope through your work and innovation.

United States and Canada

Helen St. Pierre, Behavior Consultant and Trainer (New Hampshire): *www. nomonkeybusinessdogtraining.com*

Helen St. Pierre is a New Hampshire-based professional trainer and behavior expert with 20 years of experience. She owns and operates two No Monkey Business Dog Training facilities in the state and offers a wide variety of classes and one-on-one behavior consulting. St. Pierre has a long list of national qualifications that include Certified Professional Dog Trainer (CPDT-KA), Certified Dog Behavior Consultant (CDBC), Operation Socialization Certified Trainer (OSCT), Family Dog Mediator (FDM) and Licensed Dog and Storks Educator, and she has served as the assistant director of Family Paws Parent Education. She is a professional member of the Association of Pet Dog Trainers (APDT) and is a certified member of the International Association of Animal Behavior Consultants (IAABC). She also runs a foundation that gives loving hospice home care to senior rescue dogs, called Old Dogs Go to Helen (see *www.olddogsgotohelen.com*).

Dr. Amy Pike, Veterinary Behaviorist (Virginia): *www.abwellnesscenter.com*

Dr. Amy Pike graduated from Colorado State University School of Veterinary Medicine and Biomedical Sciences in 2003. After graduation, she was commissioned as a captain in the United States Army Veterinary Corps. Working with military dogs spurred her initial interest in behavior medicine.

In 2011, Dr. Pike started seeing behavior referrals in a residency program officially approved by the American College of Veterinary Behaviorists (ACVB) under the mentorship of Dr. Debra Horwitz, DACVB. In October 2015, Dr. Pike passed the ACVB certification examination, officially becoming one of less than 100 board-certified veterinary behaviorists worldwide.

Dr. Pike owns and operates the Animal Wellness Behavior Center in Fairfax, Virginia. She is a highly sought-after speaker at behavior conferences and for animal industry organizations. Dr. Pike is a member of the Fear Free advisory committee, advising general practitioners on the art of practicing "fear free."

Dr. Laura Donaldson,
Behavior Consultant and Trainer
(New York):
www.fourpawsfourdirections.com

Laura Donaldson holds a PhD in humanities and is a professor emeritus at Cornell University in Ithaca, New York. In 2009, she graduated with distinction from the Karen Pryor Academy for Animal Training and Behavior, and she is a Karen Pryor Certified Training Partner (CTP). Dr. Donaldson is a Certified Dog Behavior Consultant (CDBC) through the International Association of Animal Behavior Consultants. She has been assessed by a board of national experts in the field of dog behavior and found qualified to become a behavior consultant. In addition, she has completed graduate (master's level) academic courses in animal learning and behavior analysis, companion animal nutrition, psychopharmacology for animal scientists and the exploration of animal behavior (all with high "A" grades).

Dr. Donaldson has also completed in-depth mentorship programs with some of the most accomplished and recognized behavior experts in the dog training field, including aggression expert Michael Shikashio and Control Unleashed creator Leslie McDevitt. She is the owner of Four Paws Four Directions training and behavior consulting in Ithaca.

Kim Brophey,
Applied Ethologist
(North Carolina):
www.dogdoorcanineservices.com

Kim Brophey, CDBC, CPDT-KA, FDM, is an applied ethologist and owner of The Dog Door Behavior Center in Asheville, North Carolina. Her commitment to Family Dog Mediation has been recognized internationally, and she was awarded APDT Outstanding Trainer of the Year in 2009 and Best Dog Trainer of WNC seven years in a row. She is a member of the International Society for Applied Ethology and the Association of Professional Dog Trainers, and is a certified member and past board member of the International Association of Animal Behavior Consultants. Brophy's L.E.G.S.(R) model of integrated canine science has been endorsed by prominent canine scientists, including the late Raymond Coppinger, and embraced by reputable academics and dog trainers worldwide. Brophey wrote the groundbreaking book *Meet Your Dog* and presented the TEDx talk "The Problem with Treating a Dog Like a Pet."

From her applied ethology module for Michael Shikashio's Aggression in Dogs Master Course to her countless radio and podcast features, Brophey's work has made profound waves throughout the dog behavior world. She continues to build bridges and invite others to contribute to a new conversation about dogs—one that challenges us to redefine how we perceive, talk about, and treat our canine companions.

Malena DeMartini-Price,
Separation Anxiety Expert
(California):
www.malenademartini.com

Malena DeMartini-Price is a world-recognized expert on separation anxiety (SA) in dogs. In 2001, she became a certified trainer and counselor from The Academy for Dog Trainers. In 2014, she founded The Separation Anxiety Certification for Dog Professionals and has certified just over 200 trainers around the world. Her program offers professional remote training help as well as self-paced options for dog owners.

Malena is the author of two books: *Treating Separation Anxiety in Dogs* and *Separation Anxiety in Dogs: Next Generation Treatment Protocols and Practices*. She has also contributed articles on separation anxiety to multiple publications such as the Association of Professional Dog Trainers (APDT) *Chronicle of the Dog*, the Pet Professional Guild (PPG) *Barks from the Guild*, and various national magazines such as *The Bark*, *The Atlantic*, and *Smerconish*. Malena is an honors graduate of the esteemed Academy for Dog Trainers, where she studied under Jean Donaldson, and she is a member of the APDT, the PPG, and the International Association of Animal Behavior Consultants.

Christine Young,
Expert Puppy Trainer
(California):
www.thepuppycarecompany.com

Certified Professional Dog Trainer Christine Young (CPDT-KA) began her training life working with horses more than 20 years ago. Young transitioned to working with dogs and fine-tuned her work with puppies. Since she opened her training business, The Puppy Care Company, she has helped more than 1,000 puppies and their owners. She is canine first aid certified and is a supporting member of the International Association of Behavior Consultants (IAABC).

She is the training director for Preston's Planet, a California nonprofit dedicated to training service dogs for women and children in need, as well as providing free dog training and behavior education for the dog foster and rescue community around the world. Each Spring and Fall, Young teaches classes at Wild Blue Dog Camp in South Lake Tahoe—the only not-for-profit training and playtime camp that funds canine cancer treatment and research.

Dr. Marty Becker,
Veterinarian
(United States, nationwide):
www.fearfreepets.com
www.fearfreehappyhomes.com

Dr. Marty Becker, "America's veterinarian," has spent his life working toward better health for pets and the people who love them. He is the founder of Fear Free, which works to prevent and alleviate fear, anxiety, and stress in pets by inspiring and educating the people who care for them. This includes veterinary and other pet professionals as well as pet parents through *FearFreeHappyHomes.com* and animal shelter and rescue group staff and volunteers through *FearFreeShelters.com*.

Dr. Becker was the resident veterinary contributor on *Good Morning America* for 17 years. He is currently a member of the board of directors of American Humane as well as its chief veterinary correspondent. His special fondness for older pets has led him to a spot on the advisory board of The Grey Muzzle Organization, which is dedicated to helping homeless senior dogs. He has written 23 books that have sold almost 8 million copies, including three *New York Times* best-sellers. He also writes the weekly nationally syndicated newspaper feature *Pet Connection* with his writing partner, Kim Campbell Thornton.

Mikkel Becker,
Trainer and Behavior Consultant
(United States, nationwide):
www.fearfreepets.com
www.fearfreehappyhomes.com

Trainer and Behavior Consultant Mikkel Becker is the lead animal trainer for Fear Free Pets. The programs and courses provide veterinary professionals, pet professionals, animal welfare communities, and pet owners with the knowledge and tools to look after a pet's physical and emotional well-being.

Becker has achieved many of the top credentials available for Unites States dog professionals. She is both a Certified Professional Dog Trainer—Knowledge Assessed and a Certified Behavior Consultant Canine—Knowledge Assessed (CBCC-KA) through the Certification Council for Professional Dog Trainers and is a Certified Dog Behavior Consultant (CDBC) through the International Association of Animal Behavior Consultants, one of the most well-known and intensive certifications available. She is a Karen Pryor Academy Certified Training Consultant (KPA CTC) as a graduate of the Karen Pryor Academy for Animal Training and Behavior and a Fear Free Certified Professional. She is the co-author of *From Fearful to Fear Free: A Positive Program to Free Your Dog from Anxiety, Fears, and Phobias*.

Lee Desmarais,
Behavior Consultant and Dog
Trainer (Massachusetts):
www.zippitydodog.net

Lee Desmarais is a trainer specializing in individual dog-centered behavioral training solutions. She is the sole proprietor of Zippity Do Dog Training and Behavior Modification based in Massachusetts. She is a graduate of the Karen Pryor Academy, a Certified Level-1 Applied Behavior Analysis Accredited Practitioner (ABAP-1), a Family Dog Mediator (FDM) and a Certified Level-1 Scent Games Instructor. She is also a Certified Dog Trainer (CDT/INTODogs) and a Certified Fear Free Professional (CFFP). Desmarais a member of the Pet Professional Guild and the Association of Professional Dog Trainers. She is also certified through the AKC as a Canine Good Citizen instructor and evaluator.

Lee has extensive experience in rescue, from emergency animal sheltering through the Medical Reserve Corps, to volunteering with the ASPCA National Field Response Team. She serves as vice chair and training advisor for PitBullary, an all-voluntary organization that advocates for pit bull–type dogs (see www.pitbullary.com).

United Kingdom/Ireland

Dale McLelland,
Behavior Consultant and Trainer
(Scotland):
https://beingcanine.co.uk and
*https://www.withoutworrycanine
education.co.uk/*

Dale McLelland is a Scottish accredited animal behaviorist who owns and operates two dog training, behavior consultancy, and boarding facilities in Ayrshire, Scotland. Through her company Being Canine, McLelland and her trainers have assisted thousands of dogs and their owners lead their best lives by implementing her training motto: "train with the brain, not with pain." McLelland is co-director of Without Worry Canine Education. McLelland is a Certified Animal Trainer, an INTODogs Certified Canine Behaviorist, and a Certified Dog Trainer. She gained an advanced diploma in canine behavior and management with distinction, and is a full member of The Association of INTODogs, a member of the International Society for Animal Professionals, and a member of the Pet Professional Guild.

Jane Ardern,
Expert Breeder and Gun Dog
Trainer (England and Wales):
https://clickertrainer.co.uk,
https://www.waggawuffins.com, and
https://smartpupbox.com

Jane Ardern is an internationally recognized breeder and trainer of gun dogs, the director of Smart Pup, and an honors graduate of canine behavior and training from Bishop Burton College in the UK. Ardern is an ICAN certified animal behaviorist and a Gundog Club accredited instructor. She is a highly sought-after speaker and workshop presenter for hunting clubs, dog training organizations, and breeding clubs. She got her first dog 37 years ago, has been training for 27 years, has shared her life with 14 dogs of 5 different breeds, and still learns something new from dogs every day. She was named the Kennel Club Accredited Instructor of the Year in 2015.

Denise O'Moore,
Behavior Consultant and
Adolescent Dog Expert
(Ireland):
www.intodogs.net and
https://www.facebook.com/
mightydoggraphics/

Irish behavior consultant Denise O'Moore is an expert at rearing service dog puppies and training adolescent dogs. She is the chair of the INTODogs Association, a signatory organization of the UK Dog Behaviour and Training Charter. Denise is the co-owner of Puppy Power Training and Behaviour, holds a distinction in pet bereavement support and assistance dog training, and is a full member of DWA, a professional member of the PPGBI, and a member of the UK Dog Behaviour and Training Charter and Pet Industry Advocacy International. She is also a talented and highly sought-after illustrator and the managing director of Mighty Dog Graphics.

Denise has unique experiences working with adolescent dogs in her role as a trainer and puppy raiser for Irish Dogs for the Disabled. She began puppy walking back in 2005 for the Irish Guide Dogs, then went on to work with the Irish Dogs for the Disabled in 2010 as a socializer, fundraiser, and freelance trainer for pilot programs.

Andrew Hale,
Behavior Consultant and Trainer
(England):
https://dogcc.org

Andrew Hale is a certified animal behaviorist with the Association of INTODogs. He is the behavior consultant for Pet Remedy and the British Isles Grooming Association. With a degree and background in human psychology, Andrew is passionate about exploring the emotional experience that lies behind behavior, both in dogs and the humans around them. Andrew was the chair of the Association of INTODogs and a driving force behind the UK Dog Behaviour and Training Charter.

In 2020, Andrew started Dog Centred Care, focused on supporting a dog-led approach to providing the best care and support for dogs. On the Dog Centred Care Facebook group, he has been hosting online conversations with some of the world's most cutting-edge trainers, scientists, researchers, trauma experts, and veterinarians. He also co-hosted the *Beyond the Operant* conversation series on Dog Centred Care's YouTube channel.

Lisa Hird,
Behavior Consultant and Trainer
(England):
www.dogbehaviourclinic.co.uk
and *https://www.*
withoutworrycanineeducation.
co.uk/

Lisa Hird is a highly certified British behaviorist and owner of The Dog Behaviour Clinic in Lincolnshire, England. She is a co-founder and co-owner of Without Worry Canine Education. Lisa has more than 30 years of experience working with dogs, and she keeps up to date with CPD courses. Her certifications include level 6 canine behavior management with distinction and Fear Free Certified Professional. Lisa is a member of many professional organizations, including The Association of INTODogs, the UK Behaviour and Training Charter, and Fear Free Certified Professionals.

Shay Kelly,
Behavior Consultant and Trainer
(England):
www.shaykelly.com
and *ShaysDogBlog.com*

Shay Kelly is an award-winning British behavior counselor and the author of two books: *Dog Training and Behaviour: A Guide for Everyone* and *Canine Enrichment: The Book Your Dog Needs You to Read*. He is a graduate of the Bishop Burton College in collaboration with the University of Hull. He holds a first-class result in BSc Canine Behavior Management. He received the Ian MacParland award for the greatest personal achievement, a 100% grade in advanced dog training, best canine behavior student award, best animal-based dissertation award, and the Richard Marginson medal for premier student of the year. Kelly has a master's degree in animal behavior. He is the founder of one of the largest and most popular canine Facebook groups, Canine Enrichment, and can be reached via his websites.

Mark Bridger-Pescott,
Behavior Consultant and Trainer
(England):
www.bonecanis.com

Expert Behaviorist Mark Bridger-Pescott is the owner of Bone Canis, a team of friendly and qualified canine-professionals based in West Sussex. His on-staff trainers and behaviorists are a modern, force-free team that uses science-backed methods. Bone Canis trainers are proud members of and have been certified by The Association of INTODogs, The Pet Professional Guild British Isles, the Dog Welfare Alliance, CAM advocate, British College of Canine Studies, Doggone Safe Educator, and the UK Dog Behaviour and Training Charter.

Mark holds a degree-level qualification in canine behavior from Animal Jobs Direct. He serves as vice-chair for INTODogs. He has worked with a variety of rescues in the local area, and his main aim is to help people and their dogs with one-on-one behavioral sessions, using a professional, force-free, kind, and safe approach of behavioral modification.

About the Author

Professional dog trainer Annie Phenix is a graduate of the University of Texas at Austin with BA in English. She grew up near Austin writing for her family's weekly newspapers (*The Westlake Picayune*, among others) and has been an award-winning, professional journalist for 35 years. Phenix was named The Austin Communicator of the Year in 2000. As a working journalist and the previous owner of a literary publicity firm (Phenix & Phenix Literary Publicists), Phenix has worked with all forms of media from small town weeklies to national programs such as "The Today Show" and the "Oprah Winfrey Show."

She began her career working with dogs in the early 1990s as a behavior consultant and trainer for a large Austin, Texas non-profit dog rescue group. She has fostered more than 400 dogs since that time. Phenix wrote a dynamic dog training column for *Dogster Magazine* for several years and she was often the most read writer for Dogster.com. She is the author of the popular book among dog trainers and owners, *The Midnight Dog Walkers: Positive Training and Practical Advice for Living with Reactive and Aggressive Dogs* (Fox Chapel Publishing, 2016). Her book was nominated for a Maxwell Award for best behavior book of the year by the Dog Writers Association of America. She recently wrote her second book on canine behavior concerns and solutions titled *Positive Training for Aggressive and Reactive Dogs: Proven Techniques to Help Your Dog from Fear and Anxiety and Enjoy Walks Again* (CompanionHouse Books, Sept. 2022). Her articles written about dogs have been printed in well over 100 publications, including *Bark Magazine, Barks from the Guild, Lucky Puppy,* INTO Dogs, *The Mountain Mail, Pet Perennials, The Durango Herald, Simply Dogs, Coast Dogs Training, Rover.com, Colorado Parks & Wildlife, Fear Free Happy Homes,* International Canine Behaviourists, Dr. Andy Roark, and others.

Over her career as a behavior counselor for troubled dogs, she has achieved many certifications including Certified Canine Behaviourist (INTODogs), Family Dog Mediator (FDM), CPDT-KA (Retired), Fear Free Certified Professional, Graduate of a Schutzhund Dog Academy, CGC Evaluator and others. She has belonged to several professional organizations such as The Pet Professional Guild, The Pet Industry Advocacy International, The UK Dog Charter, The National Association of Canine Scent Work and Fear Free Certified Professionals. She is a lifetime advocate of training dogs without the need for fear, force or pain and with compassion and science-backed methods. She divides her time between Durango, Colorado and Heber City, Utah. She loves taking long mountain hikes with her husband, Jeff, and their two sibling cattle-collie dogs, Finn and Cooper.

Acknowledgments

I didn't want to write this book. Writing a book isn't easy, especially one covering such a broad range of topics. I had a lovely, semi-retired lifestyle and was enjoying my leisure time when my acquisition editor called me in August 2021. She obviously convinced me, and I am so glad that she did—cheers to Shelley Carr. This book was much more of a transformative experience for me as a journalist and dog behavior counselor that I ever expected it to be.

There are two important reasons for this book: dogs and the owners who love them. This book is for you. When you allow animals in your life and care for them and provide for their needs, the world opens and your life is no longer quite so small, or as painful. Once you have empathy for animals, it is hard not to let a little bit of empathy for other humans sneak in as well. I care deeply about owners helping their dogs live their best lives.

I thank the one human constant in my daily life these past 25 years: my brilliant and charming husband, Jeff Hebert. He is the smartest person I know and one of the kindest. Jeff is a gift from the dog gods, I am certain of it.

I don't think this book would exist without the Irish blessing that is behaviorist Denise O'Moore. She gave me unwavering support, deep friendship, hilarious Facebook calls, and so very much more. I would not have had nearly as much fun these past few years in the dog industry if we had not become great friends. I think the positive dog training community would fall apart quickly if we didn't have Denise to unite our work. Many other industry professionals were always happy to help me research on a moment's notice and I have enjoyed getting to know each of you better! Thank you one and all.

I began writing with my search for new, effective ways to help troubled dogs. I felt quite pessimistic at first, but then I stumbled across the conversations on UK behaviorist Andrew Hale's *Beyond the Operant* YouTube channel. I stopped writing and for weeks watched every interview. I found his discussions to be enormously helpful in presenting modern approaches for helping troubled dogs by focusing on the whole dog and incorporating many scientific disciplines.

Special thanks to SilverBay Weimaraners for inclusion of their beautiful dogs in this book and many thanks to Midway, Utah, professional photographer Shawna Henrie and her company, Bleudog Fotography (*www.bleudogphotography.com*).

I have non–dog trainer friends who have been my "besties" and who always support my work. They make me laugh and we all share a love of dogs and good meals. They've also been the first readers of nearly everything I have written for years and years: Jessica Burwell, Renee Hendley, and Jan Williams—you are my tribe and I love you! I am also thankful that my father, George Phenix, knew about this book before he passed away while I was in the middle of writing it. He would call me and ask over and over again: "So the acquisition editor called you or you called her? How did it happen—tell me everything!" Thanks to my editors Sherry Vitolo and Amy Deputato, two superb, patient editors who made this book stronger. And thanks to the marketing and design teams at Fox Chapel—they are true professionals.

Special thanks, as well, to behavior expert and trainer Ellen Watkins and to podcaster extraordinaire and coach Kajsa van Overbeek for to review the book in its entirety. I knew I could count on you to give me important, meaningful, and honest feedback—something every writer cherishes.

One of my personal realizations in writing this book was seeing that the positive dog training community is not as warmongering or combative as it can appear on social media. Every professional I asked for an interview has a full schedule and is busier than they've ever been, but every person said "yes" right away. I also learned that there is a definite and palpable sense of camaraderie and support among positive trainers.

Just because a trainer, behaviorist, or veterinarian is not listed or interviewed in this book doesn't mean they aren't amazing professionals doing magnificent work in their area of expertise. I could have interviewed hundreds and hundreds of experts, and I wish I had the space to do so. Dogs are so complex —they need all our expertise and collaborative efforts focused on helping them.

If you are looking to find a truly qualified, well-trained and ethical canine professional to help with your dog, I would be happy to help you find such a trainer (my search is free of charge). Please send me an email with where you are looking to find a canine professional: *annie@phenixdogs.com.*